Antonioni and the Aesthetics of Impurity

D1527780

Antonioni and the Aesthetics of Impurity

Remaking the Image in the 1960s

Matilde Nardelli

EDINBURGH
University Press

Edinburgh University Press is one of the leading university presses in the UK. We publish academic books and journals in our selected subject areas across the humanities and social sciences, combining cutting-edge scholarship with high editorial and production values to produce academic works of lasting importance. For more information visit our website: edinburghuniversitypress.com

© Matilde Nardelli, 2020, 2022

First published in hardback by Edinburgh University Press 2020

Edinburgh University Press Ltd
The Tun – Holyrood Road
12(2f) Jackson's Entry
Edinburgh EH8 8PJ

Typeset in 11/13 Adobe Garamond Pro
IDSUK (DataConnection) Ltd

A CIP record for this book is available from the British Library

ISBN 978 1 4744 4404 0 (hardback)
ISBN 978 1 4744 4405 7 (paperback)
ISBN 978 1 4744 4406 4 (webready PDF)
ISBN 978 1 4744 4407 1 (epub)

The right of Matilde Nardelli to be identified as the author of this work has been asserted in accordance with the Copyright, Designs and Patents Act 1988, and the Copyright and Related Rights Regulations 2003 (SI No. 2498).

For Giacomo and Emilio

[T]he so tender and delicate zinc, so yielding to acid which gulps it down in a single mouthful, behaves, however, in a very different fashion when it is very pure: then it obstinately resists the attack. One could draw from this two conflicting philosophical positions: the praise of purity, which protects from evil like a coat of mail; the praise of impurity, which gives rise to changes, in other words, to life. I discarded the first, disgustingly moralistic, and I lingered to consider the second, which I found more congenial.

Primo Levi, *The Periodic Table* (1975)

Contents

Figures

Acknowledgements

My first debt of gratitude is with London, and the welcoming cultural diversity and bewildering provision of arts and cinema that it offered to a young Italian au pair on a three-month stay. It had to become my home; and it has. And I know (or hope) that it will continue to feel like home even as the UK's imminent departure from the EU contributes to consign the time of my arrival here over two decades ago to a historical past.

If I discovered Antonioni's films as double bills at the Riverside Studio in Hammersmith, my second debt of gratitude goes to David Forgacs and Briony Fer, who first encouraged and enthused me to write about Antonioni academically. Their support and ideas have shaped, and continue to shape, my thinking in fundamental ways. I am very grateful to Laura Rascaroli, John David Rhodes, Karl Schoonover, Pierpaolo Antonello, Robert Lumley, Geoffrey Nowell-Smith, Angelo Restivo, Karen Pinkus, Rosalind Galt, Francesco Casetti, Ara Merjian, Stephen Connolly, Flavia Frigeri, Romy Golan, Teresa Kittler, Giuliana Pieri and Emanuela Patti. The boundary-crossing work of these scholars and colleagues has done much to help me think about the 'impurity' of Antonioni's modern, and modernist, cinema, and continues to inspire reflection and admiration. I feel very fortunate to have been able to discuss Antonioni, and several other things besides, with many of them over the years and to have forged long-lasting friendships with some of them.

Another significant debt of gratitude is with Francesca Gavioli and Federica Sani at the Gallerie d'Arte Moderna e Contemporanea in Ferrara, where the Michelangelo Antonioni Archive is. Their knowledge and generous help have been precious. Heartfelt thanks go to my colleagues at the University of West London, and especially to Garin Dowd, Michelle Henning (who has since moved on to pastures new) and Theresa Mikuriya for inviting me to join their 'Thinking the Image' research group. Aga Baranowska and David Somerset at the British Film Institute gave me the opportunity to host and take part in a number of classes and events during an Antonioni retrospective in early 2019. The discussions that arose there were incredibly energising. Invaluable feedback and suggestions were offered by the anonymous readers and series editors, Martine Beugnet and Kriss Ravetto, at different stages of this project.

I am very grateful to Gillian Leslie and Richard Strachan at Edinburgh University Press for all their help and support, and to Sarah Meaney for the impeccable copy-editing. This book would probably never had got finished without the nudging of my 'writing buddy', and friend, Nina Lager-Vestberg. My last but crucial thanks go to a small number of friends and family: Silvia Montes, Paola Ianes, Eleanor Chiari, Karl Schoonover and Lloyd Pratt, Tory and Oliver Harud, Eugenio Lorenzi, Sam Halliday and, above all, my sister Anna Nardelli, who has always been there for me. This book is for Giacomo and Emilio, whose curiosity towards the world is a never-ending source of energy.

* * *

Portions of Chapter 4 have previously appeared as '*Blow-Up* and the Plurality of Photography', in Laura Rascaroli and John David Rhodes, eds, *Antonioni: Centenary Essays* (London: Palgrave Macmillan/BFI, 2011), pp. 185–205, reproduced here with permission of Palgrave Macmillan.

Where available, I have referred to both English and Italian versions of Antonioni's published writings and interviews, and used and translated from the Italian where the English translation seemed somewhat distant from the original meaning or missed some of its nuances. Occasionally, passages in the original Italian are not present in the English translation. Unless otherwise indicated, all translation from Italian and French elsewhere are also my own.

Introduction: Antonioni and the Aesthetics of Impurity

This is why it seems more important to me today to seek to make a cinema that may even be 'literary', or 'figurative'. (I'm expressing myself paradoxically, evidently, because I categorically do not believe that there exists such a thing as a literary cinema, a figurative cinema. Only cinema exists, which encloses within itself the experience of all the other arts, and can use them freely.)

Michelangelo Antonioni, 'La malattia dei sentimenti' (1961)[1]

If . . . we establish the discussion on the basis of media, we recognize that they form a continuum, a spectrum . . . [T]here are two fallacies of interpretation in connection with the matter under discussion. One is to keep the arts wholly separate. The other is to run them altogether into one.

John Dewey, *Art as Experience* (1934)[2]

The question proposed for our consideration is not so new; first of all, it is the problem of the reciprocal influence of the arts.

André Bazin, 'Pour un cinéma impur' (1951)[3]

[N]o medium has its meaning or existence alone, but only in constant interplay with other media.

Marshall McLuhan, *Understanding Media* (1964)[4]

Michelangelo Antonioni's films of the 1960s are widely recognised as exemplars of cinema and key in realising its 'new', 'modern' or 'art' incarnation around 1960. While these attributes also partly crystallise around Italian neorealism, the premiere of *L'avventura* in Cannes in May 1960 is often invoked as one of the inaugural moments of this new kind of cinema. According to Geoffrey Nowell-Smith, that first screening was 'the watershed separating the world of new cinemas from that of the old'.[5] Even though the film famously provoked scepticism, if not scorn and hostility among portions of that first audience (several viewers booed and cried 'Cut!'), its importance 'as a defining moment in the history of film', as Laura Rascaroli and John David Rhodes have written, 'became immediately evident'.[6] Antonioni and Monica Vitti left the screening in tears on that night, but the next morning they found a collective letter of support and admiration pinned by their hotel room, signed by a long roll of critics, filmmakers and actors praising a work of 'exceptional importance', and the film was subsequently awarded the Jury Prize 'for a new cinematic language'.[7]

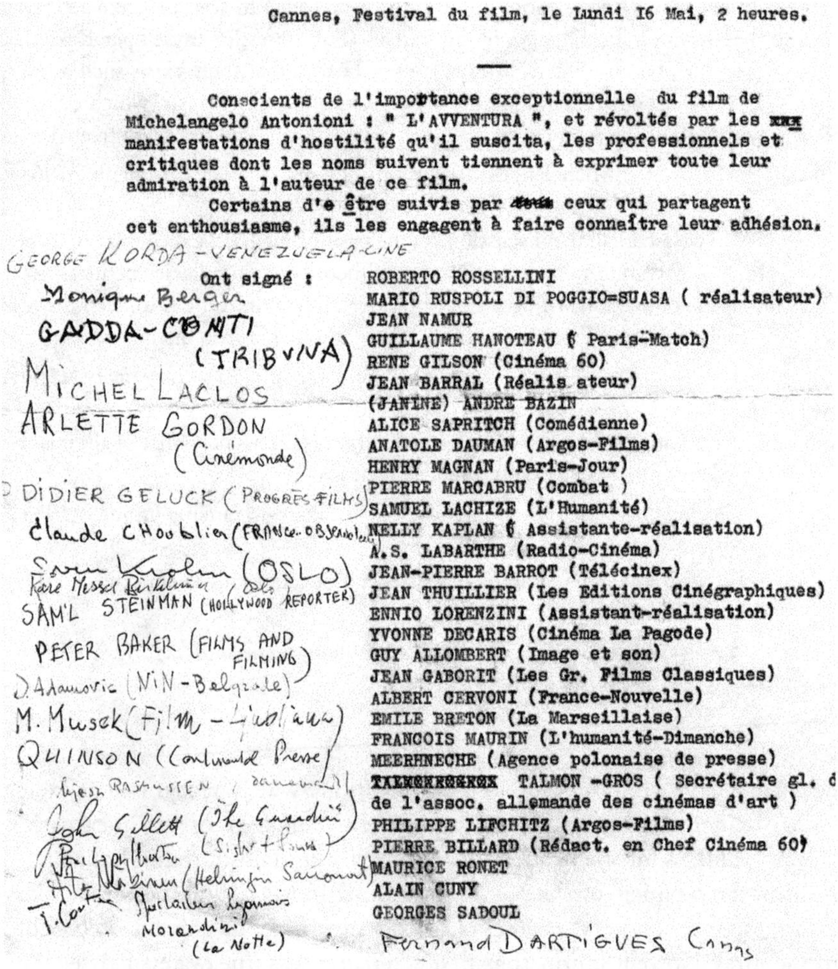

Cannes, Festival du film, le Lundi I6 Mai, 2 heures.

Conscients de l'importance exceptionnelle du film de Michelangelo Antonioni : " L'AVVENTURA ", et révoltés par les manifestations d'hostilité qu'il suscita, les professionnels et critiques dont les noms suivent tiennent à exprimer toute leur admiration à l'auteur de ce film.

Certains d'être suivis par ceux qui partagent cet enthousiasme, ils les engagent à faire connaître leur adhésion.

GEORGE KORDA - VENEZUELA-CINE

Ont signé :

ROBERTO ROSSELLINI
MARIO RUSPOLI DI POGGIO-SUASA (réalisateur)
JEAN NAMUR
GUILLAUME HANOTEAU (Paris-Match)
RENE GILSON (Cinéma 60)
JEAN BARRAL (Réalisateur)
(JANINE) ANDRE BAZIN
ALICE SAPRITCH (Comédienne)
ANATOLE DAUMAN (Argos-Films)
HENRY MAGNAN (Paris-Jour)
PIERRE MARCABRU (Combat)
SAMUEL LACHIZE (L'Humanité)
NELLY KAPLAN (Assistante-réalisation)
A.S. LABARTHE (Radio-Cinéma)
JEAN-PIERRE BARROT (Télécinex)
JEAN THUILLIER (Les Editions Cinégraphiques)
ENNIO LORENZINI (Assistant-réalisation)
YVONNE DECARIS (Cinéma La Pagode)
GUY ALLOMBERT (Image et son)
JEAN GABORIT (Les Gr. Films Classiques)
ALBERT CERVONI (France-Nouvelle)
EMILE BRETON (La Marseillaise)
FRANCOIS MAURIN (L'humanité-Dimanche)
MEERHNECHE (Agence polonaise de presse)
TALMON -GROS (Secrétaire gl. de l'assoc. allemande des cinémas d'art)
PHILIPPE LIFCHITZ (Argos-Films)
PIERRE BILLARD (Rédact. en Chef Cinéma 60)
MAURICE RONET
ALAIN CUNY
GEORGES SADOUL

Monique Berger
GADDA-CONTI (TRIBUNA)
MICHEL LACLOS
ARLETTE GORDON (Cinémonde)
DIDIER GELUCK (PROGRÈS FILMS)
Claude Choublier (France-Observateur)
SAM'L STEINMAN (HOLLYWOOD REPORTER)
PETER BAKER (FILMS AND FILMING)
M. Musek
QUINSON
John Gillett (The Guardian)
Fernand DARTIGUES Cannes

Figure 0.1 Statement in support of *L'avventura*, Cannes Film Festival, May 1960, courtesy Gallerie d'Arte Moderna e Contemporanea: Fondo Michelangelo Antonioni, Ferrara

As the premiere of *L'avventura* demonstrates, Antonioni's 1960s films were almost immediately recognised for bringing a newness to cinema, whether positively or negatively assessed. This book accepts the awareness that they inspired. While this is not the same as saying that the films made a complete break with the past (which is arguably always a disproportionate claim), I seek, in what follows, to acknowledge and work with the sense of difference that these films, as Nowell-Smith among others reported, provoked in viewers. A postcard from the sculptor Arnaldo Pomodoro sent to the director after the release of *Il deserto rosso/Red Desert* (1964) crystallises, with flattering wit, the kind of qualities that many viewers recognised in Antonioni's films.[8]

Figure 0.2 Arnaldo Pomodoro, postcard to Antonioni after the release of *Il deserto rosso*, 1964) courtesy Gallerie d'Arte Moderna e Contemporanea: Fondo Michelangelo Antonioni, Ferrara

The postcard features a young couple in the top left, above which Pomo-doro's handwriting reads 'Today they have seen *Il deserto rosso*'. This is jux-taposed with an elderly couple in the bottom right, whom Pomodoro's writing fictionally presents as a view of the formerly young couple projected several decades into the future, to a 'today' (yet to come in the writer's own present, but that could more or less coincide with mine, looking at the card a couple of decades into the twenty-first century) when 'they remember *Il deserto rosso*' and are still – as their happy, dreamy smiles suggest – mes-merised by it. By playing with time, this postcard encapsulates how, when they came out, Antonioni's films appeared not only modern but, somewhat paradoxically, modern in a way that may last. In fact, confirming Pomo-doro's prediction, they arguably, if in different ways, still appear 'modern' now, as their overt legacy in some of the most innovative filmmaking and moving-image forms to date – from the work of directors as diverse as Paolo Sorrentino, Claire Denis, Ruben Östlund, Wong Kar-wai, Lee Chang-dong and Apichatpong Weerasethakul, to experimental filmmakers and visual artists including Rodney Graham, Shezad Dawood, Marco Poloni, Stephen Connolly and Eric Baudelaire – contributes to suggest.

Perhaps the newness, modernity and art quality of Antonioni's cinema can, above all, be brought back to matters of temporality and timing. In the 1960s, films such as *L'avventura* and *Il deserto rosso* belonged to their present and seemed modern thanks to attributes (of subject matter, narration and aesthetics) that made them feel 'ahead' of the times. But, to some extent, this also generated a sense that their modernity may not wear out. In this respect, they are exemplary of art cinema as a category that, as Rosalind Galt and Karl Schoonover have argued, is both historical *and* current, something that helps specify a historically defined, if loose, cinematic corpus, but that also summons still appreciable, pursued and pursuable attributes or features in films.[9] If Pomodoro's postcard seems such a fitting tribute to *Il deserto rosso*, it is also in part because – although not necessarily intentionally – it manages to evoke the remarkable temporal 'dyschronies' of the film. The film's take on Italy's then modernising – or already modern – present makes it look at once futuristic and about what is already past, consumed and in ruins.[10] (When, in 1967, the American conceptual and land artist Robert Smithson saw a 'future "out of date"' in his tour of the industrial landscape of Passaic, New Jersey, occupied by what he called '*ruins in reverse*', structures which not so much '*fall* into ruin *after* they are built' but '*rise* into ruin *before* they are built', I cannot but think that, as an avid movie-goer, he must, at least in part, have had *Il deserto rosso* in mind.)[11]

In considering the work of one of the revered masters of modern art cinema, *Antonioni and the Aesthetics of Impurity* takes a perspective that, while keeping the 'author', also displaces Antonioni from the centre of his films, so to speak. This book seeks to understand the perceived newness and difference of Antonioni's 1960s films, not by singling them out from their social, cultural and artistic context as the work of a visionary *auteur*, but by exploring the conditions of their dynamic immersion in such context. One of the ways that I do this here is by pursuing overlooked affinities with ideas and practices not generally associated with his cinema, whose renewal or, even, 'purification' of the moving image is often attributed to an engagement with the traditional fine arts, perhaps painting above all.

As I discuss more fully in the next chapter, Antonioni's admiration for Mark Rothko is, in this context, presented as exemplary of a symmetry of intents, whereby a Greenbergian model of 'pure' painting is matched by an equivalent one of 'pure' cinema (albeit elevated through a pictorial comparison).[12] While salutary in certain respects, this selective scope lifts Antonioni's highly innovative films of the 1960s out of the richer and more complex ferment of their historical time, strangely denying engagement with the present to a director who is otherwise praised for his perceptiveness of the cultural, social and psychological realities around him. As well as a time of innovation in cinema, this was a time during which both art and culture more broadly underwent radical transformations. With media such as television, sound and videotape, as well as early computers, joining the established media technologies of photography, film and radio, mass-media culture boomed and seeped into everydayness to an unprecedented degree, precipitating that sense of a simultaneous shrinking *and* expansion of the world that Marshall McLuhan started to describe in the 1960s as a 'global village'.[13]

In the 1940s, Theodor W. Adorno and Max Horkheimer had condemned the 'culture industry' as a 'mass deception'. In the early 1950s, Dwight McDonald juxtaposed 'high' with 'mass' culture, and deemed the latter, which he distinguished into 'midcult' and 'lowcult', to be unworthy of the full word 'culture'.[14] Yet, by the early 1960s, more sympathetic observers such as Edgar Morin in France and Umberto Eco in Italy started to take more seriously mass culture itself. Indeed, as Morin put it in *L'Esprit du temps* (1962), 'the distinction between culture and mass culture is purely formal' in a world where so-called high culture is 'democratised via the paperback, the music record, image reproduction'; '[Malraux's] *The Human Condition*, [Sartre's] *Nausea* or [Camus's] *The Plague* can enter mass culture without leaving high culture'.[15] A few years later, the art critic Lawrence Alloway reasoned along similar lines with respect to visual art: 'the alignment of art and news services', while not 'reduc[ing] the specialized content of new work', he noted, 'exposes the "advanced" to a "mass"', making the very 'term avant-garde, so potent . . . as recently as the 1940s . . . obsolete'.[16]

In this context, even as ideas of purity and clear-cut disciplinary or competence boundaries were still critically the most prominent, contrary or alternative positions were gaining ground. In the same years during which Antonioni was hailed as a key initiator of a 'new' cinema, practices including those of John Cage, pop, kinetic art, happenings, minimalism, structural cinema, *arte povera*, conceptual and land art increasingly shunned traditional formats, techniques and skills – particularly those of painting – and opened out to mass culture and mass (re)production technologies, as well as to highly experimental and boundary-crossing forms such as 'mixed media', installation and performance. The thrust of artistic and cinematic production seemed geared not so much towards (quixotic) *purification* but, rather, *renewal* – a renewal whose very feasibility appeared crucially dependent on acknowledging, if not indeed intermedially engaging with the new forms, technologies and media transforming and informing culture and life. When minimal artist Donald Judd began his text 'Specific Objects' (1965) by saying that 'half or more of the best new work in the last few years has been neither painting nor sculpture', and Fluxus co-founder Dick Higgins opened his essay 'Intermedia' (1966) in a similar tone by saying 'much of the best work being produced today seems to fall between media', they were both taking a swipe at Greenbergian criticism, parroting its style but subverting its substance, and contributing to the articulation of a critical alternative to the rhetoric of purity, division and separation.[17]

If this intermedial process of aesthetic renewal was on a par with the discursive articulations of media theorists such as McLuhan, and philosophers of technology such as Gilbert Simondon, bound up with it was the attempt to explore and understand the crucial role of technological mediation in the shaping of experience and the very definition of 'the human'.[18] Contemporary media-philosophical positions, such as those of Bernard Stiegler or, more recently, of Timothy Barker, for whom 'being now involves a relationship with technical media' and 'is given its attributes through this nexus', find their roots in this moment.[19] A manifesto such as Stan Vanderbeek's 'Culture: Intercom and Expanded Cinema' – first published in Jonas Mekas's *Film Culture* in 1966 – speaks of the growing awareness of the magnitude of transformations wrought by mass media technologies, as well as of a utopian optimism about the possibility of harnessing them to humanity's advantage for an expansion of intercultural communication and collective knowledge.[20] Although this is not a pairing that one would make instinctively, Vanderbeek's views on the distance between 'technological research' and the 'emotional-sociological . . . comprehension of this technology' resonate with Antonioni's ideas on such a relationship between technological development and psychology. For, as he started to express during an important talk given at the Centro Sperimentale di Cinematografia (CSC) in Rome in 1961 – also first published in English in *Film Culture* in 1962 – and returned to more insistently when making *Il deserto rosso*, Antonioni similarly understood the human to be in a critical phase of evolutionary adaptation as a consequence of the radical technological and mediatic changes underway.

It is this richly transmedial and transnational context, as well as the impetus of experimentation, enquiry and critique that animated it, that this book lays out and investigates for Antonioni's 1960s films. From the initially bewildering 'slow' aesthetics of *L'avventura, La notte* (1961) and *L'eclisse* (1962) to the surprising use of colour in *Il deserto rosso* – and, in fact, beyond the 1960s, as the camera work of *The Passenger* (1975) and the colour manipulations of magnetic videotape in *Il mistero di Oberwald/The Mystery of Oberwald* (1980) suggest – Antonioni's pursuit of experimentation is constantly evident. Despite such indefatigable commitment to formal research and a penchant for pushing beyond the boundaries of the cinematic medium itself, Antonioni's films do not tend to be associated with that transgressive, experimental, boundary-crossing 'new sensibility' that Susan Sontag identified as a revolutionary cultural and artistic tendency in her eponymous essay of 1965 (and in which, in fact, Antonioni features as an example).[21] Yet, the 'new sensibility' whose emergence Sontag diagnoses in the wake of the crisis of traditional fine-art disciplines and the demotion of painting from its privileged position as a paradigm for all the arts is, I believe, a crucial context for Antonioni's 'new' films (and Antonioni himself referred to Sontag's attack on established aesthetic forms as obsolete in her 1964 essay 'Against Interpretation').[22] There are enticing affinities to be explored between Antonioni's films of the 1960s and the contemporaneous non-traditional art practices that flourished in that decade, when artists engaged with mass culture and mass media as fundamental in the shaping of contemporary reality and key to its understanding.

It is precisely a condition of dynamic immersion in such context that contributes to make Antonioni's cinema of the 1960s modern, or even 'contemporary', in the sense evoked by the philosopher Giorgio Agamben of a 'relationship to one's own time' which is at once of adherence *and* disjunction.[23] Antonioni, whose path into cinema in the mid-1940s was via documentary and what he frequently described as his own modulation of a neorealist sensibility, observed and absorbed the changing reality surrounding him with tireless and often enthusiastic curiosity. But he did so without *completely* adhering to it. It is through such a gap of adherence to their own present that Antonioni's films manifest that quality of 'contemporariness' which, according to Agamben, is the ability 'to firmly hold [one's] gaze on' the present rather than being 'blinded by' it.[24] This gaze, that is not blinded by what it sees, constitutes a subtle 'disjunction' for which the philosopher also accounts in temporal terms, as a kind of 'anachronism' – perhaps like the disorientating, already worn out yet futuristic, present of *Il deserto rosso*.[25]

'By beginning to understand the world through the image, I began to understand the image', wrote Antonioni in 1964.[26] The cinematic image is the tool of 'contemporaneity' for Antonioni: at once the element of adherence to the present and of disjunction from it. In this respect, Antonioni's analysis is twofold: it explores the function of mediation performed by the image (as a tool for seeing and showing) in a general sense; and it reflects on the ways in which the cinematic image more specifically performs such a function as a mass medium 'in constant interplay with other media', as McLuhan puts it.

PURITY AND IMPURITY

When *L'avventura* premiered at Cannes, notions of purity, specificity and clear-cut distinctions between media, disciplines and levels of culture (such as mass entertainment and art) that had shaped much of the critical discourse in the first half of the century, were still rhetorically dominant. The diffusion of cinema in the first decades of the twentieth century had itself contributed to rekindling debates on 'limits' and 'boundaries'. Cinema demonstrated not only a profound aesthetic hybridity that confounded the influential division between 'arts of space' and 'arts of time' offered by Gotthold Lessing in his 'Laocoön' essay (1766), but was also one of those technologies and industrially produced mass entertainments that could contaminate art *tout court* and lower taste. Whether by replacing established forms, or gaining recognition in its own right among the other arts for its unique and specific contribution (as the early film theorist Ricciotto Canudo argued by baptising the medium the 'Sixth Art'),[27] cinema may lead to an erosion of art's putative total or relative autonomy from capitalist production and consumption.

If Clement Greenberg had occupied himself with the problem of keeping mass media out of art in 'Avant-Garde and Kitsch' (1939), and then turned his attention to the shortfalls of a 'confusion of the arts' in 'Towards a Newer Laocoön' (1940), during the post-war decades, with influential texts such as 'Modernist Painting' (1961), Greenberg became more specifically focused on individual disciplines *within* the fine arts. In the camp of cinema, advocates would try to identify attributes that were *purely of* cinema, partly with the aim of gaining the status of (an) art for (certain) cinema, and some distance from mass spectacle. As a film critic in the 1930s and 1940s, Antonioni was partly involved in such debates. In a 1949 article titled 'Pazienza del cinema [Cinema's Patience]', he voiced his dissatisfaction with the 'reluctance' to take cinema seriously, 'borne of a conception of art in abstract terms' on the one hand and, on the other, due to the lack of seriousness of cinema itself, whose products all too often are condemned to being 'magic windows', and mere ways 'to pass the time'.[28]

While scepticism towards 'filmed theatre' – or, as in art documentaries, 'filmed painting' – would be a recurrent trope, the endeavour to establish the distinctive parameters for cinema's identity would not be free of problems and contradictions.[29] Cinema's ability, like photography and other lens-based media, to automatically produce likenesses of 'reality' could be counted as a contaminating factor. Although it might also go the other way and be taken as its 'specific' trait, as Siegfried Kracauer or Maya Deren, among others, reiterated in the early 1960s.[30] Often, cinema's 'purity' may turn out to be precisely its in-between-ness or hybridity – a notion that even informs much more recent positions, such as Alain Badiou's sense that cinema 'is the great "impurifier"', and which Jacques Rancière reads as a problematic way of concentrating and securing impurity *within* cinema, as its domain of specificity.[31] For Rudolf Arnheim in *Film as Art* (1932), film came 'midway between theater and the still picture'.[32] However, such midway-ness, as he specified in an essay first published in the Italian journal *Bianco e nero* in 1938 (whose title, 'The New Laocoön', makes obvious its reference to Lessing just as Greenberg's does) was still, crucially, based on a separation rather than an interpenetration of attributes. It was more like a 'successful marriage . . . where the personality of the two partners remains intact', as he put it, than 'the child that springs from that marriage, in whom both components are inseparably mixed'.[33] In this vein, theories of film centred on the notion of 'filmic' or 'cinematographic specificity' – '*specifico filmico*' or '*specifico cinematografico*' – were articulated well into the 1960s. In Italy, these were the positions of leading figures such as Luigi Chiarini and Umberto Barbaro. In addition to being editorially involved in key publications such as the aforementioned *Bianco e nero* and *Filmcritica*, Barbaro and Chiarini taught at CSC (of which Chiarini was in fact also a founder), where many important directors including Antonioni studied.[34]

But even if these aesthetic models of the arts and cinema that centred on purity were more nuanced or contradictory than they might at first seem, and had started to come under attack by the late 1950s, Antonioni's films would tend to be presented and upheld as quintessentially, *purely*, cinematic. This dominant critical framing has more or less overtly continued to inform accounts of their newness, art and modernity – if not, indeed, of their mod*ernism*. When, in a recurrent trope in Antonionian discourse – modulations of which have been articulated by Pascal Bonitzer, Gilles Deleuze and, more recently, the historical geographer Matthew Gandy, among others – the director is seen to take the cinematic image towards abstraction, if not emptiness, the implication is not quite, as it might intuitively be, that he is negating cinema but, rather, that he is reducing it to its specific, pure essence. The 'empty shot' that, according to Bonitzer, has been 'Antonioni's great project' since *L'avventura*, is a kind of 'non-figurative' limit – or, as Gandy puts it, a 'cinematic void' – whereby cinema itself is clawed back to its bare essentials: the abstract or empty image stands in for the screen itself, 'blends into [its] white surface', in Deleuze's words.[35]

Immersing Antonioni's 1960s films in their historical and cultural context thus also means linking them to reflections which, as the epigraphs at the beginning of this Introduction show, had begun to articulate alternatives to critical positions invested in upholding notions of aesthetic 'purity' and precise formal and disciplinary boundaries determined on the basis of attributes unique to given media or arts. John Dewey's experiential, empirically phenomenological approach, for instance, was crucial to thought such as that of Eco.[36] Another such alternative position was expressed by André Bazin in his 1951 essay 'Pour un cinéma impur', whose still current English translation of 1967, as Lúcia Nagib and Anne Jerslev have noted, avoided the dramatic force of the word 'impure' by opting for the softer 'mixed'.[37] Not only, Bazin insists throughout the essay, has cinema itself – an exemplarily hybrid form in its combination of image, word and sound, and temporal and spatial attributes – always taken from the other arts, 'just as the education of the child derives from imitating the adults around him', but all of the arts ultimately owe their transformation to their 'reciprocal influence'.[38] From this perspective, the endeavour to outline Antonioni's 'aesthetics of impurity' is not so much a 'new' reading of his films, but rather a reading that reconnects them with ideas and critical debates, as well as practices, whose importance for his work – as well as, in fact, for the work of many *auteurs* and masters of modern or art cinema – generally tends to be downplayed, if not ignored.

Rascaroli and Rhodes have provocatively observed in the introduction to their volume *Antonioni: Centenary Essays* (2011) that Antonioni's films can appear 'rather uncinematic – too fascinated by other forms . . . using cinema less as a specific medium (with its 'own' laws) and more as a way of bringing various media into contact with one another'.[39] *Antonioni and the Aesthetics of Impurity* takes up this provocation and seeks to argue that the very sense of newness or modernity accruing in Antonioni's 1960s films is due to their hybridisation and exchanges with other arts and media. It is not through pursuit of a putatively greater cinematic purity and closure onto their own medium and its 'specific' qualities but, rather, precisely through an openness to *other* forms and media that Antonioni's films contributed to a new kind of cinema. In his essay, Bazin notes that while in the first few decades of the medium's development, experimentation with its technical and formal limits might have been sufficient to produce valuable and innovative films, by the time of his writing in 1951, 'cinema has no longer anything to conquer' in that respect. Its only hope for something new lay in its ability 'to irrigate its banks, to insinuate itself between the arts among which it has so swiftly carved out its valleys, subtly to invest them, to infiltrate the subsoil, in order to excavate invisible galleries'.[40] In the mid-1960s, a somewhat surprising supporter of this 'impure' approach can be found in Adorno who, in an essay in which, as we will see, he also writes about *La notte*, he argues that 'film's most promising potential' with regard to its 'radical intentions . . . lies in its interaction with other media, themselves merging into film'.[41]

In many ways, Bazin's and Adorno's positions adumbrate what I argue that Antonioni's 1960s films do. I explore how, in Bazin's expression, they 'irrigate [their] banks' in other arts and media, but I also want to suggest that Antonioni's films, just as in the mode of their receptiveness to 'reality' more generally, are not simply 'intermedial' but engaged in a *critical intermediality*. While Adorno, who does not call it so, finds film's possibility for critical inter-mediality in an opening out to the 'progressive tendencies in the visual arts', I think that Antonioni's cinema also finds it in a wider, less selective openness to both established and emerging art and mass media forms, which it both *absorbs and resists*. Returning to Agamben's notion, we could say that what I call 'critical intermediality' is a particular manifestation of what the philosopher describes as 'contemporariness'. It is indeed with this media-focused and mediated manifestation of 'contemporariness' in Antonioni's cinema that this book is primarily concerned.

To account for the newness and art quality of Antonioni's 1960s films in terms of impurity and dialogue with other art and media forms is to go against the grain of what are still entrenched ways of thinking not only about his cinema in particular but also about modern art cinema more generally. Thus, in doing so, I side with Galt and Schoonover's broader proposal that 'impurity' may be a defining 'principle' of art cinema itself, wedged as it is between Hollywood and the avant-garde, aesthetically and institutionally belonging fully to neither the world of experimental nor mainstream cinema; an interstitial, hybrid and international category that, in important ways, shows us the uselessness of 'constant melodramatic binary opposition[s]' such as the one between modernism and realism.[42]

In profound ways, as Noa Steimatsky in particular has argued, both 'modernism' and 'realism' co-exist in Antonioni's cinematic (and in fact, also pre-cinematic) career.[43] In this respect, what is often seen as his tendency towards 'abstraction' is perhaps none other than a manifestation of an assiduous, active engagement with the reality around him, and therefore also with the forms of expression developed to address our world (even if such forms may ostensibly seem to be departing from, or rejecting, representation of the world). In an essay that ended up in *The Open Work* (1962/1967), and in which *L'eclisse* features as an important example, Eco argued for an understanding and employment of 'form' – and experimental, seemingly less realistic, if not abstract or abstract*ing* form in particular – in terms of a 'commitment to reality':

> [T]he only meaningful way in which art can speak of man and his world is by organising its forms in a particular way and not by making pronouncements with them. Form must not be a vehicle for thought. It must be a way of thinking . . . The real content of a work is the vision of the world expressed in its way of forming.[44]

If this sounds Adornian in some respects, there is a more active sense of involvement and engagement with reality *through* form in Eco's notion, which resorts to the word '*impegno*' (meaning 'commitment', 'pledge' or 'obligation') than in the critique by withdrawal hypothesised by Adorno. Eco's understanding of form – or 'the way of forming' – as a dynamic, experimental process that develops in response to a changing reality chimes with how Antonioni would (as he started doing during his talk at CSC in the early 1960s) continue to talk of his sense of the inadequacy of established 'forms' throughout and beyond the decade. 'Traditional images', he noted in 1970, 'are no longer capable of representing the world . . . There is a need, I think, to recommence from zero to experiment with new ways of representation. It is a process already under way'.[45] These 'new ways of representation' being tried out cannot, in turn, be other than provisional themselves, open to change: 'We no longer know what to call "art", what its function is and even less what function it will have in the future. We only know that it is something dynamic'.[46] So, in profound ways, the impurity of Antonioni's aesthetics – and one must also think of how such aesthetics changed *throughout* his career, and *after* the 1960s – stems from an enduring commitment to reality, a changing reality whose expression or 'thinking', as Eco puts it, requires formal experimentation. Form itself cannot be other than a perpetual work in progress. Looking back to Antonioni's career in the mid-1980s, in light of the director's forays into 'impure' forms of painting that embraced photography as well as cinema with the series *Le montagne incantate* [*The Enchanted Mountains*], the Italian art historian Giulio Carlo Argan noted that Antonioni preferred to be a 'prisoner' of cinema rather than a 'master' of it. The idea of the prisoner of a medium may seem to run counter to a pursuit of hybridity and impurity. Yet, what Argan perceptively suggests is that it is only by approaching cinema with the mindset of a 'prisoner', 'living it from the inside', that Antonioni could recurrently plot and practise his escape from it, 'reserv[ing] to himself the unlimited right to transgress it'.[47]

THE MASS IMAGE

Galt and Schoonover note that 'art cinema' is often seen 'as elitist and conservative', if not 'retrograde'.[48] This perception began to emerge in the course of the 1960s and 1970s, just as art cinema itself fully coalesced into a discernible category. Caught between (re)considerations of Hollywood and mass media culture on the one hand, and movements such as 'direct cinema' and 'third cinema' on the other, art cinema was often seen as 'the kind of cinema to be fought', as Steve Neale put it in 'Art Cinema as Institution' (1981), the Eurocentric 'bastion of "high-art" ideologies'.[49] At face value, the minimal, yet sleek style of Antonioni's 1960s films might well embody the 'perfect cinema – technically and artistically masterful', which Julio García Espinosa, in his manifesto 'For an Imperfect Cinema' (1969) defines as 'almost always reactionary'.[50] Yet, not only were Antonioni's films of the 1960s themselves films of relatively modest means (budgetary constraints afflicted both *L'avventura*, which almost never got finished, and *Il deserto rosso*). They were also, as mentioned, the product of the spirit of experimentation, unafraid of commerce and contamination with the world in the broadest sense of the word, while simultaneously trying to understand it.

Antonioni and the Aesthetics of Impurity looks at Antonioni's dialogue with other, traditionally defined arts such as painting (post-war abstraction in particular) in Chapter 1, and music in Chapter 3. But even as it does so, it is the renewed attention to, and preoccupation with, the mass image in the decades after the war which constitutes the crucial aspect of the context to which this book links Antonioni's films of the 1960s, and seeks to account for their innovative impurity and critical intermediality. The horrors of World War II contributed to a sense of the 'inadequacy' of mechanically produced images, such as photography and film, to represent reality: for many, 'the photographically generated image came to be seen forever doomed by its inherent paucity'.[51] But in the wake of the boom of what, even before the full diffusion of television, had been labelled the 'culture industry', such concerns about a structural insufficiency of the image were yoked to anxiety about the proliferation and ubiquity of images in an age of visual mass media and the emergence of a global visual culture.

If in the 1920s and 1930s critics such as Kracauer had worried about the 'blizzard' of photographs in print media, the degree of concern hit a whole new level in the ensuing decades because of television's invasion of the home with an overabundant 'flow' of images.[52] About a decade before McLuhan popularised the idea of an age of visuality in *The Gutenberg Galaxy* (1962), whose long-view of culture dates such dominance all the way back to the invention of print media, Lewis Mumford had noted the 'ubiquitous' distribution of 'the picture' with palpable alarm. Humanity had not only become progressively more 'picture-oriented', but 'overwhelmed' by this mode of relating to the world, to the point that 'an ever-rising flood of images . . . in every sort of medium – the camera and printing press, by motion picture and by television' was replacing 'actual experience' of the world and damaging the ability for 'attentive concentration'.[53] If for McLuhan television in fact held the promise of a rebalancing of culture towards the auditory, more or less overt reflections on the primarily visual orientation of mass media and mass culture – by Henri Lefebvre, McDonald, Morin, Eco – abounded in the wake of the medium's diffusion.[54] As the Heideggerian author of a treaty 'against the image' that Antonioni had in his library put it in 1963: 'modern man feeds on images' (see Chapter 4).[55] And, indeed, in that same year, the *Almanacco letterario Bompiani*, an annual volume dedicated to a round-up of cultural, literary and artistic trends (of which, unsurprisingly, Marcello Mastroianni's Giovanni in *La notte* is a reader) was dedicated to this 'civilisation of the image [*civiltà dell'immagine*]'. In his contribution to the volume, the philosopher and painter Gillo Dorfles wrote: 'No epoch before ours has seen any given image – the face of a famous actress, a king in exile, a dictator, a box champion, a two-headed calf – multiplied by a thousand, by a million as in our age. The power, the impact of such images is proportional to the volume of their repetitions and to the rapidity of their replacement.'[56] *Antonioni and the Aesthetics of Impurity* seeks to outline an Antonioni that, through his films, participates in these debates and thinks about the image in *mass* media – as well as *inter*-medial – terms. Indeed, as the book suggests, this engagement on Antonioni's part makes mass visual culture both an object of critique and, somewhat counter-intuitively perhaps, a tool of cinematic renewal and self-critique.

CHAPTERS

While this book can, of course, be read sequentially, the chapters are arranged thematically and do not necessarily require it. The exception might be Chapter 1, on Antonioni and pictoriality, which conceptually precedes and contextualises the others. Here, I consider how the trope of cinematic purity attached to Antonioni's 1960s films is intertwined with another persistent critical trope: that he approaches cinema like a painter. Yet, I argue that despite still dominant paradigms of pictorial purity, Antonioni approached painting not only as a concrete, material activity in which he himself was engaged, but also as a category that, around the mid-twentieth century, was itself in profound transformation and often ostentatiously 'impure'. Impure pictoriality, as I argue, provided Antonioni with the conceptual means to renew, rather than purify, cinema, through an exchange with a form already contaminated by the cinematic and other forms of mass media culture. Chapter 2 addresses the perceived turn to 'interiority' of Antonioni's cinema during the course of the 1960s, often described as an 'interior neorealism' or a quintessentially psychological cinema. Such turn, often associated with a breakdown of narrativity and a changed temporal economy, is generally enlisted as another factor fostering increased cinematic purity. Yet I consider how it can be better understood by examining its entanglement with the diffusion of television. In the wake of its mass diffusion in the 1950s, this new medium, transmitting an externally generated 'flow' of images inside the home, gave rise to new temporal and viewing economies, as well as preoccupations about its effects on viewers' interiority: their minds. Starting with a discussion of *L'avventura* and *La notte*, I consider how the new temporal aesthetics of Antonioni's cinema may be both a consequence of and a reaction to the televisual. I then conclude with *Il deserto rosso* to address how television's dynamics of interiority and exteriority are in turn connected with the then-emerging fields of cybernetics and early computers, with which Antonioni, like other 'moderns', was fascinated. Chapter 3 turns to relations between sound and image. It explores how the ostensibly quieter films of the 1960s – in which dialogue becomes sparser and from which extra-diegetic musical soundtrack is all but eliminated – have crucial affinities with contemporaneous transformations in music itself, where the diffusion of new mass media technologies, such as audiotape and television, acted as powerful catalysts for experimentation with noise and attention to soundscape. In particular, I trace here a connection with the experimental practices of John Cage, *musique concrète*, and composers including Luciano Berio, Bruno Maderna and Luigi Nono associated with RAI Studio di fonologia musicale. Chapter 4 considers Antonioni's thematisation of photography in and beyond *Blow-Up* (1966), in the context of the post-war proliferation of media images and image culture. It argues that if photography and what Vilém Flusser more broadly terms 'technical images' affect Antonioni's cinema, his cinema in turn also demonstrates a commitment to reflect on such proliferation, and engage film, as itself a medium of technical images, in a self-critique of the role of the image in mass media culture. Chapter 5 concludes by exploring how Antonioni's engagement with photography also produces an aesthetics: an aesthetics that may be seen as provocatively *uncinematic*. I consider how photography and its characteristic stillness are implicated in an intermedial re-articulation of the cinematic image through which means – or, in fact, media – usually called upon to alleviate boredom are harnessed to make boredom manifest aesthetically, and even to encourage its production during consumption of the work as a form of resistance and critique.

NOTES

1. Antonioni, 'La malattia dei sentimenti', p. 27. The text was first published in *Bianco e nero*, no. 2–3 (February–March 1961) from a talk delivered at the Centro Sperimentale di Cinematografia in Rome on 16 March 1961. It appeared in English as 'The Malady of Feelings' in *Film Culture* (Spring 1962), and under the title 'A Talk with Antonioni on His Work' in Antonioni, *The Architecture of Vision*.
2. Dewey, *Art as Experience*, pp. 235, 237.
3. The essay was translated as 'In Defense of Mixed Cinema' by Hugh Gray, in Bazin, *What Is Cinema?* Vol. 1, from which I quote, p. 55.
4. McLuhan, *Understanding Media*, p. 35.
5. Nowell-Smith, *Making Waves*, p.159. See also Nowell-Smith, *L'avventura*.
6. Rascaroli and Rhodes, 'Interstitial, Pretentious, Alienated, Dead' in Rascaroli and Rhodes, *Antonioni: Centenary Essays*, esp. pp. 3–4; Betz, *Beyond the Subtitle*, p. 2.
7. See also Rascaroli and Rhodes, 'Interstitial, Pretentious, Alienated, Dead', p. 3.
8. 9C, fasc. 109, Michelangelo Antonioni Archive, Ferrara.
9. Galt and Schoonover, 'Introduction: The Impurity of Art Cinema', in Galt and Schoonover, *Global Art Cinema*, p. 5.
10. Agamben uses the term 'dys-chrony' in 'What is an Apparatus?', p. 41.
11. Smithson, 'A Tour of the Monuments of Passaic, New Jersey' (first published in *Artforum*, December 1967), in Flam, *Robert Smithson*, pp. 73, 72.
12. Antonioni's famous exchange with Rothko was first reported by Gilman, 'About Nothing – with Precision'.
13. McLuhan popularised the term with *The Gutenberg Galaxy* and *Understanding Media*. See also Mirzoeff's *How to See the World* for a reflection on 'global visual culture'.
14. Adorno and Horkheimer, 'The Culture Industry'; McDonald, 'A Theory of Mass Culture'.
15. Morin, *L'Esprit du temps*, p. 65.
16. Alloway, *The Venice Biennale 1895–1968*, p. 149.
17. Judd, 'Specific Objects' (1965), p. 181; Higgins, 'Intermedia' (first in *Something Else Newsletter*, 1966), p. 49.
18. See, for example, Simondon, *On the Mode of Existence of Technical Objects*.
19. Barker, *Against Transmission*, p. 123.
20. VanderBeek, 'Culture: Intercom and Expanded Cinema', p. 15.
21. Sontag, 'One Culture and the New Sensibility'.
22. Tinazzi, 'The American Experience' (first published in *Jeune Cinéma*, March 1969), p. 313.
23. Agamben, 'What Is the Contemporary?', p. 41.
24. Ibid., pp. 41, 45.
25. Ibid., p. 41.
26. Antonioni, *Sei film*, p. xvi ('Cominciando a capire il mondo attraverso l'immagine, capivo l'immagine'). Cf. 'Preface to Six Films', p. 66.

27. Canudo, 'The Birth of the Sixth Art'.
28. Antonioni, 'Pazienza del cinema' (first in *Cinema*, January 1949), pp. 148, 149.
29. See, for example, Pirandello, 'Will the Talkies Abolish the Theatre?' and Bazin 'Painting and Cinema'.
30. Kracauer, *Theory of Film*; Deren, 'Cinematography: The Creative Use of Reality'.
31. Badiou, 'The False Movement of Cinema', p. 88; Rancière, *Aesthetics and Its Discontents*, p. 83.
32. Arnheim, *Film as Art*, p. 25. (The essays in the first part of this book first appeared in German in 1932, but the English language book, published in 1957, also contains a selection of later essays.)
33. Arnheim, 'The New Laocoön', p. 208.
34. Greenberg, 'Avant-Garde and Kitsch' was first published in *Partisan Review* in Autumn 1939 and 'Towards a Newer Laocoön' followed a year later. Greenberg, 'Modernist Painting', which was first a talk in a radio broadcast as part of *Forum Lectures: Voices of America* in 1960, and then published in *Arts Yearbook* in 1961, is one of the exemplary texts of his position. For Barbaro and Chiarini's positions, see Barbaro, *Poesia del film*, and Chiarini, *Arte e tecnica del film*.
35. Bonitzer, *Le Champ aveugle*, p. 88; Deleuze, *Cinema II*, pp. 5–9 (p. 5 cited); Gandy, 'The Cinematic Void'.
36. Eco pitted the then dominant idealist aesthetics of Benedetto Croce against Dewey's philosophy in his *Opera aperta*. The book, itself an 'open work', went through three different editions in Italian (1962, 1967 and 1971). No integral translation of it has appeared in English, but a selection of the essays has been published as *The Open Work*.
37. Nagib and Jerslev, 'Introduction', p. xvii.
38. Bazin, 'In Defense of Mixed Cinema', p. 56.
39. Rascaroli and Rhodes, 'Interstitial', p. 7.
40. Bazin, 'In Defense of Mixed Cinema', p. 74.
41. Adorno, 'Transparencies on Film', p. 203.
42. Galt and Schoonover, 'Introduction: The Impurity of Art Cinema', pp. 6, 7 and 17. See also King, *Positioning Art Cinema*.
43. Steimatsky, *Italian Locations*, esp. pp.1–39. Steimatsky also considers Antonioni's photo-essay 'Per un film sul fiume Po [For a Film on the River Po]', published in *Cinema* (25 April 1939).
44. Eco's essay 'Del modo di formare come impegno sulla realtà' first appeared in the Italian journal *Menabò* in 1962. It was not included in the first Italian edition of *Opera aperta* (1962), but it featured in the substantially different second edition of 1967, which is still largely the edition currently in print. The essay was translated into English as 'Form as Social Commitment', and is included in the English version of Eco, *The Open Work*, from which I cite here, p. 142.
45. Antonioni, 'Let's Talk about *Zabriskie Point*', p. 100.
46. Antonioni, 'Apropos of Eroticism' (originally in *Playboy*, November 1967), pp. 154–5.

47. Giulio Carlo Argan in *Antonioni: Le montagne incantate*, p. 13.

48. Galt and Schoonover, 'Introduction: The Impurity of Art Cinema', p. 5.

49. Neale, 'Art Cinema as Institution', p. 12.

50. Espinosa, 'For an Imperfect Cinema' (first published in *Cine Cubano*, 1969), p. 24. Rocha, 'An Aesthetic of Hunger'.

51. Schoonover, *Brutal Vision*, p. xiii.

52. Kracauer, 'Photography', p. 58. Williams, *Television*.

53. Mumford, *Art and Technics*, p. 96.

54. McLuhan, *The Gutenberg Galaxy*, pp. 24–31; and McLuhan and Powers, *The Global Village*, esp. pp. 37–46. See Lefebvre, *The Critique of Everyday Life*, vols 1–3. McDonald, 'A Theory of Mass Culture'; Morin, *The Stars* and *L'Esprit du temps*; Eco, *The Open Work* and *Apocalypse Postponed*.

55. Munier, *Contre l'image*, p. 21.

56. Dorfles, 'Civiltà (e inciviltà) dell'immagine', p. 67.

CHAPTER 1

Impure Pictoriality: The Matter of Painting

Alongside purity, one of the most frequent tropes that critics would attribute to Antonioni's cinema is pictoriality.[1] Not unlike Pier Paolo Pasolini, Andrei Tarkovsky and Ingmar Bergman, Michelangelo Antonioni is a director whose films are insistently associated with painting. Whether because of the care that Antonioni is seen to take in composing his images, or – starting with *Il deserto rosso/Red Desert* (1964) – the distinctive use he makes of colour, film scholars have often attributed a 'pictorial style' or 'pictorial effect' to his cinema, as Seymour Chatman and Sam Rohdie, among others, have put it.[2] The film director, in short, is seen to approach cinema *like a painter*, or, as the critic and curator Dominique Païni recently argued, through the 'constant perspective of a painter. Of an abstract painter, to be precise'.[3] In fact, these two persistent critical tropes are also persistently intertwined: it is not so much *despite* but, rather, precisely *because of* its pictorial qualities that Antonioni's cinema is also associated with ideas of purity, seen to be engaged in a cleansing of film that leads it towards the abstraction, if not the 'emptiness', of the image.[4] Thus, echoing the comparison that Antonioni allegedly drew between the 'nothing' in the colour-field canvases of Mark Rothko and in his own films, scholars including Angela Dalle Vacche and Steven Jacobs have associated the director with an 'abstract sensibility' in pursuit of 'the sublimity of emptiness' closely attuned to mid-twentieth-century painting.[5]

Yet, if Antonioni 'does approach cinema like a painter', as Laura Rascaroli and John David Rhodes have recently concurred, then this is indeed one of the factors, as they also point out, that makes his films 'impure'.[6] Given these premises, what might it mean to re-assess the critical trope that Antonioni's perspective is that of a painter – if not, more specifically, as Païni puts it, of 'an abstract painter' – by taking it as literally as possible? This is not a wild suggestion, for painting was undeniably very important to the director, as he himself acknowledged on repeated occasions, not only as something *to look at*, but also as something that he *did* – an activity in which he engaged more or less throughout his whole life.[7] The Antonioni archive holds a collection of approximately 400 pictorial works by the director. The best-known part of this oeuvre is *Le montagne incantate* [*The Enchanted Mountains*], first exhibited at the Museo Correr in Venice in 1983.[8] This and later exhibitions notwithstanding, Antonioni engaged with painting without overt artistic ambitions (a modality of approach which, I believe, is also significant, as we shall see): 'I'm not a painter, more a filmmaker who paints', as he would tend to put it.[9] As he painted assiduously in the late 1950s and early 1960s, partly as a way of experimenting with colour as he was preparing to turn to colour film, it is presumable that he thought about the paintings around him in their materiality and as the result of the practice of painting too.[10] Certainly, as Antonioni explained in the 1980s, his fascination with the 'matter of painting' – the material qualities of paint and its support, such as texture – was one of the reasons for resorting, not without paradox, to photographic enlargements of portions of his own pictorial work in *The Enchanted Mountains* series.[11]

It is chiefly by maintaining focus on a material concreteness of painting and, because of this, a continuing connection of the medium with external reality even in its most abstract forms, that I seek here to reconsider a still dominant understanding of Antonioni's cinema as both pure, if not abstract, and indebted to painting, if not itself pictorial. Certainly, at a first level, what Antonioni described as his 'great love for painting' and 'modern art' constitutes one of the ways in which he continued to observe, absorb and reflect on reality and the world around him.[12] It is within this broader perspective that this chapter considers how, conceptually and materially, Antonioni *used* painting as an object and activity through which to think about and practise cinema. In this respect, even if Antonioni, so to speak, took abstraction *from* painting *for* his cinema, abstraction itself is not opposed to or incompatible with realism or reality. On the contrary, it may be a mode of realism, a way of engaging with reality – and not only a transcendental or spiritual reality, à la Wassily Kandinsky or Piet Mondrian, but also an external reality, à la Fernand Léger, or a material reality, as in the various concrete-art movements, such as the Italian MAC (*Movimento arte concreta* or Concrete Art Movement), that flourished in the inter and post-war periods. If, more than simply keeping 'in touch with the latest work being done in art', as he said, Antonioni actively pursued the pictorial in his cinema, then such intermedial transit also offers itself as an articulation of what Agamben – as I mentioned in the Introduction – terms 'contemporariness'. Antonioni's cinematic absorption of painting constitutes a way of being immersed in his reality through a position of dissymmetry: a 'diffraction' rather than a 'reflection', as Karen Barad might put it, critically aware of one's own formative role in the re-production of reality.[13]

In fact, as I want to suggest, Antonioni's interest in painting, materially real and concrete (as both an object of contemplation and an activity that he himself pursued) even when abstract, attuned him to the fact that painting itself was not static, unchanging or lacking in movement, so to speak, but, particularly around the mid-twentieth century, a category in profound, radical transformation. Indeed, much of the painting around – and the kind of painting for which Antonioni seemed to have a predilection – might even have been called, as someone put it in a question to him in 1961, 'non-painting'.[14] Notwithstanding critical attempts to dematerialise painting, abstraction in particular, and present it in terms of purity, from the late 1940s there had been much pictorial work (including, possibly, Rothko's own) that displayed its physical concreteness and impurity. If the pursuit of pictoriality is one of the factors that makes Antonioni's cinema impure, perhaps 'impurity', and intermediality, is also what Antonioni observed in, and took from, painting itself.

PICTORIAL PARADIGMS

It is especially the films from the central period of Antonioni's career, in the 1960s, that tend to be aligned with notions of cinematic purity. As mentioned above, this is the chief quality that may lead them towards 'abstraction' – by which, ostensibly, is meant a degree of disengagement from realistic representation (or from the so-called 'illusion' of reality), in favour of a concentration on cinematic form *per se*, irrespective of its referential or depictive content. Indeed, abstraction in this sense may even be associated (as commentators from a diverse range of fields, including Pascal Bonitzer, Gilles Deleuze and, more recently, the historical geographer Matthew Gandy, have put it) with a drive to 'void' the cinematic image, push it towards 'emptiness' – often by filming fog, mist, blank walls or deserts.[15]

While still part of the critical tropes about Antonioni's work, these interpretations were delineated and cemented at the time of the films' original releases, when debates about the defining, unique or essential attributes of film that had occupied avant-garde filmmakers and early critics in the 1920s, were still raging – or raging with renewed energy.[16] (Of course, part of the problem for the inability to settle such debates, and for the co-existence of wildly competing notions and definitions, lay in the very hybridity of cinema in the first place, a medium that confounded Gotthold Lessing's influential division between 'arts of space' and 'arts of time', could combine visual, narrative, textual and aural elements and, moreover, 'captured' likenesses of reality automatically through photochemical technology.) In the 1960s and early 1970s then, enthusiasts including Georges Sadoul and Alberto Moravia might extol films as different as *La notte* (1961) and *Zabriskie Point* (1970) as paragons of a 'pure' art, while sceptics such as Edoardo Bruno, the editor of the Italian journal *Filmcritica* – in principle not hostile to the quest for the 'specifically filmic' – might condemn *L'avventura* (1960) for its 'formal drifts' away from realism and towards 'empty and unconsidered abstraction'.[17]

Given the emphasis on what may be purely or specifically *of* a given medium, it is certainly interesting that such qualities accrue to Antonioni's cinema even if – or perhaps, paradoxically, because – it is also at the same time deemed to be strongly linked to painting, aligned with a 'pictorial style' or 'effect'.[18] While seeing Antonioni's cinema as both 'pure' *and* 'pictorial' engenders a conceptual difficulty or contradiction, given that the alleged pursuit of the pictorial in the moving image is an inherently intermedial strategy, the contradiction or difficulty is not generally noted as such. Rather, painting seems to function not only as a paradigm *of* purity, but also as a tool *for* cinematic purity. In the (not always spoken) context of a hierarchy of art forms, the finest of the fine arts, that is, might provide a boost to cinema, helping to elevate and decontaminate it from its mass-medium connotations.

Often, Antonioni's affinity with fine art is demonstrated by pointing to the influence of paintings by Mario Sironi, Giorgio De Chirico and Giorgio Morandi in the 'tetralogy'.[19] Besides the actual presence of work by these artists in the films, Antonioni's dialogue with them is seen to reside in the way in which the director's images appear emphatically arranged and composed – indeed, in this sense, more like a painting that one 'makes' than a photographic or filmic image that, especially before digitality, was felt at least in part to be 'found' in or 'taken' from reality. Although Antonioni himself would, unsurprisingly perhaps, deny framing a shot with 'a particular painter or painting in mind',[20] De Chirico's 'pittura metafisica' of nearly empty townscapes, for instance, seems undeniably evoked in the very way in which the director captures and works on (even if only through framing, angle and lens used) a location he finds, such as the modern, yet abandoned Sicilian village in *L'avventura*, or the Via Pietro Alighieri in the historic centre of Ravenna in *Il deserto rosso*, whose pavement and buildings, moreover, were painted white and filmed with blue filters on the camera lens so as to appear greyish.[21] But if Antonioni's 'pictorial style' or 'effect' is thus understood in the sense of flaunting the composition of cinematic images *as pictures* – to give them the look of having being *made* – it is also seen to distance such images from more conventional representational or realistic ends. It is in this respect that his cinema's dialogue with painting is generally seen to reach an apex at the high-modernist moment of abstract expressionism, if in its post-gestural or, as Clement Greenberg described it, 'post-painterly' manifestation in the work of artists such as Rothko, Barnett Newman and Clyfford Still, where the paint on the canvas does not overtly bear the expressive gestural marks of its application by the artist's hand.[22] As a 1965 review of *Il deserto rosso* in *Sight and Sound* put it, the film sought to achieve 'purely pictorial effects the way an abstract, modernist artist wants to paint about painting itself'.[23] Indeed, despite the fact that in the early-1940s Antonioni had already seen in the abandonment of black and white 'a new gleam of hope for cinema's future',[24] the much-reported admiration for Rothko's large canvases is deemed to have contributed to Antonioni's turn to, and peculiar use of, colour for *Il deserto rosso*.[25] The director himself wrote to the painter that he had seen the latter's 1962 retrospective in Rome four times. In this context, the meeting during which, as Richard Gilman first reported in 1962, Antonioni allegedly said to Rothko: 'your paintings are like my films – about nothing, with precision', is thus taken as the expression of a profound correspondence.[26]

While such correspondence may have both formal and metaphysical connotations (the latter of which Gilman warns against by pointing out that 'nothing' is not 'nothing*ness*'), its main pivot is the alignment of an exemplary model of 'pure' painting with an equivalent one of 'pure' cinema – through which the latter is also elevated to the prestige of the former. The equation may seem to be between Antonioni's cinema and Rothko's paintings, yet the unspoken mediator for such alignment is modernist art criticism, particularly that of Greenberg. Twenty years after essays such as 'Avant-Garde and Kitsch' (1939) and 'Towards a Newer Laocoön' (1940) on the dangers of confusion *between* art and non-art, and *within* the arts, Greenberg was reinforcing and finessing his position through a focus on painting (and sculpture).[27] In 'Modernist Painting' (1961), 'purity' is a goal at both trans-disciplinary and intra-disciplinary level: something that modernism seeks to achieve in general, but through the particular, individual discipline, as a search for 'the unique and proper area of competence of each art' that acknowledges the 'limitations' or 'boundaries' of the medium.[28] In painting, such limitations – which Greenberg identifies with the two-dimensionality and the shape of the canvas, 'flatness and the delimitation of flatness' – find exemplary realisation in abstraction.[29] While such realisation is not exclusive to abstraction, abstraction itself guarantees most easily the exclusion of 'effects' 'that might conceivably be borrowed from or by the medium of any other art' – such as literature, theatre or sculpture when paintings depict events, objects or people as if in time or three-dimensional space.[30]

It is this model that Gilman implicitly uses when he aligns Antonioni's cinema and Rothko's painting, assigning to them a rejection or loosening of representation in a realistic or mimetic sense. There is, however, a slight frisson. For it is not so much that each medium pursues such a path in its own way, but that painting provides a model that cinema seeks to approximate. Although not as abstract as Hans Richter's *Rhythmus 21* (1921) might be (their difference from 'the purely abstract film and the work of the American underground' is mentioned at a point), Antonioni's films are, according to Gilman, 'about nothing *in particular*, being instead, like most recent paintings, self-contained and absolute'. It is such being 'about nothing *in particular*' that endows Antonioni's films with a pictorially inspired path towards abstraction that makes them, in this assessment, paradoxically 'more purely cinematic' and thus 'revolutionary' in their achievement.[31]

Although over fifty years old now, Gilman's contemporaneous assessment – in its absorption of then prevalent models of purity and separation of the arts, and eulogies of abstraction – remains representative of the way in which purity, painting, abstraction and even emptiness are put in relation to each other when talking about Antonioni's cinema. For Bonitzer writing in the 1980s, Antonioni's cinema is that of a 'modern painter' because of what the French critic sees as a search for the 'formless' (intended as an avoidance of clear-cut, realistic representation, perhaps in the gestural manner of *art informel*), if not even, as we have seen, 'empty' images.[32] Not unlike the colour-field or (near-)monochromatic paintings of some abstract expressionism, where even geometrical or vaguely biomorphic shapes seem to have vacated the canvas, colours in Antonioni (including the blacks and whites of his pre-1964 films) are not simply attributes of the image, but intrinsically part of what the image is made of, according to Bonitzer. *La notte*, he writes, is not simply 'a film *in* black and white but *of* blacks and whites'. In *Cinema and Painting* (1996), Dalle Vacche, while suggesting that the influence of painting is 'baroque' as well as 'modernist' in *Il deserto rosso* (where, in her view, it is aligned with madness, excess and femininity through the character of Giuliana), remains anchored to the idea that it dislodges the cinematic image from realism, as a mode of engagement with external reality, and heightens its abstraction, formal purity and emptiness.[33] Thus *Il deserto rosso*, according to Dalle Vacche, is a 'double transgression': 'from a cinema of architecture to a cinema of painting, and . . . from neorealist documentation to pictorial abstraction', which offers 'visions so pictorial and so abstract that they push outward the boundaries of what until now we have considered acceptable for the visual track of a European art film.'[34] A few years later, Jacobs too sees a drive towards abstraction and, in fact, emptiness, in Antonioni's movies; and the way in which he describes it follows closely Greenberg's account of the 'limitations' – above all, the flatnesss – of painting. According to Jacobs, there is an equivalency between the pictorial, often wall-sized, flatness of Rothko's and Pollock's abstract paintings and the 'abstraction' 'realized by the two-dimensionality of many of Antonioni's images', focused as they are on large flat surfaces, such as walls and austere facades of modernist buildings, and on compressing optical distance between planes, through camera angles or even, in *Il deserto rosso*, the use of telephoto lenses.[35] Furthermore, through such strategies, Jacobs concludes, '[L]ike Rothko and Newman, Antonioni is an artist who explores the sublimity of emptiness'.[36] In essence, this is also the reading that Païni offers in his attribution to Antonioni of the 'constant perspective' of 'an abstract painter'.[37] Or that, in an essay specifically on Antonioni and Rothko, curator Jeffrey Weiss provides when (enticingly but also somewhat impressionistically) he suggests that the director's visual and narrative 'abstraction' might be an 'appropriation of Rothko's compositional image', albeit one that articulates the temporal dimension of the artist's abstract painting above all: a translation of the 'empty' canvas into 'empty' cinematic duration, or *temps mort*.[38]

From Gilman's early report onwards, what painting is seen to have provided to Antonioni is both a paradigm *of* purity for cinema and, perhaps more contradictorily, a vehicle *for* cinematic purity, if not emptiness. In other words, what pictorial abstraction – or, rather, a certain Greenbergian model of it which sees it as a pinnacle of achievement and critical self-definition – has recurrently been deemed to offer Antonioni's cinema is the ideal of, and the tool for, a loosening of realism, a disengagement with external reality and its materiality.

Yet abstraction and realism are not mutually exclusive or irreconcilable. Indeed, perhaps Antonioni's 'vision' has always been animated by a synthesis of the two, as Noa Steimatsky has argued by referring to his essay 'For a Film on the River Po' (1939), on which his first documentary film *Gente del Po* (1943–7) is based. In this illustrated essay, she suggests, a 'neorealist' content is articulated in 'modernist', and even 'abstract' terms. This interpenetration of modes is vividly clear in the format – that of the photographic essay – and the images used, the last one of which especially is an aerial view that 'abstracts' landscape into cartography, a high-angle view that returns in the film *Gente del Po* as a 'grasp of the landscape *as* cinematic image *in the process of being drained*'.[39] Or, as Karl Schoonover, Martine Beugnet and John David Rhodes have – differently – suggested, the impulse towards 'abstraction' in Antonioni might itself be a mode of representation of and engagement with reality, albeit one that does so through a kind of reduction and simplification of form.[40] For Schoonover, the walls so insistently recurring in Antonioni's films are not so much vehicles for emptiness and abstraction, but surfaces. Indeed, they are surfaces whose state of ruination and decay (Schoonover focuses on the example of *I vinti*/*The Vanquished*, 1948) brings forth their physical materiality.[41] According to Rhodes, Antonioni 'instructs us that abstraction is already promised by and embodied in the concretion of the particular, whose ipseity both hides and discloses the universal'.[42] In this respect, as both Rhodes and Beugnet consider, Antonioni's abstraction might be close to that described, before the emergence of abstract – or non-figurative – art as such, by the art-historian Wilhelm Worringer. In his 1908 book *Abstraction and Empathy*, Worringer sees 'abstraction' as a historically and culturally recurrent mode of coping with the torment generated by 'the unending flux of being', that enables 'wrest[ing] the object of the external world out of its natural context' and 'purifying' it through geometric stylisation and simplification.[43] Within this broader context, what I want to suggest here is that Antonioni engaged with painting – *abstract* painting, most often – with a clear awareness of its concrete materiality, entanglement with external reality and, even, impurity at a moment when the category of painting itself was in radical flux and transformation.

In painting, forms of abstraction have recurrently been understood or defined in terms of realism. 'Realism = Abstraction; Abstraction = Realism', Kandinsky wrote in *The Blue Rider Almanac* (1912).[44] If the reality at stake is supra-sensible and metaphysical for artists such as Kandinsky or Mondrian, it is an external or material one not only in the 'new realism' of Léger's near-abstract paintings of the 1920s but also, in the 1950s and 1960s, in Yves Klein's blue monochromes (included in the 'nouveau réalisme' movement that the critic Pierre Restany founded in 1960), and the 'concrete abstraction' of artists including Lucio Fontana, Bruno Munari and Alberto Burri.[45] Indeed, in this respect, Burri's practise of titling his works according to the materials and procedures employed (as in the series *Sacks, Plastics, Combustions*, etc.) outlines his ostensibly 'abstract' work, in the sense of being non-figurative, as what Emily Braun has called a 'material-based realism' and Germano Celant has described as 'a pleasure in the concrete'.[46]

Greenbergian criticism was a balancing act between acknowledging the materiality of the medium whose 'limits' gave painting definition, and deflecting attention from what, within it, may risk sallying that definition; such as the fact, as the critic admitted in 'Modernist Painting', that 'the first mark made on a canvas destroys its literal and utter flatness'.[47] Even as he was finessing it, Greenberg's model was far from solid or resistant to challenge or internal contradiction. To circumvent this, Greenberg had to offer a somewhat *de*materialised view of painting's materiality, one that shifted attention away from a close haptic engagement with surface and texture that may reveal a fundamental non-flatness, if not impurity, and towards 'strictly optical' qualities.[48] Thus, work such as Pollock's was described by Greenberg in terms of the 'all-over' quality of the surface.[49] The optical 'all-overness' ('a unity that should be immediately evident') of pictorial work would correspond to an 'at-onceness' of experience on the part of the viewer, able – and enabled by the work itself – to take it in 'only with the eye', 'at a glance . . . in an indivisible instant of time'.[50]

By the mid-twentieth century, however, many of the paintings around were ostentatiously material – even haptic rather than optical – *and* impure.

These characteristics could, in fact, apply to Pollock's own work (shown in Italy at the Venice Biennale in 1950), whose paint drips are not only thick and encrusted but also often embedded with 'foreign' stuff (like the cigarette butts, nails, buttons and key detectable in *Full Fathom Five,* 1947) visible when looked at up close. They would also describe a plethora of ostensibly 'pictorial' work, including: the scratches and graffiti of '*informel*' artist such as Jean Dubuffet and Wols; the punctured surfaces of Lucio Fontana's early *Spatial Concepts*, the *Buchi [Holes]* (1949–); the detritus of mass culture and printed matter in Robert Rauschenberg's *Red Paintings* (1953–) and *Combines* (c. 1954–); the rugged burlap and burnt plastic of Burri's aforementioned *Sacchi [Sacks]* (c. 1953–) and *Plastic Combustions* (c. 1957–); the seventy-four-metre canvas on rolls of Pinot Gallizio's *Industrial Painting* (1958); the bulges and creases of Piero Manzoni's kaolin-dipped canvases of the early *Achromes* (c. 1958–) and the estranged ordinariness of the cotton, fibre-glass and bread-rolls-based slightly later ones (c. 1961–2); and even Michelangelo Pistoletto's *Quadri Specchianti [Mirror Paintings]* (1962), that go beyond the 'limits' of painting by including viewers, and the temporally-extended performance or performativity of the encounter with art, in their mirror surfaces. This was all work that, in different yet connected ways, put pressure on notions of purity and separation of the arts by exploring the possibilities of contamination and boundary-crossing *between* art, mass media and 'life', as well as *within* art's various disciplines. Indeed, some of it did not look like a painting in a traditional sense, or even had any paint on it, let alone being compliant with Greenberg's requirement of two-dimensionality.[51] 'They were already the end of painting', Fontana later explained to Carla Lonzi of his late-1940s *Spatial Concepts*, reprising an often repeated declaration in the twentieth century.[52] At more or less the same time, an Italian art critic echoed this by reporting that, 'in the early 1960s', rather than 'paintings' (or 'sculptures'), 'all the younger artists were making "things", "objects", or "visual machines"'.[53] Along similar lines, in his 1969 book on the significance of the Venice Biennale as a 'communication system' for art, the British critic Lawrence Alloway remembered how, moving through the exhibition's 1958 edition, 'the effect of Fontana, Wols and Rothko', though in different pavilions, 'combined' to make it clear that something 'different' had started to emerge.[54] This was something that the 1964 Biennale's presentation of Pop art, where Antonioni, as David Alan Mellor has put it, had an 'epiphany on seeing Robert Rauschenberg's silkscreen paintings with their cornucopia of profane modern images', showed to be developing in further, yet still connected, directions.[55]

This is not to say that Antonioni cited from one – however diverse – group of paintings (or even 'things') rather than others. It is not, that is, to replace a pictorial model for another in his cinema, to substitute Rothko with Rauschenberg, or even Burri, whom, however, we know that the director also admired (the script for the unrealised film *Tecnicamente dolce* [*Technically Sweet*], drafted in 1966, at a point refers to walls 'like Burri's').[56] It is rather to say that Antonioni, as an avid observer of 'reality', assiduously 'absorbed contemporary visualities', as Mellor writes in relation to *Blow-Up* (1966) and its diffused pop sensibility.[57] As Mellor's sense of an aesthetic shift from Rothko to Rauschenberg (or Pop) between *Il deserto rosso* and *Blow-Up* suggests, perhaps Antonioni 'took' from all of the paintings he saw around him, and to seek to point to how a shot might be framed with 'a particular painter or painting in mind' would be somewhat to miss the point.[58] The pictoriality of Antonioni's cinema might be best understood not by focusing on individual paintings but by considering how the director confronted a category in radical transition. Indeed, rather than static pictures (and some of them were not even so any longer, for kinetic artists such as Gianni Colombo had sought to animate them via mechanical or other means by the late 1950s), Antonioni faced a pictorial in movement.[59]

The art historian Briony Fer has talked of Antonioni's films of the 1960s in terms of a migration of 'pictorial concerns' from art to cinema: that is, precisely at the moment when artists were turning against painting as traditionally defined, precipitating a crisis of the medium and that 'confusion of the arts' against which Greenberg warned, Antonioni seemed to be taking up the pictorial baton.[60] Yet, what Mellor calls the director's 'incorporation of contemporary visualities' means that, rather than from a clear-cut, stable and established sense of what painting might be, Antonioni was already 'taking from' a contested terrain undergoing radical reconfiguration (indeed, a reconfiguration to which mass media images – including cinema – were themselves, in different ways, contributing). Just as the 'purity' of painting was a rhetorical mirage rather than an actuality, so the definition and actual manifestation of painting were in flux. In this context, if the 'pictorial' having migrated to cinema is necessarily transformed by the very move itself, and thus intrinsically hybrid, the notion of a pictorial paradigm, or of pictoriality, does not emerge as an avenue for the purification and closure of (Antonioni's) cinema onto its own medium, or for its elevation through contamination with a 'higher' or 'fine' art at the most. On the contrary, it broaches the prospect for an even more complex, radical intermediality.

VERNACULAR PAINTING, 'PEDESTRIAN COLOUR'

As 'a filmmaker who paints', Antonioni's engagement with painting was doubly literal: he was absorbed by it as a material object of contemplation but, also, as a concrete activity that he himself pursued. There is a curious image in the Antonioni archive in Ferrara which helps to bring into focus the specific aspect of Antonioni's interest in the material reality of painting that I want to discuss. It is a postcard sent to the director by Richter, the avant-garde painter and filmmaker who, with *Rhythmus 21*, had produced what is often seen as one of the first examples of a 'pure', as well as 'abstract' cinema.[61] While the immediate occasion is to compliment the director on *Zabriskie Point* and what the German calls its 'good' style, Richter's own artistic pedigree is play- fully self-mocked in the card, which shows him up a ladder, propped against the façade of a house, wall-brush in hand.

To the sides of the image, the handwritten text remarks on the activity: 'Caro Antonioni, you see that I am not "only" making pictures'. The term 'pic- tures' is ambiguous, and could refer both to film (such as *Dreams That Money Can Buy*, 1947) or *Dadascope*, 1961 and painting – or, in fact, the painted wood reliefs Richter was mainly working on by that time, one of which, fixed to the outer wall of the house as a curious decorative feature or blind window, seems to be at the receiving end of Richter's brush. In any case, Antonioni must have tried to bring together both the postcard image and the surreal- dada vein of Richter's later work, for a subsequent letter by the German artist notes: 'Your suggestion to paint together your house or to tape a surrealistic dialogue is very enticing'.[62]

Figure 1.1   Hans Richter, postcard to Antonioni after the release of *Zabriskie Point*, 1970, courtesy Gallerie d'Arte Moderna e Contemporanea: Fondo Michelangelo Antonioni, Ferrara

So, here we are: on the one hand, a cult figure of the historical avant-garde, a largely abstract painter *and* 'father' of abstract cinema, champion – as he wrote in 1955 for the first issue of Jonas Mekas's *Film Culture* – of film 'as an original art form' focused on the 'essentially cinematic'.[63] On the other, one of the masters of modern(ist) art cinema, similarly routinely extolled – or criticised – for the cinematic purity, if not abstraction, of his films, who was also in his own turn, as we have seen, a painter. Yet, here, the two are wittily inviting each other to something as unartistic and vernacular, materially concrete and engaged with external reality as *decorating* (even, indeed, a decorating that has subsumed 'art' into itself, and which may be accompanied by a verbal modulation of surrealist-inspired chance encounters and juxtapositions).

While it is likely that the two never realised their plan, the image resonates with another, slightly earlier, image of vernacular painting involving Antonioni.

Figure 1.2 Painting the trees, *Il deserto rosso*, production still, 1964, courtesy Gallerie d'Arte Moderna e Contemporanea: Fondo Michelangelo Antonioni, Ferrara

The kind of painting going on here is a peculiar equivalent of the decorating captured in Richter's postcard. What is shown is the application of paint to a patch of trees in the industrial port of Ravenna where Antonioni shot *Il deserto rosso*, so that the pro-filmic reality that the director found could better fit the polluted, washed-out and decayed reality of the world that the director wanted to portray – or *make* – on screen. Antonioni's recourse to this kind of procedure, for *Il deserto rosso* and *Blow-Up* especially, is a well-publicised fact. The results of it are clearly visible at specific points in both films (with stretches of roads, buildings' facades, fences, and even grass and water, coloured according to the director's mandate), even if most flaunted in the earlier one.[64]

Figure 1.3a   Examples of pro-filmic paint in *Il deserto rosso* and *Blow-Up* (white-painted fruit)

Figure 1.3b   Examples of pro-filmic paint in *Il deserto rosso* (1964) and *Blow-Up* (1966) (red-painted shopfronts)

Antonioni, however, famously never got to shoot the white-painted forest captured in this photograph, as the lighting was not right on the morning of the shoot (he needed bad weather and it was sunny). So, he wrote about it, in fairly extensive detail, and published the short text as a preface to the book of the film script.[65] What the photograph, with the long extendable ladder and the person climbing up it to make the hose of the paint pump reach the tree top, begins to suggest, Antonioni's text makes clear. The painting at issue here is not abstract in any sense, nor particularly pure. As a painting *of* things – of 'nature', even – it is very concrete, and literally bound up with external reality, a reality which it contaminates (although Antonioni tells us that the paint is water-based), and by which it is also in turn, if not contaminated, then rendered prosaic even in its peculiarity. It is a complex operation and physical activity, and also indeed, as he writes, 'exhausting' labour, carried out through the night in sub-zero temperatures.[66] It is telling, I believe, that Antonioni did not seek to hide or be mysterious about his interventions with paint on the pro-filmic, but in fact liked to attract attention to them in their vernacular, material qualities, as with the vendor's painted fruit and cart in the film.

The materiality of paint and painting (as activity or, indeed, labour) which Antonioni's 'white forest' text seeks to capture, resonates with the high number of small pictorial compositions which, though undated, are deemed to have been produced in the period between the late 1950s and early 1960s (c. 1957–62).

Figure 1.4 Michelangelo Antonioni, *Untitled* (c. 1957–62), oil on paper, 167 mm × 120 mm, courtesy Gallerie d'Arte Moderna e Contemporanea: Fondo Michelangelo Antonioni, Ferrara

As Antonioni was hoping, and preparing, to shoot his first film in colour, he 'took up [his] brushes again to refamiliarise [himself] with colour', as he explained.[67] Generally in sizes of 35×25 centimetres or 16×12 centimetres, these small abstract compositions appear as a work of *working through*: pictorial techniques, styles, textures, juxtapositions of colours. In their totality, they present an 'image' of painting understood in terms of concreteness: materials and procedures which are tried out, tested, experienced *through practice*. This engagement of, and with, the materiality of painting, and colour, is also what *Il deserto rosso* itself does, in many ways.

The film's opening titles credit the use of 'Tintal' colours, a line of washable household paints launched by the manufacturer Max Mayer in the early 1950s (and whose development and specific function, as an industrial product for consumer use in the improvement of property, is emblematic of Italy's economic miracle and building boom in those years). If the relation of these colour-paints to Antonioni's interventions on the pro-filmic is not spelled out, the mention nevertheless attracts attention to colour as material – even, indeed, as product.[68] This materiality is foregrounded in the fictional world of the film, where Giuliana's project to open a shop offers occasions to see her surrounded by cans of paint (Tintal, presumably) and colour swatches on the walls (in what to some extent may also function as a self-reflexive enfolding of Antonioni's own pictorial interventions in the film's diegesis).

Figure 1.5a   Giuliana in the shop that she plans to open, with cans of paint and swatches on walls, *Il deserto rosso* (1964)

Figure 1.5b   Giuliana in the shop that she plans to open, with cans of paint and swatches on walls, *Il deserto rosso* (1964)

Put provocatively: if *Il deserto rosso* is informed by fine-art painting, it is also 'about' paint and painting in a more vernacular sense. Widely seen as the most pictorial and abstract of Antonioni's films because of its particular use of colour, the film is also profoundly engaged with the material reality – the prosaic concreteness – of painting. The recurrent colour swatches, paint cans and painted surfaces stand out as examples of, and attract attention to, the prosaic, quotidian, material reality of colour in the modern world that the film addresses. Indeed, in this sense, household paint, as a product *of* industry and *for* consumption, is exemplary not simply of a materiality of colour, but of its manifestation and circulation as, or within, mass-produced commodities.

Interviewers, including Jean-Luc Godard, would insistently try to attribute Antonioni's interventions on the pro-filmic and sometimes non-naturalistic use of colour to the 'spirit' of a painter seeking to move away from realism, if not reality, and towards abstraction.[69] Yet, Antonioni would consistently reply not only by denying any sort of 'pictorial research' ('we are far from . . . painting', he said to Godard) but also by placing emphasis on reality rather than abstraction – particularly the reality of colour, as an effect or product of industry that, from the emergence of colour printing in the inter-war period to the diffusion of colour plastics after the war, had fast become absorbed into the materiality of everydayness.[70] 'In *Red Desert*', as he explained after the film's release:

> we are in an industrial world which every day produces millions of objects of all types, all in colour. Just one of these objects is sufficient – who can do without them? – to introduce into the house an echo of industrial living. Thus, our houses are full of colour, and our streets and public spaces are full of colourful posters. With the invasion of colours, we have become addicted to them.[71]

He elaborated further after the release of *Blow-Up*, when quizzed about his dislike for 'real colours':

> It's untrue to say that the colours I use are not those of reality. They *are* real: the red I use is red, the green, green, the blue, blue, and the yellow, yellow . . . Think of what factories were like, especially in Italy at the beginning of the nineteenth century, when industrialisation was just beginning: grey, brown, and smoky. Colour didn't exist. Today, instead, almost everything is coloured. The pipe running from the basement to twelfth floor is green because it carries steam. The one carrying electricity is red, and that with water is purple.[72]

So, the colour at issue is a colour that is real but *made*, rather than *found*. It is a product of the 'industrial world', which has in turn coloured the world of industry, its factories, as *Il deserto rosso* shows, and our everyday reality: it has 'filled our homes, even revolutionised our taste'.[73] From this perspective, the famous party scene in the hut by the port, in which the use of red in particular, for the walls of the wooden shack, has drawn comparisons with the work of Rothko and Burri, is not merely a display of pictorial sensibility. If it points to the awareness of a pictorial paradigm in transformation, it does so above all through an attunement to the materiality of these practices. At a point when even fine-art painting was meeting, or even willingly going towards, the industrial and the prosaic, this is a materiality that, notwithstanding the works' abstraction or seeming withdrawal from representational content, bears the marks of its entanglement with reality. While this entanglement is less evident – to some extent resisted – in the work of Rothko, it is overt and literal in what Braun, as we have seen, calls Burri's 'material-based realism'.[74] If in Burri's works such as *Sacco e rosso* [*Sacking and Red*] (1954) or *Rosso plastica* [*Red Plastic*] (1961) paint is no more important than the humble and industrial materials of burlap and cellotex overtly displayed for what they are, what Antonioni calls 'the echo of industrial living' is present even in Rothko's work, where, as analyses have shown, diluted household paints, as well as more traditionally 'fine art' oils, are employed for the translucent layering on his canvases.[75] The tendency is to see the red in the shack especially as exemplary of Antonioni's pursuit of abstract painting, 'a highly abstract pictorial ground on which [the characters] can act', as Fer describes it.[76] Yet, for all its abstractness, it remains, unmistakably, vernacular red paint – unevenly applied, damaged and visibly touched up with different hues – on wooden planks; planks, in fact, that the characters at a point tear down to burn in the stove for warmth, in what David Forgacs has described as a 'happening-like' performance.[77]

Even though Antonioni might not have been familiar with Rauschenberg's work before seeing it at the 1964 Biennale, the director's attitude to colour and paint resonates with what the American artist described as 'pedestrian colour' – a description which in turn encapsulates the new ways of relating to the activity and materials of painting on the part of many artists in the post-war decades. The expression 'pedestrian colour' – which Rauschenberg used, for instance, for his *Red Paintings* of the early 1950s – evokes at least two ideas at once, as Helen Molesworth has suggested. On the one hand, the proximity to the word colour may make us read 'pedestrian' in the sense of ordinary, prosaic, even 'dull, average, not special'.[78] But this meaning stems from, and must be related to, pedestrian's primary meaning as 'on foot'. In this sense, the expression evokes the idea of colours experienced while walking and in 'movement through urban space'.[79] As in the *Red Paintings* layers of unevenly applied red paint cover, but do not completely hide, the fragments of consumer culture (advertising, print media, packaging) which Rauschenberg included in the works, 'pedestrian colour' thus evokes both the 'movement' through which such colourful materials are experienced on the street, and the sense of dreariness that insistent, repetitive presence engenders.

In many ways, Antonioni talked of colour in similar terms. He related it to ordinary – and, in both senses of the word, pedestrian – life (in the 'street' and 'public places', as well as the 'home', as we have seen above). A letter of 1962 (to his first wife Letizia Balboni) describes a temporary 'abstract painting' made of colourful 'rubbish' – 'pieces of paper: white, black, red, yellow, blue' – Antonioni one morning caught sight of, as the wind swept it up and pushed it against a metal-wire fence, along one of his 'usual' routes to work.[80] The image above encapsulates vividly how Antonioni understood colour as an experience of and in movement – even, indeed, routine or habitual movement. In this context, he also considered colour in relation to its functionality in daily existence. Remarks such as the one quoted above on the colour-coding of pipes or on the 'psycophysiology' of colour (raised with Godard) connect Antonioni's interests with contemporaneous debates on colour's practical role in modern living – and working.[81]

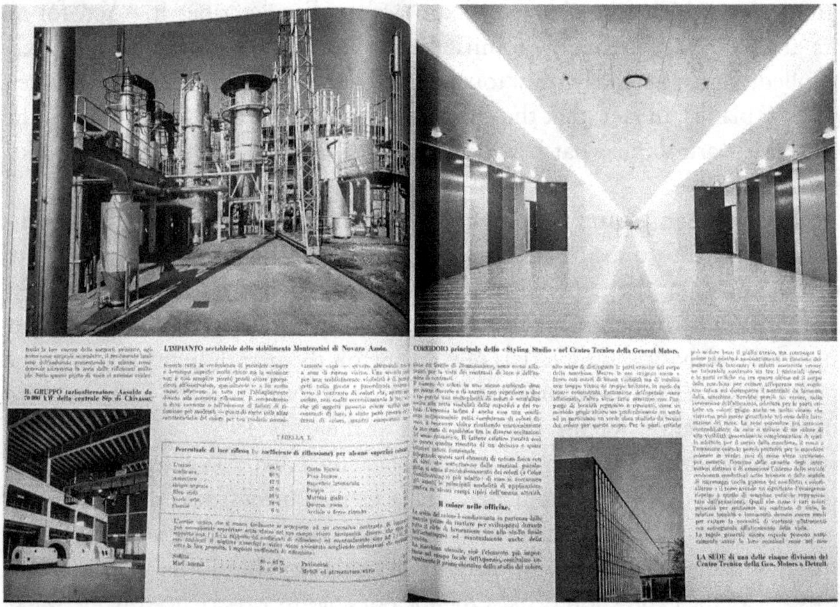

Figure 1.6 Double-page spread from article 'Funzione del colore [The function of colour]', in *Civiltà delle macchine* 6/2, (March–April 1958)

From the bright colours of factory machinery and pipes, to Giuliana's discussion with Corrado about the most suitable décor for her shop (whose colours, as she explains, should be neutral so as not to distract buyers from the merchandise), this functionality is addressed in *Il deserto rosso*, even if couched in what is generally understood to be Antonioni's aesthetisation of industrial modernity.

Writing as a film critic in the 1940s, Antonioni had invoked 'three-colour ads in illustrated magazines' not only because of their 'visual succulence', which could serve as a model for colour in film, but also because of their valence as 'impressions'.[82] 'Impressions last such a short time. Colours also last but a short time', he wrote.[83] In an earlier essay, Antonioni had drawn on Hegel's *Aesthetics* (1835), seeking to adapt the philosopher's attention to the interrelationship of colours in painting to cinema, where such 'dynamics' would be literally in movement, both within and between film frames.[84] If this awareness of colour being in movement *in film* recurs in film writing – from Sergei Eisenstein and Béla Balázs, whom Antonioni himself read, to Deleuze – the director seems to draw the understanding of colour as movement *from life itself*, where colour is encountered pedestrianly.[85] By the time of *Il deserto rosso*, where Antonioni addresses some of the consequences – if not the aftermath – of Italy's rapid industrialisation and economic miracle (which was itself slowing down by the early 1960s) in what is also in important respects a proto-ecological film, colours might have lost some of their prelapsarian succulence but are still 'impressions'.[86] Of his recourse to out-of-focus images, such as those filmed with a telephoto lens of Ravenna's industrial port in the opening-credits sequence, and short shots (very different from the generally longer takes of the trilogy, or the famous 'sequence shots' of *Cronaca di un amore/Chronicle of a Love Affair*, 1950), Antonioni explained: '[p]erhaps it was colour that engendered this requirement, this profound need to treat it in blots, as if they were pulsations penetrating confusedly into the character'.[87] Through the blur and short shots, Hegel's description of 'colour as an echo', by which Antonioni had been attracted in the 1940s, is brought to the service of the director's intention to render colour as 'an echo of industrial living' in *Il deserto rosso*.[88] Rather than a means for moving away from external reality and materiality, colour is rather a key conduit for an engagement with the world and its matter: 'What interests me now is to put the characters in touch with things, because today what counts are things, objects, matter'.[89]

The materiality of external reality – in both its ordinariness and fleetingness, as the expression 'pedestrian colour' may suggest – is overtly incorporated in the work of Rauschenberg, Burri or, to add a new example, Mimmo Rotella, whose torn posters and *décollages* came, quite literally to start, in the early 1950s, from the street. In the work of Rothko, however, this materiality, in its prosaicness and ephemerality, as well as for the 'impurity' it may bring to painting, seems more elusive, if not absent. How, then, might Antonioni's intense admiration for this artist's work, especially around the time that he was thinking about colour film and working on *Il deserto rosso*, be squared with the kind of understanding of painting, and pursuit of impure pictoriality, I have sought to attribute to Antonioni? I want to suggest not only that Antonioni perhaps appreciated precisely the material concreteness of Rothko's abstract paintings (aspects which were important to Rothko himself and, if more obliquely and tacitly, even to Greenberg's critical model), but also that he possibly saw in them an 'absorption' of that modern reality – and the world of mass media in particular – which they nevertheless so forcefully reject.

SCREEN/CANVAS: IMPRESSIONS AND DURATION

In May 1962, presumably after he had visited Rothko's studio in New York earlier in the year or in late 1961, when he had travelled there for the US premieres of *L'avventura* and *La notte* respectively, Antonioni wrote Rothko a letter.[90] The immediate reason for the correspondence is the communication of his preferences with regard to a painting that the artist had 'agreed to give' to the director. Antonioni wrote that, on hearing the news, he 'hurr[ied] back to Rome, to see one more time your exhibition [at the Galleria Nazionale d'Arte Moderna], which closes today'. He goes on to explain that '[t]his was the fourth time' he had visited the exhibition, a retrospective of the American artist's work curated by the gallery's director Palma Bucarelli in 1962: 'and each time, in these pictures that seem to be made of nothing, that is, made only of colour, I discover something new'.[91]

Where 'made of nothing' suggests that Antonioni is thinking of these paintings' abstraction, 'made only of colour' evokes the colour paint that they are made of, their materiality – albeit indeed a materiality in which the overt gesturality or evidence of personal execution à la Pollock or Willem De Kooning is absent. Rothko himself often insisted not only that his pictures were 'not abstract', but that he was a 'materialist', whose 'new areas of color are things', not symbols or forms of self-expression ('I express my not-self', he once said).[92] 'Mondrian divides a canvas', Rothko explained in an interview in 1952, 'I put things on it'.[93] Bucarelli took up this 'materialist' emphasis in her essay for the catalogue accompanying the exhibition, and even drove it towards the prosaic. In Bucarelli's view, the experience of Rothko's canvases, even though 'plain coloured surfaces', was 'plastic, tactile'.[94] Remarking on the luminosity emanating from the artist's canvases, she rejected 'mystical' connotations: for 'light . . . if the most subtle and rarefied of matters, is still nevertheless matter', and 'the film of oil paint . . . however thin, still has a body: like mica . . . or cellophane'.[95] Rothko's 'gesture', if there was one, was 'the ancient, confident, constant one of someone who decorates a wall'.[96]

But, as Bucarelli in fact also says in her essay, there is another aspect of the encounter with Rothko's work that Antonioni's account points to as important: temporality. Not unlike the painter's own prolonged contemplation of Henri Matisse's *Red Studio* (1911) at the Museum of Modern Art in New York in the late 1940s (which Rothko credited for the breakthrough in 1949 into his distinctive colour-field compositions), Antonioni's encounter is a repeated and protracted looking: he not only visited four times but, as he also writes, 'spent several hours in the exhibition'.[97] If Antonioni had talked of colour as movement, 'last[ing] but a short time', here, it seems, duration is key to the discovery of this work 'made only of colour'. Although there are various, slightly different accounts of Antonioni's visit to Rothko's studio, the duration of looking at the painter's colours is something that they all place emphasis on: 'Antonioni is capable of staying two hours in front of a painting', remembers Furio Colombo, the journalist who organised the meeting, while according to Robert Motherwell, who might also have been present on the occasion, 'Antonioni must have sat there an hour and a half without speaking a word'.[98]

What Antonioni seems to appreciate in Rothko's canvases, and how, is slightly different from the dominant critical model of the time. For Greenberg, work such as Rothko's or Newman's testified to 'a vision keyed to the primacy of color', but in a different sense from how Antonioni – as we saw earlier – thought of colour as 'real', concrete and even, as I suggested, pedestrian.[99] Writing about the exhibition of Rothko's work at the Biennale in 1958, the Italian art critic Gillo Dorfles presented them as 'the beginning of a new tonalism', 'completely different' from 'colour-material' and 'colour-pigment'.[100] Even nearly fifty years later, revisiting his encounter with the artist and his work in the United States, Dorfles stressed the way in which they constituted a '"return" to pure painting' – 'none of Pollock's tangles or dripping' – and 'achieved absolute abstraction'; a metaphysical or spiritual form of abstraction whose concreteness, as a concrete-art painter himself, Dorfles seems able to ignore or, indeed, transcend.[101] This echoes with Greenberg's sense that it was precisely the 'repudiation of virtuosity of execution' (in favour of what he also described as an 'anonymous' style), and renunciation of 'tactility' or 'painterliness' ('loose, rapid handling, or the look of it') in these colour-field paintings that contributed to increase their 'purity', 'optical clarity' and 'intensity'.[102]

Greenberg's disciple Michael Fried and the philosopher Stanley Cavell would, a few years later (in reference to work by Morris Louis, Kenneth Noland and Frank Stella, among others), harness these attributes, as well as

Greenberg's notion of 'at-onceness', to refine the idea of the aesthetic encounter with 'pure', modernist art as somewhat out of time. Since such art is 'wholly manifest' at 'every moment', as Fried put it, such encounter would be *in*tense, not *ex*tended: an 'instananeousness' and 'presentness' lifting the viewer *out of* the mere present.[103] By withdrawing gestural rhetoric and playing down execution, such works, as Cavell saw it, looked 'as if they might as well have been made instantaneously, and that their use should take no longer'.[104] The experience that they generate or encourage, even in the case of series, is one of 'total thereness' and 'simultaneity'.[105]

But what if, in this context but also against its grain, not unlike in Bucarelli's slightly divergent account, Antonioni saw in Rothko's work precisely a framing of colour in time, a durational unfolding of colour that the eye *watches*? Perhaps this experience of colour as something that unfolds and needs to be looked at over a period of time, counterbalanced, but also completed, his own understanding of colour as brief bursts, pulsations. In fact, as I want to suggest, there is a reciprocity between pictoriality and cinematicity in these artists' work, in the sense that they both absorbed the pictorial and the cinematic respectively while also, at the same time, resisting them. Where Rothko absorbed yet resisted the cinematic in his painting, so Antonioni absorbed yet resisted the pictorial in his cinema.

This reciprocity is implicitly summoned by Fer in her book *The Infinite Line: Remaking Art After Modernism* (2004). On the one hand, as we have seen (not unlike several other scholars), Fer sees Antonioni's cinema to be animated by pictorial concerns – or, as she puts it, by 'a persistent recall of the pictorial' in his cinematic 'procedure' at a time when artists seemed to be abandoning, dismantling or (remember Fontana) burying painting itself.[106] On the other hand, earlier in the book, she writes about Rothko in terms highly evocative of cinematic qualities in the painter's oeuvre. Citing Rothko, who wrote that 'by saturating the room with the feeling of the work the walls are defeated', she explains that the artist sought to 'prolong the encounter' with his work, 'as if entering a mesmeric world'.[107] 'This desire to "defeat the wall"', Fer continues, 'was at the same time the drive to create a scene of entrapment': through the work, the wall is turned into a kind of 'screen'.[108]

Of course, it is not possible to imagine Rothko, in his constant focus beyond 'material needs' and rejection of commercialisation and consumerism, as either a lover of movies or mass culture.[109] Indeed, though he admired *L'avventura* and *La notte*, precisely because he saw something different in them, Rothko, according to Colombo, 'did not have a relationship with cinema before, or after, Antonioni'.[110] However, the way in which he talked of painting in general and his work in particular is often very evocative of the cinematic. In his posthumously published writings on art (probably dating

to the early-1940s, just before the move to abstraction), he described painting in terms of both motion and duration. Pictorial plasticity, as he explains,
needs to engender 'movements' or 'rhythmic intervals' able to entertain what
he called not a viewer but a 'spectator':

> In painting, plasticity is achieved by a sensation of movement both into the
> canvas and out from the space anterior to the surface of the canvas. Actually,
> the artist invites the spectator to take a journey into the realm of the canvas.
> The spectator must move with the artist's shapes in and out, under and above,
> diagonally and horizontally; . . . This journey is the skeleton, the framework
> of the idea. In itself it must be sufficiently interesting, robust and invigorat-
> ing. That the artist will have the spectator pause at certain points and will
> regale him with especial seductions at others is an additional factor helping to
> maintain interest. In fact, the journey might not be undertaken at all were it
> not for the promise of these especial favors.[111]

As he subsequently elaborated, such durational journey inside the 'realm of
the canvas', 'with especial seductions' 'to maintain interest' works better with
large sizes. 'I paint very large pictures', he declared in 1951. 'The reason I
paint them, however', Rothko explained, 'is precisely because I want to be
intimate and human': just as he himself had to be 'in' the picture to paint it,
so the viewer – or spectator – should not be left 'outside' the experience, but
drawn in.[112] To this end, Rothko, who famously had exacting requirements
for the installation of his work, sought to hang 'his biggest paintings in the
smallest rooms in order to increase the sense of intimacy', seeking to set-up
what Fer – again, cinematically – calls a 'close-up view'.[113] Interviewed in the
mid-1950s, Rothko described the ideal installation of his work as 'like a little
chapel where the traveler, or wanderer, could come for an hour to meditate
on a single painting hung in a small room, and by itself'.[114] And of the late-
1950s murals which he famously withdrew from the Four Seasons restaurant
of the Seagram building in New York for which they had been originally
commissioned, he said that his aim had been 'to make a place rather than
pictorial vestiges'.[115] It seems irreverent towards Rothko to suggest that the
places – the chapels – that he endeavoured to create, with large pictures for
the 'traveler, or wanderer' to come and ponder on 'for an hour' recall cinema,
not only as a durational unfolding of large images, but also as a place (not
small, but made 'intimate' by the darkness) and mode of consumption. But
this is not to say that his work willingly and enthusiastically pursued the
cinematic – or the movies. Rather, if Rothko's paintings invite comparisons
with cinema or cinematic descriptions, it is not so much that they pursue
cinematic concerns, but that they absorbed the cinematic, some of its traits
and modalities, while also – indeed, because of – being concerned *about* it.

Although their work is very different, it may be interesting to think about Rothko's canvases in relation to the series of pictorial works called *Schermi* [*Screens*] that Fabio Mauri started making in 1957 and continued to make up to a few years before his death in 2009. Mauri's *Screens* speak both of a concern about cinema, and of an attempt to absorb it: 'cinema', as Mauri put it, 'was an imaginary that had to be reckoned with'.[116] Indeed, though invoking its 'imaginary', Mauri himself reckoned with it mostly by withdrawing its images. Some of his *Screens*, like the ones that Antonioni is photographed in front of at a gallery private view of the artist's work in Rome in 1969, include 'transfer' images (à la Rauschenberg) of cinema stars, but the vast majority of them are abstract.

They are generally white-painted (sometimes black) or blank surfaces: sometimes containing the writing 'The End' in English (or '*Fine*' in Italian) in black; sometimes simply canvas pulled over a structure of two, differently sized, wooden stretchers so as to produce a bulging shape; sometimes paper torn and ripped so as to reveal the underlying 'scaffolding'.[117] By contrast with the large sizes of Rothko's canvases, the size of Mauri's *Screens* is relatively small: more like that of a television screen, which Mauri overtly invoked at times, as a site that, while in competition with cinema in some respects, is also

Figure 1.7 Antonioni at *Fabio Mauri 1959–69*, Studio d'Arte Toninelli, Rome, 1969.
Photo: Claudio Abate. Courtesy the Estate of Fabio Mauri and Hauser & Wirth

a fundamental vehicle for its products. In the very constancy and insistence on the 'screen', across more than five decades, Mauri's oeuvre plays out overtly the artist's concern about cinema, and television, as visual mass media. This is a screen that returns but that also, by mostly being blank or 'representing' the moment of 'the end', frustrates the very entertainment of cinema and television. Mauri absorbed the image in the sense of withholding it or negating it. Rothko absorbed it (Bucarelli said that his rectangles were 'never completely in focus'),[118] but was also after something *absorbing*, which he pursued by seeking to 'manipulate the encounter' with the work, as Fer puts it, recourse to large sizes and a complex – and famously secretive – method of paint layering that secured a translucency through which even the weave of the canvas might still be seen.[119] In the explicit critique of cinema (and television) of Mauri's *Screens*, the medium is addressed plainly but its conditions are rejected. In Rothko's work, on the other hand, it is more like a tension between resistance and incorporation. It seems, even, a subtle resistance *via* incorporation, a hijacking of some of the mass medium's conditions for ends alternative to the ones most commonly associated with it.

This tension, if implicitly evoked by Bucarelli in her essay for the 1962 Rome exhibition, was overtly addressed by the novelist and critic Michel Butor, in an essay first published in 1961 in French (and in 1962 in Italian), and about which Antonioni asks Rothko in the first few lines of his letter to the artist ('Have you read Michel Butor's critical essay on your work?').[120] Where Bucarelli concludes that a painting by Rothko 'is *not* a screen',[121] Butor emphatically argues the contrary. Rothko, he says, is among those ('most sensitive' and 'most contemporary') painters who started to approach 'the theme of the screen' and, indeed, 'to conceive of their own canvas *as a screen*'.[122] This canvas screen is both cinematic and televisual (at a point Butor likens Rothko's paintings to the 'phosphorescent wall of the television screen', 'emanating' light from within), and, not unlike Bucarelli's invocation of a blurriness of colour, Butor's links the veils of colour of Rothko's abstract work to the 'fog' of the earlier figurative work, which 'subtracted' or absorbed the represented objects. Butor's understanding of Rothko's canvas as a screen forms the basis of a very political reading of his work as a critique of America's capitalist culture, culminating in his suggestion that the withdrawal of the Seagram Murals from the Four Seasons Restaurant in fact ensures the continued presence within those very walls of the work's condemnation and rejection of the place ('the most expensive restaurant ever built') for which they were originally made.[123]

In the broad context of European 'resistance' to American cultural and economic hegemony, the criticality that Butor reads in Rothko's work might have held a certain appeal for Antonioni, who was to cast his own critical gaze on it with *Zabriskie Point* and, in the post-war years, had joined the chorus of voices expressing concern about 'Americanisation', writing of American cinema, for instance, that it was 'attempting to supplant our industry and industrialise our fantasy'.[124] But a more significant part in his appreciation of Rothko's work might have been played by the emphasis on duration in Butor's – and Bucarelli's – readings. For these resonated, by contrast, with emerging debates on the proliferation and, consequently, the *lack of duration* of the image in mass culture, which may have contributed to attune Antonioni to the temporality of Rothko's ostensibly image-less work. If the time of looking – if not, indeed, of watching – that Rothko's overtly prescribed for his work resonates with the time necessary for the experience of cinema – the consumption of movies – it is also, at the same time, in contrast with the increasingly faster tempo of the image in post-war mass culture. One year before the release of *Il deserto rosso*, the yearly publication *Almanacco letterario Bompiani* (for which Mauri worked as co-ordinator in the 1960s), was dedicated to 'The Civilization of the Image'. Dorfles launched an appeal for the production of images 'destined to last' – beyond their 'utilitarian', 'informative moment' – in the midst of the 'uninterrupted and unstable flow of images mechanically produced and reproduced'.[125] Without the anxiety evident in Dorfles's call, Antonioni too had an awareness that, in a media landscape where television had joined photography, print and cinema, images do not last: '[T]he image ages immediately', he wrote.[126] Dorfles and Antonioni are describing an awareness of what Francesco Casetti, invoking Benjamin, has described as 'a loss of the rituality of vision' in the age of mass media, and that, in the early-1980s, scholars such as John Ellis and Cavell, in reference to television in particular, have described in terms of 'the glance' or 'monitoring', rather than attentive viewing or a prolonged 'gaze' (see Chapter 2).[127] Antonioni's durational appreciation of the 'nothing' 'made only of colour' in Rothko's paintings suggests that he saw – or *watched* – how they embraced but also rejected cinema, in an attempt to hold on to a kind of rituality of vision, restoring time (in the sense of duration, if not slowness) to it through a paradoxical withdrawal of the image itself. This perhaps resonated with the way in which Antonioni, on his part, embraced the pictorial in his cinema, while also resisting it. Antonioni, did not want, as he often insisted, his cinema to enter the territory of painting.[128] Yet, what he perhaps saw and found inspiring in the wide range of contemporaneous painting about which he kept informed, was precisely an 'impure pictoriality' that provided him with a conceptual means with which to *renew*, rather than purify, cinema, through an exchange with a form in turn already exposed to the cinematic and other mass media. As the absorption and resistance informing Rothko's empty screens suggest, Antonioni might also have found in such impure painting a form of critique of the cinematic image itself. If he drew on the mid-twentieth century's impure pictoriality, it was not so much to make cinema pictorial but, somewhat paradoxically, via this already-contaminated painting, to pursue a form of intermedial reflexivity – or, indeed, a *critical intermediality* – that may make cinema and its experience more self-critical.

This continued even when, with *Il mistero di Oberwald/The Mystery of Oberwald* (1980), he turned to video cameras to make what, thanks to the electronic manipulation of luminance and colour signals, may appear not simply as a 'pictorial' but also a 'painterly' film, in the sense of 'painterly' described by Greenberg (on the basis of Heinrich Wölfflin's earlier concept) for work by artists such as Pollock and De Kooning. '[W]ith video', as Antonioni himself once put it, 'you can, as it were, paint a film with electronic colours, even as you are filming it'.[129] While this was in 1975, before *Oberwald*, it also points back to the fact that the director had planned to experiment with magnetic video cameras as soon as they became available in the mid-1960s – just after *Il deserto rosso* – for the never-completed film *Tecnicamente dolce [Technically Sweet]*.[130] Yet, in contemplating the possibility of 'paint[ing] a film', Antonioni is not only calling into play a third medium, video, but suggesting that whatever 'painterly' qualities such endeavour might yield, they would be due to operations other than brushstrokes: the appeal is that '[y]ou just push a button and you get the tone of colour you want'.[131] Not only is this automated operation very different from the manual work of applying paint with the brush and any model of painting traditionally understood, it is also radically intermedial, like Antonioni's other 'pictorial' work of the 1980s, *The Enchanted Mountains*. Painting is pursued and resisted here too, absorbed and transformed through means of mechanical reproduction, as small details of abstract watercolour compositions are photographically enlarged, in an operation that 'zooms in' into their materiality, making it 'real', if not, indeed, figurative – turning blots of colour into mountainous landscapes. Furthermore, as the art historian Giulio Carlo Argan pointed out, *The Enchanted Mountains* also belong to cinema, not only because of the procedure of enlargement that recalls the mechanics of cinema as the images on tiny film frames are made large during projection, but because, perhaps not unlike Rothko's work, they 'visualise durations', they 'don't have the object-like two-dimensionality of the picture but the fluctuation and luminosity . . . of the screen'.[132]

Notes

1. In their introduction to *Antonioni: Centenary Essays*, Rascaroli and Rhodes have critically outlined these and other tropes ('Interstitial, Pretentious, Alienated, Dead', p. 1).
2. Chatman, *Antonioni*, for example, p. 87; Rohdie, *Antonioni*, for example, pp. 3, 51 and 91.

3. Païni, 'Ritratto di cineasta in veste di pittore', p. 28. This essay is in the catalogue of the exhibition *Lo sguardo di Michelangelo: Antonioni e le arti* that Païni curated at the Palazzo dei Diamanti in Ferrara, Italy, 10 March – 9 June 2013.

4. Bonitzer in *Décadrages* has associated Antonioni's cinema with painting and seen its images in pursuit of representational abstraction and emptiness, pp. 97ff. See also Bonitzer, *Le Champ aveugle*, p. 88.

5. Dalle Vacche, *Cinema and Painting*, p. 44 ('abstract sensibility'); Jacobs, 'Between EUR and LA', p. 332 ('the sublimity of emptiness').

6. Rascaroli and Rhodes, 'Interstitial, Pretentious, Alienated, Dead', p. 6.

7. See, for example, Antonioni, 'A Talk with Michelangelo Antonioni on His Work', esp. p. 44; Tassone, 'Conversation' (originally in *Positif* 292, June 1985), esp. p. 230; Lannes and Meyer, 'Identification of a Filmmaker' (originally in *L'Express* 9–15 August 1985).

8. Antonioni, *Antonioni: Le montagne incantate*; Farina, *Michelangelo Antonioni. Le montagne incantate*; Antonioni's paintings have been catalogued and analysed by Vitale, *Michelangelo Antonioni. Schedatura e analisi del fondo pittorico*.

9. Tassone, 'Conversation', p. 231.

10. Ibid., p. 230.

11. Ibid., p. 231, the English text translates as the 'materials of painting', the Italian has 'la materia del dipinto', literally 'the [physical] matter of painting'. See also Lannes and Mayer, 'Identificazione di un regista', p. 217.

12. Antonioni, 'A Talk', p. 44.

13. Ibid. Agamben, 'What Is the Contemporary?'; Barad, *Meeting the Universe Half-Way*, pp. 29–30 and ch. 2.

14. Antonioni, 'A Talk', p. 42.

15. Bonitzer, *Le Champ aveugle*, p. 88; Deleuze, *Cinema I*, pp. 119–20; *Cinema II*, pp. 5–9; Gandy, 'The Cinematic Void'.

16. Rascaroli and Rhodes, 'Interstitial, Pretentious, Alienated, Dead', p. 1.

17. Sadoul, 'Puro come *La notte*'; Moravia, 'È esplosa pura l'arte di Antonioni'; Bruno, 'Le responsabilità della Biennale', p. 456. For further contemporaneous discussion on these themes, see, for example, Plebe, 'Forma e contenuto nel linguaggio filmico'.

18. Chatman, *Antonioni*, for example, p. 87; Rohdie, *Antonioni*, fr example, pp. 3, 51 and 91.

19. Among others, Sironi's *La caduta (La notte)* [*The Fall (The Night)*] (1933–5) and Morandi's *Natura Morta* [*Still Life*] (1960) feature in *La notte* (1960), Ian Stephenson's *Still Life Abstraction* (1957) in *Blow-Up* (1966); and Giacomo Balla's *Ballafiore* (1924) in *Identificazione di una donna/Identification of a Woman* (1982).

20. Antonioni, 'A Talk', p. 44.

21. The abandoned village has been identified by Rosalind Galt as Schisina, near Messina (rather than Noto, as it is presented in the film). As Galt discusses, Schisina was built in 1950 to house peasants who had been assigned expropriated and previously uncultivated land in the context of the post-war land reforms, but by the end of the 1950s it was completely uninhabited. Galt, 'On *L'avventura* and the Picturesque', esp. pp. 146–7. David Forgacs offers a detailed

discussion of the use of paint and lens filters in his commentary to the BFI's DVD edition of *Red Desert* (2011).

22. See Greenberg, 'After Abstract Expressionism' (*Art International*, October 1962) and 'Post-Painterly Abstraction' (*Art International*, Summer 1964).
23. Roud, '*The Red Desert*'.
24. Antonioni, 'On Color', p. 112 cited. The text was first published in Italian as 'Del colore' in *Cinema* (December 1942), and is available in the collection Antonioni, *Sul cinema*. In a non-dated (but probably written in the late 1930s) letter to Letizia Balboni (who was to be his first wife), Antonioni wrote: 'Io diventerò matto se non farò un film a colori [I'll go mad if I don't make a film in colour]', see Di Carlo, *Il mio Antonioni*, p. 44.
25. Most recently, this has been suggested by Weiss, '*Temps mort*: Antonioni and Rothko'; Antonioni's letter to Rothko, dated 27 May 1962, is published just after Weiss's essay in Wick, *Mark Rothko*, p. 56.
26. Gilman, 'About Nothing – with Precision', p. 11. Benci, '"All that Is Behind Colour": Antonioni and Painting' provides a carefully researched reconstruction of Rothko and Antonioni's encounter.
27. Greenberg, 'Avant-Garde and Kitsch' and 'Towards a Newer Laocoön' (*Partisan Review*, in 1939 and 1940 respectively).
28. Greenberg, 'Modernist Painting' (radio broadcast at *Forum Lectures: Voices of America* 1960, printed *Arts Yearbook* 4, 1961), p. 86.
29. Greenberg, 'After Abstract Expressionism', p. 131.
30. Greenberg, 'Modernist Painting', pp. 81–2. These ideas were also in 'Towards a Newer Laocoön'.
31. Gilman, 'About Nothing', pp. 11 and 12.
32. Bonitzer, *Décadrages*, pp. 100 and 97. Bonitzer, *Le Champ aveugle*, p. 88.
33. Dalle Vacche, *Cinema and Painting*, ch. 2.
34. Ibid, p. 44.
35. Jacobs, 'Between EUR and LA', p. 331. From a literal point of view, the film image is always flat, while, as Greenberg himself had noted, a mark of paint on a canvas destroys its flatness.
36. Ibid., p. 332.
37. Païni, 'Ritratto di cineasta in veste di pittore', p. 28.
38. Weiss, '*Temps mort*: Rothko and Antonioni', pp. 46, 45 and 54 cited. While Weiss's reading is suggestive, it is not wholly convincing on Antonioni's films, whose consideration is impressionistic if not inaccurate, especially with regard to the *temps morts* that Weiss generically assigns to *Red Desert*, and which are in fact hard to find in this film in particular, which, with the transition to colour, also inaugurates the use of an editing pace faster than previous films.
39. Steimatsky, *Italian Locations*, pp. 1–14, 35.
40. Beugnet, *L'attrait du flou*, p. 102; Rhodes, 'Abstraction and the Geopolitical: Lessons from Antonioni's Trip to China', considers the relation between abstraction and reality/realism in Antonioni via a focus on his 1972 documentary.
41. Schoonover, 'Antonioni's Waste Management', esp. pp. 243–7.

42. Rhodes, 'Abstraction and the Geopolitical', p. 56.
43. Worringer, *Abstraction and Empathy*, p. 36. Chatman also draws on Worringer in his discussion of Antonioni's 'flat "abstract" style', in *Antonioni*, p. 118.
44. Kandinsky and Marc, *Der Blaue Reiter Almanach*, p. 85.
45. See Foster, Krauss, Bois and Buchloh, *Art Since 1900*, pp. 434–8. On Fontana, Munari and MAC, see White, 'Bruno Munari and Lucio Fontana: Parallel Lives'. For in-depth accounts of these movements see Caramel, *M. A. C.: Movimento Arte Concreta 1948–1952* and Ameline, *Lex Nouveaux Réalistes*.
46. Braun, 'Aftermath', p. 42; Celant, 'Alberto Burri and Material', p. 7.
47. Greenberg, 'Modernist Painting', p. 90.
48. Ibid.
49. Greenberg, '"American-Type" Painting' (*Partisan Review*, Spring 1955), p. 217.
50. Ibid., p. 218; Greenberg, 'Modernist Painting', p. 90 ('only with the eye'); and 'The Case for Abstract Art' (*Saturday Evening Post*, August 1959), pp. 81 and 80. For an important critical study of Greenberg's model, see Jones, *Eyesight Alone*.
51. Theorisations promoting a 'confusion of the arts' come somewhat later, in the mid-1960s. See, for ecample, Higgins, 'Intermedia', first published in 1966 in *Something Else Newsletter*; and Judd, 'Specific Objects', first published in 1965 in *Arts Yearbook*.
52. Lonzi, *Autoritratto*, p. 125.
53. Fagiolo dell'Arco, *Rapporto 1960*, quoted by Christov-Bakargiev, 'Thrust into the Whirlwind: Italian Art Before Arte Povera', p. 35.
54. Alloway, *The Venice Biennale*, pp. 15, 144.
55. Ibid., p. 150. Morris Louis and Kenneth Noland, promoted by Greenberg, were also at the Biennale – and, in fact inside the American Pavilion – while Rauschenberg (who won that year) and Jasper Johns' works were exhibited *outside* the Pavilion, in a temporary structure. Mellor, '"Fragments of an Unknowable Whole"', p. 126.
56. Antonioni, *Tecnicamente dolce*, p. 87. Although the script was published in 1976, the treatment for the film was first developed at the same time as *Blow-Up*, around 1964–5. On Burri and Antonioni, see also Braun, *Alberto Burri*, p. 63.
57. Alan Mellor, '"Fragments of an Unknowable Whole"'.
58. Antonioni, 'A Talk', p. 44.
59. Christov-Bakargiev and Scotini, *Gianni Colombo*.
60. Fer, *The Infinite Line*, pp. 170–3.
61. On Richter's *Rhythmus 21* and abstraction see, among others, Turvey, *The Filming of Modern Life*, ch.1.
62. Typewritten letter from Richter to Michelangelo Antonioni, 30 November 1970, 9B_1, fasc. 80, Archivio Michelangelo Antonioni, Servizio Gallerie d'Arte Moderna e Contemporanea, Ferrara.
63. Richter, 'The Film as An Original Art Form' (originally in *Film Culture* 1, January 1955), p. 19.
64. In *Blow-Up*, for instance, the facades and shop fronts of the buildings along an entire road (in Brixton) the photographer drives along on the way to Maryon

park have been painted red. Generally, as Antonioni has explained, the rationale and aesthetics of colour in the two films is different, and the interventions were more naturalistic in *Blow-Up* (such as spraying the grass or fence with green paint to make it greener). Reneé Tobe considers *Blow-Up* and the difference between the physical, material landscape and the cinematic landscape assembled by the director in '*Blow-Up*: Who Owns the City', paper delivered at *Landscape and Architecture in the Cinema of Michelangelo Antonioni: Study Day*, BFI Southbank, 16 February 2019 and *Film, Architecture and the Spatial Imagination*, ch. 4.

65. Antonioni, *Il deserto rosso*, pp. 9-13 ('Il bosco bianco').

66. Ibid., p. 12.

67. Tassone, 'Conversation', p. 230.

68. As Pomerance writes in his fascinating article 'Notes on Some Limits of Technicolor: The Antonioni Case', Alfred Hitchcock had his assistant make enquiries ('What exactly is "TINTAL"?'), as he thought that maybe it referred to a manipulation of Technicolour film stock itself.

69. Godard, 'The Night, The Eclipse, The Dawn' (first in *Cahiers du cinema*, November 1964), pp. 293, 296. Antonioni, 'A propos of eroticism', p. 160.

70. Godard, 'The Night, The Eclipse, The Dawn', p. 296.

71. Maurin, '*Red Desert*' (first in *Humanité Dimanche*, 23 September 1964), p. 283.

72. Antonioni, 'A propos of eroticism', pp. 160–1.

73. Ibid., p. 161.

74. Braun, 'Aftermath', p. 45.

75. On Burry and paint see Braun, 'Aftermath'. Though proverbially secretive about his materials and methods, Rothko also used household paints, diluted with turpentine, in the various layers he applied to his canvases. See Barker and Ormsby, 'Conserving Rothko's *Black on Maroon* 1958'.

76. Fer, *The Infinite Line*, p. 173.

77. Forgacs, *Red Desert* DVD commentary.

78. Molesworth, '"Pedestrian Color": The *Red Paintings*', pp. 120–1. Seckler, 'The Artist Speaks: Robert Rauschenberg', p. 84.

79. Molesworth, '"Pedestrian Color"', p. 121.

80. Antonioni in Di Carlo, *Il mio Antonioni*, p. 181 (letter to Letizia Balboni, 5 April 1962).

81. Godard, 'The Night, the Eclipse, the Dawn', p. 294. On colour's functionality, see d'Ayala Valva, 'Funzione del colore'.

82. Antonioni, 'Color Does Not Come from America' (originally in *Film rivista*, 18 December 1947), grouped under the title 'On Color' with two other essays, 'On Color' (originally in *Cinema*, December 1942) and 'Suggestions from Hegel' (originally in *Corriere Padano*, 2 June 1940), in *October*, p. 119 cited. In Italian in Antonioni, *Sul cinema*, pp. 193–6.

83. Ibid.

84. Antonioni, 'Suggestions from Hegel' in 'On Color', esp. pp. 115–16. In Italian in Antonioni, *Sul cinema*, pp. 187–92.

85. See Everett, 'Mapping Colour: An Introduction to the Theories and Practices of Colour', esp. p. 25.

86. For ecological readings of the film, see Pinkus, 'Antonioni's Cinematic Poetics of Climate Change'; and Schoonover, 'Antonioni's Waste Management'.

87. Maurin, '*Red Desert*', p. 286. (I have modified the translation a little, cf. Maurin, '*Il deserto rosso*, p. 253.) Note how Antonioni's account of the treatment of colour as external stimuli 'entering' the character is different from accounts that see it as a projection of Giuliana's mind, her psyche or interiority (e.g. Pasolini, 'The "Cinema of Poetry"').

88. Antonioni, 'Suggestions from Hegel', in 'On Color', p. 117; Maurin, '*Red Desert*', p. 283. For Beugnet, in *L'attrait du flou*, the 'blur' in Antonioni takes the image towards abstraction, but an abstraction which, unlike the one described by Worringer, manifests not an attempt to apprehend and order the world but the very inability to do so (pp. 102–3).

89. Jean-Luc Godard, 'The Night, The Eclipse, The Dawn' p. 294.

90. According to Benci's meticulous reconstruction and analysis of accounts, the meeting between the two is likely to have taken place in either April 1961 (on the occasion of the US premiere of *L'avventura*) or February 1962 (for the US premiere of *La Notte*). The encounter was organised by the writer and journalist Furio Colombo, who moved to New York in 1959 to work for the Olivetti Corporation of America, but his accounts over the decades have been inconsistent with the dates. See Benci, '"All That Is Behind Colour"', esp. p. 82.

91. Antonioni, 'Letter to Rothko', p. 55.

92. Rothko quoted in Rosenberg, 'Rothko', p. 94.

93. Rothko interviewed by William Seitz in 1952, cited by Breslin, *Mark Rothko: A Biography*, p. 276. See also Lopez-Remiro, *Mark Rothko: Writings on Art*, p. 119 (which cites Rodman, *Conversations with Artists*).

94. Bucarelli, 'Mark Rothko', p. 10.

95. Ibid., pp. 9 and 10.

96. Ibid., p. 11.

97. Antonioni, 'Letter to Rothko', p. 55. For Rothko on Matisse's painting, see Breslin, *Mark Rothko*, p. 283; and Ashton, *About Rothko*, p. 61.

98. Spurrell, 'Interview with Furio Colombo', p. 209; Weiss, 'Temps Mort: Rothko and Antonioni', p. 45. Weiss cites from an unpublished obituary by Motherwell on Rothko. As Benci points out, Weiss provides no bibliographical details for it, although he may be referring to a commemoration of the older artist that Motherwell held at the National Institue of Arts and Letters in New York on 28 January 1971. See Benci, '"All That is Behind Colour"', p. 82.

99. Greenberg, 'After Abstract Experssionism', p. 129.

100. Dorfles, 'Biennale' (1958), now in Oliver Wick (ed.), *Mark Rothko*, p. 3.

101. Dorfles, 'A Song without Words', p. 41.

102. Greenberg, 'After Abstract Expressionism', pp. 130–1.

103. Fried, 'Art and Objecthood' (originally in *Artforum*, 1967).

104. Cavell, *The World Viewed*, p. 116.
105. Ibid., pp. 110 and 111.
106. Fer, *The Infinite Line*, p. 172.
107. Fer, *The Infinite Line*, p. 13. Fer cites Rothko in Anfam, *Mark Rothko*, p. 75.
108. Ibid., pp. 13 and 14.
109. Rothko, *The Artist's Reality*, pp. 9–10.
110. Furio Colombo, interviewed in Gianni Massironi, *Dear Antonioni* (*Arena*, BBC, episode 33, 18 January 1997), cited by Benci, 'All That Is Behind Colour', p. 77.
111. Rothko, *The Artist's Reality*, pp. 46–7.
112. López-Remiro, *Rothko: Writings on Art*, p. 74.
113. Fer, *The Infinite Line*, p. 12.
114. Rothko cited in Breslin, *Mark* Rothko, p. 375.
115. Rothko's Note on the Seagram mural commission, in Wick, *Mark Rothko*, pp. 169–70. See also Anfam, *Mark Rothko: The Work on Canvas*, p. 96.
116. Fabio Mauri, *Arte per legittima difesa*, p. 13.
117. On Mauri's screens see among others: Christov-Bakargiev and Cossu, *Fabio Mauri. Opere e azioni, 1954–1994*.
118. Bucarelli, 'Mark Rothko', p. 10.
119. Fer, *The Infinite Line*, p. 13.
120. Antonioni, 'Letter to Rothko', p. 55.
121. Bucarelli, 'Mark Rothko', p. 10.
122. Butor, 'Le moschee di New York' (in French in *Critique*, October 1961, and in Italian in *L'Europa letteraria*, 1962), now in Butor, *Saggi sulla pittura*, p. 140 cited. (In English in Butor, *Inventory*, pp. 260–77.)
123. Ibid., p. 151.
124. Antonioni, 'Color Does Not Come from America' in 'On Color', p. 118.
125. Dorfles, 'Civiltà (e inciviltà) dell'immagine', p. 74.
126. Typewritten note, 8d1/fasc. 56 (n.d., early 1960s?), Michelangelo Antonioni Archive, Ferrara.
127. Casetti, 'Back to the Motherland', pp. 3–4. Ellis, *Visible Fictions*, esp. p. 137; Stanley Cavell, 'The Fact of Television', p. 85.
128. For example, Godard, 'The Night, The Eclipse, The Dawn', p. 296.
129. Ongaro, 'An In-Depth Search' (originally in *L'Europeo*, 1975), p. 350.
130. For a mention of video experimentation and *Tecnicamente dolce*, see Steimatsky, 'Pass/Fail: The Antonioni Screen Test', esp. p. 196. The script for the film was published in the late 1970s but, as Antonioni explains in the preface to *Tecnicamente dolce*, the treatment for it was pitched to Carlo Ponti together with *Blow-Up*, the film that got chosen.
131. Ongaro, 'An In-Depth Search', p. 350.
132. Argan, in Antonioni, *Antonioni: Le montagne Incantate*, p. 14. See also Arrowsmith, 'Translator's Preface', in Antonioni, *That Bowling Alley on the Tiber*, pp. xvi–xviii.

CHAPTER 2

Performing the Mind: Interiority, Television and Artificial Brains

> As pure as *La notte*. Is this not the adjective best suited to Antonioni's film? . . .
> Purity is truly in Antonioni's exquisite art. Already with *L'avventura* one could
> have thought that the director had reached the apex of his burning and arid
> discourse, of his 'interior realism', which is distant and detached so as best to
> enter inside the heart of individuals . . . But with *La notte* he has gone even fur-
> ther . . . in reaching an examination of consciousness, in the anxious research
> of a meticulous purification . . . Everything thus seems as pure as water. Not
> the impetuous water of streams that drag with them sand, mud, stones and
> detritus; but the water of a liquid ten times distilled.[1]

The excerpt above from the metaphorically heavy review of *La notte* by the
film historian Georges Sadoul (published in French and Italian in early 1961)
may not itself display the qualities of which it speaks. Yet, it is exemplary
of how the cinematic purity which contemporaneous critics often extolled
in Antonioni's post-1960 films is often presented in co-dependence with a
shift, widely noticed by critics and overtly declared by Antonioni himself,
from exteriority to interiority. The critic Guido Aristarco articulated this even
more strongly when, also writing after the release of *La notte*, he concluded
that in Antonioni's new films 'the problem consists less in characterising
the individual personality than in making a precise analysis of the psychic
machinery itself'.[2]

Already in the 1950s, with films such as *Cronaca di un amore/Chronicle of a
Love* (1950) and *Il grido/The Outcry* (1957), critics had started to talk of a move
away from a 'neorealist' exploration of the relationship between the individual
and external reality, and towards an engagement with the psychological, psychic
or mental reality of the characters in what they termed an 'interior neorealism'.
While possibly disagreeing with the terminology, Antonioni would agree with
the essence of this explanation and often refer to it. During the talk at CSC in
March 1961, to which I have already referred more than once in this book,
Antonioni confirmed that the new social and historical situation of the 1950s
and 1960s, with respect to that of the immediate post-war period in which

neorealism had emerged, had required 'a turn towards [an] internal form of film-making', a cinema which is not so much concerned with externals as it is with those forces that move us to act in a certain way and not another'.[3] Pointing to the intensification of his efforts in this direction, he noted that while in *Cronaca* he had opted to 'keep the camera on the actors even after the prescribed action was complete . . . to capture their thoughts, their states of mind' by 'follow[ing] them around physically with the camera' as the 1950s wore on, he had come to realise that 'this was not the best method after all'. For, as he explains, 'I was concentrating too much on the external aspects of the actor's states of mind and not so much on *the states of minds themselves*'.[4] Pushing further in the endeavour to develop a cinema of interiority, to find a 'method' for conveying 'the states of minds themselves', may in many ways be seen to reach an apex with *Il deserto rosso/Red Desert* (1964).[5] As Pier Paolo Pasolini suggested when he spoke of the 'free indirect subjective' as the stylistic mode of this film, here the disturbed mind of the neurotic Giuliana is conveyed via its distinctive, at times non-naturalistic, use of colour, and disorientating, and at times frenzied, framing and editing.[6] But even a film seemingly as straightforwardly focused on external reality – if not on the reality of appearances – as *Blow-Up* (1966) has been seen as a study of interiority, with 'the camera', as Dudley Andrew wrote, 'literally building the character's psyche': 'we are in his mind'.[7] In this respect, contemporaneous critics' frequent and recurrent attribution of this effort to Antonioni is as interesting as the director's own declaration of such endeavour. What deserves attention is the context in which such externalisation of interiority, or, as Aristarco put it, of the 'psychic machinery itself', is deemed both a topic of interest and something in which cinema may be actively involved.

Whether the concern with interiority is the result or the cause of cinematic purity is not always necessarily clear. But the rhetoric is the familiar one of a reduction, rarefaction, 'meticulous purification', as Sadoul put it, and abstraction of the cinematic image: a move from representation or 'strictly figurative' results, as Antonioni himself explained, towards a primary concern with formal rendering.[8] While in this context intermedial associations with painting (as we saw in Chapter 1) or literature may be permissible and even courted, one of the media that Antonioni's cinema is generally felt to be pure *of* is television.

Thus, in an article titled 'Il film letterario [The Literary Film]' which, again, appeared in early 1961, Antonioni's *La notte* is praised as at once a 'literary film' – the same category to which Aristarco assigns it – and an exquisite example of a 'pure cinema' that opposes television.[9] The crux of such differentiation is interiority. In an article featured, not without irony, adjacent to the second of a special section dedicated to 'Television and Culture' in the *Pirelli* magazine, *La notte* is presented as exemplary of a cinema that, to differentiate itself from the threatening competition of this newly popular source of moving images, 'to the wholly *external* and anecdotal temporality of television substitutes its own *interior* temporality more akin to that of the novel'.[10] If the novel in question is not so much the classic, 'realist' one of the nineteenth century but rather its twentieth-century 'modernist' modulation, even in its pursuit of inner monologues or streams of thought, the gist of the point made is that to the exteriority – and anecdotal superficiality – of television and its temporality is opposed to the interiority of Antonioni's pure (yet literary) cinema.

But if the turn to 'interiority' in Antonioni's cinema has been used to corroborate notions of cinematic purity, the attempt to analyse – if not enact – the mind cannot be, almost by definition, simply or *purely* cinematic.[11] In what follows, I want to argue not only for its entanglement with television, and the new kind of narrative, temporal and viewing economies that the medium introduced, but also, relatedly, with the multifarious thinking about interiority and the psyche in which television (as well as cinema) was itself entangled. Both the media landscape that television was crucially transforming, and broader debates about the mind and consciousness – from the possibility of their control by mass media, to analyses of their functioning and malfunctioning or, even, projects for their artificial (re)production – constitute an important but generally unacknowledged context for Antonioni's turn to 'interiority'.

Starting with television, this chapter considers how Antonioni's cinema may in fact be informed by the medium, and such attributes as superficiality, externality and 'flow' which accrue to it despite, or perhaps because of, the very position of the TV set *inside* the home and the connection with the outside world that it provides. It then goes on to consider how such concern for mental and psychological reality can be connected to the then-emerging medium of the computer and fields such as cybernetics, in which Antonioni was keenly interested. In their turn informed by televisual ideas around notions such as 'scanning' and 'monitoring', early computing and cybernetics did much to popularise the very idea of the mind as mechanism, and the possibility of externalising it and studying it. Now iconic devices or 'thinking machines' such as William Ross Ashby's homeostat and William Grey Walter's tortoises Elmer and Elsie contributed to propel these fields into the limelight from the late-1940s. Thus, despite a long-held association between cinema and the mind – whose point of origin may indeed reside in the temporal coincidence between the development of moving-image technologies and modern sciences of the mind such as psychology and psychoanalysis in the late nineteenth and early twentieth centuries – even Antonioni's turn towards what he described as 'an internal form of filmmaking' does not testify to the increased purity, or withdrawal onto itself, of the director's medium.

On the contrary, it provides further evidence of Antonioni's cinema commerce with the world and profound entanglement with other media, as its aesthetics react to the televisual and take on board ideas of exteriorisation articulated in cybernetic and computational sciences.

MINDING TELEVISION

Unlike in the United Kingdom and United States, where experimental or local transmissions date to the 1930s, television broadcasting in Italy only started in earnest in 1954. From that moment, ownership and viewing rose dramatically in the space of a few years. When trial broadcasting began in 1953, 12,000 licences were issued; this number had risen to 80,000 by the end of 1954, and to more than 2 million by 1960.[12] Television broadcasting remained a state monopoly – of RAI, Radiotelevisione Italiana – until the 1970s, but was funded via advertising as well as licence fees. Even if counterbalanced by a relatively rich portfolio of more 'cultural' offerings such as documentaries and current-affairs debates, from the start, the most popular programmes tended to be variety and quiz shows modelled on American counterparts, such as Mike Bongiorno's *Lascia o raddoppia* [*Leave It or Double It*].[13]

By the early 1960s, several Italian critics and scholars had turned, not without a palpable sense of alarm, to analysing the mass medium and its incredibly rapid growth – often referring to the Anglophone, and mostly American, literature that had emerged in the previous decade.[14] Conferences and books started to appear, and many major cultural publications, including the magazine *Pirelli*, *Almanacco Letterario Bompiani* and *Civilta' delle macchine*, dedicated special issues or lengthy essays to the televisual phenomenon.[15] While debates and legal rulings on television's function as a public information and educational service would inform programming, it is perhaps not wholly surprising that anxious analyses on the detrimental effects of television inspired by the contemplation of the American deregulated and commercial model, or by critical commentary on such model, might inform the outlook of many commentators, even if only as something that should be avoided. Even though surprisingly contained in its pessimism, a representative example might be Theodor Adorno's American-period essay 'How to Look at Television' (1954), in which he suggested that to consider the 'effect' of the medium, and 'expos[e]' its profound 'socio-psychological implications and mechanisms', psychoanalysis's rationale of searching for hidden and overt meanings, as in Freud's distinction between the 'latent' and 'manifest' content of dreams, should be kept in mind.[16]

To an even greater degree than cinema, because of its domestic instalment inside the home, television is generally addressed in these early years as a form of mental addiction and even 'conditioning' (to use a term in vogue at the time), something with hypnotic, absorbing, doping – and duping – effects on its audiences.[17] As Umberto Eco reported in a chapter dedicated to television in his 1964 book *Apocalittici e integrati* [*Apocalypse Postponed*], the epigraph to one of the first monographic studies on the medium in Italy, Adriano Bellotto's *La televisione inutile* [*Useless Television*] (1962) is a viewer's statement that reads: 'To tell you the truth, I don't like this television very much, which is often boring, not to say worse, and that obliges me to remain glued to the screen for hours and hours, when I have thousands other things to do instead.'[18] If one had to purposefully set aside leisure time and leave the home for cinema, television not only spares viewers any 'ritualistic effort', but may ensnare them surreptitiously, distracting them from necessary domestic chores.[19] In this sense, as this viewer's confession suggests, television is not only an occupation of the interiority of the house, a replacement of its hearth, even, as suggested by one of the critical photo-reportages on television in the Italian press at the time, with images teleported from outside.[20] As the 'flow' of images, easily accessible at the flick of a switch, that Raymond Williams will famously theorise about a decade later, it is also an occupation of one's time, mind and even body, which, unlike with radio listening, must ideally remain stationary in front of the monitor.[21] As Marshall McLuhan wrote: 'TV will not work as background. It engages you. You have to be *with* it.'[22] Even though radio, cinema and print are part of the landscape that Edgar Morin evoked in his 1962 book *L'Esprit du temps* when he described mass media as a 'colonization of the soul', television is arguably the chief culprit.[23] Television, in other words, is seen as a new powerful tool: a medium that, while often described in terms of superficiality and externality aesthetically and content-wise, and understood to enable the transmission of an external visual stream inside the home, nevertheless *acts on* viewers' interiority, their mind and consciousness.

It is within this setting – a media and cultural landscape in which television is felt to be rapidly impressing dramatic changes – that it is interesting to think about the early 1960s' critical emphasis on 'interiority' and 'purity' in Antonioni's cinema. If television, more acutely and forcibly than other mass media, including cinema itself, is understood to *act on* viewers' interiority (to have the capability for 'undreamed of psychological control', as Adorno put it in his essay),[24] then there is a way in which Antonioni's cinema is, by contrast, upheld as an *enactment of* consciousness or the mind.

TELEVISUAL AESTHETICS: LIVENESS, FLOWS AND MONITOR(ING)

Antonioni, as is well known, came to do some work for television. In 1972, he directed for RAI the long documentary *Chung Kuo, Cina/Chung Kuo, China*.

And in 1980, as mentioned in Chapter 1, he made – again, for RAI – *Il mistero di Oberwald/The Mystery of Oberwald*, a visually experimental adaptation (shot with video rather than film cameras) of Jean Cocteau's 1946 play *The Two-Headed Eagle*. In addition, as Michael Loren Siegel has argued, the often lurid appearance of the 1982 film *Identificazione di una donna/Identification of a Woman* may invite associations with televisual aesthetics – those of the then-emerging Berlusconian commercial television especially – even though the medium itself is not overtly part of the film's subject matter.[25] Yet, in the early 1960s, the distance between Antonioni's cinema and television would generally be felt to be too great to need mention. And while TV sets feature in the *mise-en-scène* of Antonioni's 1960s films, including *La notte*, they never appear to be on.

The thought of spelling out how different from television *La notte* was probably never crossed Sadoul's mind when he wrote his appreciation of this film's 'purity'; or, for that matter, Adorno's mind, when, invoking purity less overtly, he extolled the film's paradoxical denial and preservation of cinema's quintessence in 'Transparencies on Film' (1966).[26] So it is particularly interesting, I think, that the author of the article 'The Literary Film' mentioned above, Fabio Carpi, pointedly did. As he strove to present *La notte* (and *L'avventura*) as paradigmatic of an anti-televisual type of cinema emerging in response to a crisis – of narrativity and temporality above all – precipitated by television itself, Carpi in some way hides his worst fear in plain sight. That is, the 'different rhythm' and new 'narrative time' that Carpi credits Antonioni with *inventing*, as something that radically distinguishes the director's and, with it, modern cinema from television, may actually point not to a radical avoidance and negation of emerging televisual aesthetics, as Carpi suggests, but, in some way, to an *absorption* of them.[27] When Carpi praises Antonioni's accomplishment with *La notte* as that of 'having made a two-hour film with the same thing, the same situation, even the same material', he is perhaps, and certainly inadvertently, suggesting that cinema may be renewing itself in the face of the 'competition of television' – particularly, here, its perceived redundancy and repetitiousness – *through the televisual itself*.[28] While the point that he is trying to make is that the rapid expansion of the new medium is urging a 'revision of all conventions' that might deliver a new, purer cinema, the novelty and purity of such cinema – focused, as he underlines, on interiority – may paradoxically be crucially informed by the very medium to which, in Carpi's view, it is most antithetical.[29] Could it be that it is precisely by adopting *and* adapting the exteriority and superficiality of television's flow that Antonioni's cinema succeeds in its articulation of interiority, consciousness and 'the states of mind themselves'?

There were, in fact, some critics who detected something televisual in modern cinema and in Antonioni's inner-oriented films in particular. Eco,

who worked for RAI in the late 1950s and started around then to write a
number of essays on television (versions of which ended up in his early books
Opera aperta [*The Open Work*] (1962) and *Apocalypse Postponed*), suggested
at the time that while the possibility of 'live broadcast' ('la ripresa diretta')
counted as a 'specifically televisual quality', this quality 'could perhaps be pin-
pointed as the debt of new cinema towards television'.[30] 'Cinema', he writes:

> at least in its traditional forms, had habituated the spectator to a type of linked
> narration . . . structured according to a clear beginning, middle, and end in
> which every element of the action appeared dictated by the very economy of
> the narration. Now, with live television, a radically different way of 'narrating'
> events has been asserting itself: live television broadcasts images of an event
> while the event itself unfolds. The director needs, on the one hand, to orga-
> nise a 'story' able to offer a logical and lucid account of what is happening,
> and, on the other, to be ready to accept and incorporate into such 'narration'
> all those unforeseen occurrences that the autonomous and uncontrollable
> unfolding of the actual event imposes on the broadcast . . . The result will
> unavoidably be a 'story' whose rhythm, whose balance between essential and
> inessential, is profoundly different from that pursued in cinema, and which is
> thus getting viewers used to a new type of narrative texture, a narration that
> frays continuously into the superfluous but that is, because of this, also able
> to generate a new appreciation of the complex causality of the everyday (that
> film, in its operations of narrative selection and purification, had got us to
> forget). It is not a coincidence if, after just a few years of exposure to televisual
> narration, even cinema seems to have started off on a new type of narration,
> of which a distinguished example might be Antonioni's work.[31]

   In *The Open Work*, Eco goes into some detail accounting for how films like
L'avventura and *La notte* may be informed by television, and the new attribute of 'liveness' which, unlike film, broadcasting enabled in moving images.
Indeed, with the launch of TV broadcasting, Italians had been able to see live
on screen key events such as the election of the new president of the republic,
Giovanni Gronchi (1955), the funeral of Pope Pius XII (1958) and the visit
to their country of Queen Elizabeth II (1961). While many might not have
owned a TV set to begin with, live television, as one commentator put it,
'undoubtedly had offered viewers the opportunity of seeing much more and
much better than if they had been at the event in person'.[32] (As many have
noted, 'liveness' is a quality that stuck to the perception of much of television,
and that many types of programmes, including sit-coms with their canned
laughter, seek to cultivate even when pre-recorded.)[33] Watching these films,
Eco notes, feels at several points like watching a live broadcast: '*L'avventura*
often lapses into the long, blank spells of live TV', he muses.[34]

Eco probably had in mind, above all, the long sequence immediately after Anna's disappearance, shot on the Aeolian island of Lisca Bianca. As the characters wait in vain for her reappearance, 'searching' the barren landscape against a background of rapidly changing weather conditions, and seeking refuge in a small fisherman's hut, there is indeed the sense of a 'live event' dragging out and even going wrong, because its presumed protagonist fails to turn up again.[35] In some respects, Anna's introduction on the screen at the beginning of the film adopts the conventions of televised live events, as the camera captures her, frontally, with a backwards tracking shot as she moves forwards along and around a bend on the road on which she is walking, much in the way that a favourite contender in a race might be shot in a sport broadcast. An incorporation of the 'dead times' of live television similar to that which he perceives in *L'avventura* is, according to Eco, in *La notte* too, in the scenes of the all-night party which take up most of the film, or what he describes as 'the heroine's interminable walk amid boys setting off fireworks', where it could seem that the camera trails Lidia in her noon-till-dusk stroll as live television might follow an 'event'.[36]

Eco is not, of course, saying that these films *are* live television, but somewhat like it aesthetically or experientially for the viewer. He is suggesting that both their emergence and, despite the criticisms and attacks they received, the mere acceptance of their existence as cultural (arte)facts by audiences, point to a common sensibility accustomed to 'the new logic of live TV'. This entails a mode of narration that may 'continuously gather the inessential' but in which, also, 'nothing might happen for a long time', and that, as Carpi wrote, may leave characters and viewers stuck 'with the same thing, the same situation, even the same material'.[37] This may be the case, for instance, as Eco writes:

> when the camera remains focused on the curve of a road waiting for the sudden appearance of the first runner who does not appear or, weary, it wanders on to the facades of the surrounding houses or the expectant faces of the spectators, for no other reason than this is the way things go, and there is nothing else to do but wait.[38]

The essence of this new mode of narration and temporality is not frugality or reduction, as the often-used metaphors of purification might suggest, but rather abundance or surplus. By pointing to the seeming rejection of traditional devices or *economies* of narration, the narrative mode that Eco is among the first commentators to attribute to Antonioni's films appears almost like 'observation', quintessentially focused on externality: the surface of things and the unfolding of life's events. And this is so, crucially and interestingly, *even as* their psychological dimension – their exploration of interiority – is widely acknowledged and brought into relief.

Another commentator who, albeit in different terms, articulated a suspicion that modern cinema – 'movies that look "artistic"', as she sneered – and television might in some ways be connected was Pauline Kael. 'Are Movies Going to Pieces?', she asked in a 1964 article, thinking in particular, not unlike Eco and most others, of the way in which this cinema seemed to assault narrative.[39] Answering affirmatively, she blames Antonioni (and Alain Resnais) for such attack, thus contributing, as will Christian Metz a few years later, to seal Antonioni's reputation as one of the key filmmakers who, with his tendency towards 'non' or 'de-dramatization', had 'thrown off' narrative or marked its 'breakdown'.[40] But Kael also surmises that television might have something to do with these developments. By contrast with Eco's alignment of television with extended duration, empty time, unforeseen or superfluous happenings, Kael, with the abundant choice of stations and the heavily interrupted programming of American commercial television in mind, associates it with fragmentation, and writes: '[i]t is possible that television viewing, with all its breaks and cuts and the spinning of the dial to find some action, is partly responsible for the destruction of the narrative sense.'[41]

Both Eco and Kael, then, invoke television as a way of explaining what they see as newly emerging aesthetics and concerns in modern cinema – and in Antonioni's cinema in particular as exemplary of such cinema. The attributes that they respectively identify in television, however, may seem irreconcilable at first. For, on the one hand, Eco seems to associate television – and live television particularly – with uninterrupted duration, continuity and flow. While Kael, on the other, seems to relate it to interruption, discontinuity, choppiness. Kael's impressionistic recourse to American-style television programming, and the viewing habits that this encourages, as factors in the breakdown of narrative in 1960s European cinema may perhaps sound not as culturally pertinent as Eco's reflections. Yet, besides sharing an awareness of the significance of television as a new 'cultural form', as Williams put it in his landmark study of 1974, the two positions are superficially rather than fundamentally in contrast, and can in fact be seen as complementary.[42]

In different ways, they both engage with the experience of television as *flow*, as Williams defined it, indeed in part thinking, unexpectedly or counter-intuitively perhaps, about American commercial television and its programmes routinely *interrupted* by commercials. According to Williams, 'flow' is 'the defining characteristic of broadcasting, simultaneously as a technology and as a cultural form'.[43] The concept of flow, as he suggests, is implied by the way in which, not unlike with radio, one tends to describe the activity as a whole, and generically, speaking of 'watching TV'.[44] Rather than on a specific, individual programme, the emphasis, as Stanley Cavell also argues in a slightly later essay, 'The Fact of Television' (1982), seems to be on the general experience of engaging with the medium – an experience which, elaborating on Williams's term, Michelle Henning has recently defined as a medium 'on tap'.[45] Viewers may interrupt their experience of the flow by turning off the TV set, but there is a sense that the flow 'continues elsewhere' and remains accessible.[46] More crucially, as Williams explains, broadcasting can be described in terms of flow – or, better, of 'planned flow' – because programming unfolds according to sequencing criteria seeking to connect, and carry viewers through, from one programme to another.

Even though Williams mentions the way in which on American television the transition between programmes and adverts may be 'unmarked', the point of his concept of flow is not to emphasise uninterrupted continuity and homogeneity, but precisely to draw attention to the way in which television broadcasting pieces together heterogeneity and 'miscellaneity' into a seemingly smooth continuum 'available in a single dimension and in a single operation'.[47] Without overt reference to Williams's notion of flow, Cavell makes a similar point when he observes that television programmes 'admit discontinuities both within themselves and between one another . . . so as to participate in [the] *continuity* of broadcasting'.[48] Even in a context such as Italy's first decade of broadcasting, where transmissions, during most of the week, would be limited to the latter part of the day (from the late afternoon to before midnight), and where transitions between different programmes, and between these and commercials, would be clearly identifiable (commercials would all be grouped within a self-contained, dedicated advertising show, the *Carosello*), Williams's concept is nevertheless useful for its conciliation of structural heterogeneity and discontinuity with superficial smoothness and continuity. It is precisely 'the experience of visual mobility' that the televisual flow makes domestically, daily available (if not quite 'on tap' to start) - which is one of the medium's key innovations – bringing the kaleidoscopic lure of the moving image into the interior space of the home.[49] 'TV' as John Ellis put it in *Visible Fictions* (1982), 'belongs to the everyday', and its regime is 'one of *continuous variety*, a perpetual introduction of novelty on the basis of repetition'.[50]

Despite a seeming emphasis on the continuous, the homogeneous and the visually monotonous, even Eco's discussion of television (and live television specifically) can be aligned with this understanding of televisual flow as something subsuming – *made of* – visual heterogeneities and discontinuities, not only across programmes, but also within them. As he points out, even live television is always already the production of an event, the result not only of 'interpretation' and 'choice' but, also of 'montage'.[51] At the very least, as Eco goes on to explain, the images transmitted to the television receiver, and viewable on the monitor of the home TV set, are the product of a selection on the part of the programme directors, who, however *impromptu* and simultaneously with the event itself, choose from their bank of preview monitors, relaying from the multiple cameras placed at the scene, which view to broadcast at each moment. Even the televisual flow of live broadcasting is itself – internally, as it were – made up of discontinuities (occasionally temporal as well as spatial) and visual heterogeneities (variations of focus, changes of framing or angle). In this respect, the 'experience of visual mobility' offered by the televisual flow may not appear very dissimilar from what cinema offers (and, indeed, Williams's expression recalls Walter Benjamin's famous account of cinema in terms of visual shock in 'The Work of Art' essay).[52] Yet, the way in which the images of this flow are linked, and the mode of viewing that such flow invites or presumes, are different from cinema. As Eco suggests, television has encouraged both a 'radically different way of "narrating" events' and 'new perceptive habits'.[53]

In a reasoning that resonates with Eco's earlier reflections, Cavell in 'The Fact of Television' suggests that '*monitoring*', rather than viewing, is the 'the mode of perception' that television performs and encourages, as a consequence both of its potential for liveness and of its domestic, quotidian presence inside the home.[54] Underlining, not unlike Eco, the potential un-eventfulness of the event that, thanks to liveness, viewers are enabled to witness and scrutinise on the monitors of their TV sets at home, Cavell explains:

> The bank of monitors at which a door guard glances from time to time – one fixed, say, on each of the empty corridors leading from the otherwise unattended points of entry to the building – emblematizes the mode of perception I am taking as the aesthetic access to television.[55]

That in the case of television broadcast, viewers are not given to see 'the bank of monitors the producer sees' (the equivalent of the building guard's 'bank of monitors' evoked in the passage above) but a selection of 'views transmitted to us one at a time for home consumption' is not significant.[56] The replacement of the producer's simultaneous views with a succession of views to be 'fed into our sole receiver' does not alter the essence of the operations at stake.[57] Where in theory, Cavell sustains, 'we could all watch a replica' of the simultaneous views that the producer or director sees, we should think of the changing views on our television screen as 'a switch of attention from one monitor to another monitor'.[58] Indeed, according to Cavell, it is not so much 'succession' as 'switching' that structures live television broadcasting. This 'means that the move from one image to another is not motivated, as on film, by requirements of meaning, but by requirements of opportunity and anticipation – as if the meaning is dictated by the event itself'.[59] In this sense, not unlike medical monitoring of brain or heart activity, the monitoring that (live) television itself enacts, and promotes as a mode of reception in viewers, presupposes, as Cavell suggests, 'the establishment of some reference or base line . . . of the uneventful' from which events can 'stand out with perfectly anticipatable significance'. If the warning signs that something 'eventful' is about to happen entail a 'preparing [of] our attention to be called upon by certain eventualities', outside of these required peaks of attentiveness, the average level of engagement of 'monitoring' may remain superficial: a scanning that will pause and 'go deeper' only if warning signs appear.[60]

Monitoring, then, implied by Eco and overtly described by Cavell as the form of 'aesthetic access' *of* and *to* television, outlines not so much a mode of temporality and narration in which something happens, but in which something *may* – but also *may not* – happen. One of the consequences of this form of aesthetic access is an ostensibly greater exposure to chance, which may seem crucially to inform both the content of the live televised events and the way in which they are assembled for broadcasting. In this respect, if 'long, blank spells' and 'dead times' may be part of televisual flow, so too will be the apparently casual connections between different camera views, linkages across images seemingly unmotivated by 'requirements of meaning' or narrative conventions. So, in fact, it is *both* these aspects that, smelling something televisual in modern cinema, Eco detects in 'two of its most illustrious examples . . . *L'avventura* and *La notte*'.[61] If the notions of 'flow' – as something that continues or endures – and of 'monitoring' – as a kind of looking (of both the camera and the viewer) at something uneventful out of which an event may emerge – could apply well to *L'avventura* and *La notte*, then, according to Eco, so does the sense that what happens in these films has the *appearance* of chance rather than narration, since the incidents portrayed seem lacking in dramatic links and are disconnected.[62]

This seemingly superficial, phenomenological 'monitoring' of externality that Antonioni's films attentively *construct* cinematically is not incompatible with explorations of interiority: intellectual, moral, psychological, as Eco himself acknowledges. The exteriority and superficiality of television and its (live) flow seem to be *at the service of* the 'interiority' of Antonioni's cinema. But how? As we now turn to consider, this cinema that, according to Eco's suggestion, may be seen to be informed by the televisual and its continuous, yet heterogeneous, flow is also perhaps at the same time articulating it in a different way, precisely by 'remediating' it outside of broadcasting as such.[63] In the context of anxieties about the assiduous and insidious presence and psychological impact of television inside the home, such adoption and adaptation of its flow might have been an attempt to *not act* on the interiority and consciousness of the viewer – to engender, perhaps, an attentive yet *not* absorbed viewer. Yet, at the same time, it might have endeavoured to *enact* interiority as such, offering some kind of articulation of it.

CUTS

A consideration of Antonioni's use of the cut in the 1960s offers a slightly different and generative lens through which to further consider the counter-intuitive, if not paradoxical, implications of an indebtedness to television on his part. In the 1960s, Antonioni declared that he 'could no longer stand real time', because 'there are too many useless moments'.[64] Such a remark sounds strange from a director that, as Eco suggested, absorbed the 'long, blank spells of live TV', and artfully included in his cinema, as Antonioni himself put it, 'those moments . . . when, apparently, nothing is happening'.[65] For the allusion is, of course, to a strategy of cutting and editing, which, as Antonioni noted elsewhere, already starts with filming, 'as soon as we focus our camera on something', 'making a choice' of what, how and how long to shoot.[66]

Antonioni often reiterated his passion for and fascination with editing, and was very keen to stress his hands-on involvement with it – 'from the first cut to the last of all my films' – noting how this was the case even in the bigger, MGM productions like *Blow-Up* and *The Passenger* (1975).[67] Indeed, in this respect, Antonioni's fascination and involvement with editing chimes with that of many contemporaneous experimental filmmakers, for whose 'artisanal' approach the operation had a particular allure. The American photographer and experimental filmmaker Hollis Frampton, for example, was beguiled by how 'film builds upon the straight cut'.[68] What emerges from these comments is not only a sense of the importance of operations of cutting – and of cutting *out*, perhaps – but also of the cut itself.

In a book on Antonioni of 1973, the Italian film historian Lorenzo Cuccu noted that *La notte* was the first of Antonioni's films in which straight cuts completely replaced dissolves.[69] Up to *L'avventura*, although less conspicuously and less frequently than, say, in *Il grido*, the director had tended to follow the cinematic conventions of using dissolves or fades-to-black to 'soften' the spatio-temporal transitions between different sequences, or between different moments within sequences (as, for example, in the car drive into the centre of Rome at the beginning of *L'avventura*, where a dissolve stands in for the longer duration and length of the journey not shown on screen).

For Cuccu and others, the replacement of the dissolve with the cut is one of the key identifiers of modern cinema. Alongside the abrupt, jumpy cuts of Jean-Luc Godard's *Breathless* (1960), Antonioni's change of tack coincides almost exactly, for instance, with Alain Resnais's (and Alain Robbe-Grillet's) decision to eliminate from *Last Year at Marienbad* (1961) a series of dissolves that they had initially planned. On realising that these would have brought to the film's temporality an unwanted gradualness, they replaced them with straight cuts.[70] Like Antonioni, Resnais used – and discussed – the cut very self-consciously as a crucial marker of a new cinema, even, provocatively, *within* the long, smooth tracking shots that constitute one of the key formal motifs of *Last Year*. The recurrence of gliding tracking shots 'sweeps' the viewer along, so to speak, endowing a film that pursues slowness – and even stillness, as in the insistence on tableaux-like poses on the part of its characters – with a movement that is absorbing, almost hypnotic. These tracking shots themselves are only superficially smooth and seamless. With a strategy that occurs again and again in the film, the long tracking sequence along the corridor towards the beginning of *Last Year at Marienbad* is not only, on attentive viewings, interrupted by cuts, but actually a montage of several quite different corridors. As at other points in the film, this is a heterogeneity that Resnais did not want to disguise but that is not necessarily always easy to pay attention to or spot, especially on a first viewing.[71] In a way, the aesthetics of the film is one that encompasses and reconciles both flow and interruptions. More strongly, it is a flow that incorporates and subsumes interruptions (visual, temporal and spatial discontinuities) within itself, not unlike Williams's televisual flow that carries the viewer through different segments of programming by offering a variegated 'experience of visual mobility'.

For Cuccu, Antonioni's turn from dissolve to cut makes *La notte* and the subsequent films appear, paradoxically, like 'one very long sequence'.[72] In a way, he is right. As Antonioni, in his own words, decides to throw out of the window 'all those connective links between sequences, where one sequence served as the springboard for the one that followed', the very idea of 'transition' is eliminated.[73] If this, also in view of the added 'carry-through' effect generated by the tracking shots, can be said of *Last Year at Marienbad* too, then perhaps it is not preposterous to see both as partly responding to television in their turn, and the absorbing, sweeping, yet also potentially dazzling and disorientating, *superficial* smoothness of its *structurally* heterogeneous and discontinuous flow. Despite the fact that Robbe-Grillet (who wrote *Last Year*'s screenplay) will a couple of years later write of a time that 'doesn't flow anymore', the paradox, in profound ways, is that similarly to cinematic movement, televisual flow functions because of – rather than despite – the interruption and discontinuity that the cut introduces and simultaneously bridges over.[74] But, at the same time, as Alain Badiou noted more recently, '[i]t is in movement that the effects of the cut become incarnate'.[75]

If the replacement of the dissolve with the cut contributes to the transformation – or, in the view of some, the undoing – of conventional cinematic narrative, rhythm and temporality, the cut also acquires a new presence.

According to Gilles Deleuze, the cut as such plays a crucial role in the emergence of modern cinema, where, in contrast to its function in classical cinema, it acquires a kind of autonomous presence.[76] Indeed, modern cinema for Deleuze marks a moment when 'the cut' shifts from being understood as an operation or technique (often invisible or discreet) for 'the linkage of images', to acquiring 'an importance in itself', not as *part of* the images, but *on a par* with them.[77] '[T]he cut', Deleuze writes, 'no longer forms part of one or the other image', 'included as the end of the one *or* as the beginning of the other', but 'stands on its own'.[78] It comes to be valued as an 'interstice' if not even, almost, as a thing or image 'in its own right', as when the cut is 'extended [to] appear . . . as the black screen, the white screen and their derivatives and combinations'.[79] While for Deleuze this may be more a sign of cinema's refusal of the televisual than of its absorption ('it is not cinema which needs television', he declares in the preface to the English edition of *Cinema II*), black screens and white screens, like unplanned moments of interruption of transmission, are instances of 'extended' cuts which could occur fairly frequently in television broadcasting.[80]

With *L'avventura*, even if dissolves still feature, cuts begin to attract attention to themselves, to acquire presence in the terms evoked by Deleuze. In this respect, if the modern cinema of Antonioni and others, as Eco perceptively suggested in the early 1960s, owes some of its stylistic and formal innovations to its porousness towards – rather than impermeability from – television, it also, in absorbing some of the qualities of television's flow, appears to play up the discontinuities and interruptions within it. As Antonioni recounted in the 1960s, in his first ever film project, a since-lost short produced at the Centro Sperimentale di Cinematografia in 1941, he had pursued an utter transparency of the cut. Assigning the parts of a respectable woman and of a prostitute to the same actress, he had striven to make the interruption between filming the actress impersonating one and then the other *invisible*.[81] By contrast, in the unusual angles and radical re-framings of films such as *L'avventura*, cuts are propelled into *visibility*. Think, for instance, of the famous scene in which Sandro and Claudia make love in the grass before reaching Noto, as the camera alternates between close-ups of their faces and wide-angle shots of the landscape traversed by the train. Or, in *L'eclisse*, think of the cut that, standing for an un-signposted – and fairly lengthy – temporal ellipsis, introduces Vittoria's 'African' dance (see Chapter 5). And in *Il deserto rosso*, in ways that have some affinity with Resnais's *Last Year at Marienbad* or *Muriel* (1963) and their effort to find a cinematic articulation of memory and its ambiguities or failures, the visibility of the cut is overtly associated with an articulation of Giuliana's disturbed mental state. As Giuliana's malaise worsens in the wake of her son's (feigned) leg paralysis, the cutting becomes more visible. This is so from the cut that introduces the fable – or 'fantasy' – about a solitary girl on a picture-perfect desert island that she tells her son (a famously odd interlude that Millicent Marcus has described as 'an anti-film within the film'[82]), to the frenzied and disorientating editing used just afterwards for the scene of her lovemaking with Corrado in his hotel room. Counter-intuitively, in all these examples, it is through a particular way of rendering external reality, the place and time the characters observe and inhabit, that interiority – the character's states of mind of disorientation, unease, apathy, crisis – is pursued and articulated. But if in *L'avventura* and *La notte* the pursuit of interiority is indebted to televisual aesthetics, with *Il deserto rosso*, as I want to suggest, cinematic form also absorbs another emerging techno-cultural register, that of cybernetics and early computer sciences. While the interrelation of interiority and exteriority is still central, these fields' approach to mental or brain activities is different. To prepare the ground for this, however, I first move the discussion of flow from television to consciousness itself, and the perceived affinity with cinema, its dynamics, and its 'cuts', in particular.

(DIS)CONTINUITIES

Before being associated with broadcasting, the notion of 'flow' had been associated with understandings of consciousness and the mind. Eco alludes to this as he mentions modernist literature's 'stream of consciousness' as a partly related precursor to the uninterrupted, dilated duration of live television.[83] The narrative methods of James Joyce or Italo Svevo in the early twentieth century had been influenced by William James, who in *The Principles of Psychology* (1890) had presented thought as 'a stream'. 'Consciousness', he wrote, 'does not appear to itself chopped up in bits. Such words as "chain" or "train" do not describe it fitly . . . It is nothing jointed; it flows'.[84] Similarly, for Henri Bergson, who was strongly indebted to James's ideas, consciousness was chiefly explained as an internal durational flow, a heterogeneous yet indivisible 'lived time' different from the external, measurable and mechanistic time of science.[85]

This model of consciousness as a continuous stream, however, co-exists with another, outlined at more or less the same time and that, even while possibly hoping in the possibility of free-wheeling streams of thought (as Svevo's 1923 psychoanalytical novel *La coscienza di Zeno/Zeno's Conscience* might suggest), emphasised interruption, discontinuity, removal or blockage. In the Freudian model, consciousness is not an uninterrupted flow, but discontinuous and riddled with holes, because of competing forces such as the unconscious, repression and memory.[86] In the short 1925 essay 'A Note Upon the Mystic Writing Pad', using the example of a very elementary organism not unlike the 'living vesicle' he had used in 'Beyond the Pleasure Principle' (1920), Freud considers consciousness in its most basic but also most general manifestation.[87] Strictly dependent on perception, it is characterised as a 'flickering up and passing away', a discontinuous process whose gaps and interruptions are not accidental but constitutive.[88] 'Like a light ceaselessly turning off and on', as Jean Laplanche has put it, consciousness, in Freud's model, is interrupted by pauses, cuts – or, in its human manifestations, by repressions and absences.[89]

As psychoanalysis itself became institutionalised and more mainstream in the post-war decades, its concepts and model of the mind came to be articulated – if not popularised – via cinema (think, among others, of Alfred Hitchcock's films such as *Spellbound* (1945) or *Marnie* (1964)) and absorbed by film theory. In this respect, more than simply using psychoanalysis to read individual films and their narratives, the so-called 'apparatus theory' of Jean-Louis Baudry and others in the 1970s, pursued a nexus *between* cinema *and* the mind.[90] It is in this context, for instance, that filmmaker and theorist Thierry Kuntzel returned to Freud to suggest that, despite Freud's own scepticism towards the possibility of using cinema to explore the 'abstractions' of the psyche, 'the functioning of the [cinematic] machine itself' might have been of interest to him. For, as Kuntzel explains in the essay 'A Note Upon the Filmic Apparatus' (1976), the machines and mechanics of cinema might have provided a better illustrative model of the basic activities of what Freud calls the 'mental apparatus' than the one he himself resorts to in 'A Note Upon the Mystic Writing Pad' when he uses a wax-based, 'Etch-a-Sketch'-kind of children's toy to illustrate the intermittent reception of external impressions on the part of the system of perception and consciousness.[91]

In a context not as overtly informed by apparatus theory as Kuntzel's, Frampton perhaps also had Freud's essay in mind when he wrote that cinema had 'discerned and enunciated for itself a task, namely, the founding of an art that is to be fully and radically isomorphic with the *kineses* and *stases* – in short, with the dynamic "structure" (if one may still dare use that word) – of consciousness itself'.[92] When, interviewed in London in 1972, Frampton was asked: 'Your films are about the consciousness of the people who are looking at them, aren't they?', his quipping answer was: 'I would like to believe that they're about consciousness, period'.[93] This terse reply is representative of how an appreciation of cinema as an activity engaging the viewers' consciousness cohabited with the notion that cinema itself could function as a dynamic 'mimesis' or 'incarnation' *of* consciousness, as Frampton himself put it.[94] The unusual, cognitively challenging, structures of Frampton's *Zorns Lemma* (1970) and *(nostalgia)* (1971), and Michael Snow's *Wavelength* (1967), to an extent both address *and* represent cinematically – through structure and dynamics rather than visual content as such – their viewers' minds. If for Baudry and other 'apparatus theorists' the cinematic apparatus was a model of the psyche as a site of ideological manipulation, illusory representation and psychic repression, for experimental filmmakers such as Frampton and Snow the way in which '[f]ilm, even in its physical attributes' could 'become a kind of metaphor for consciousness' had more positive implications.[95] As well as addressing and activating viewers' consciousness – rather than *acting on* it like certain kinds of film-spectacle or television (a medium that Frampton described as a system of 'affections') – cinema could also function as a model for it in a very didactic way according to these filmmakers.[96]

Arguably, this is what Frampton's *Zorns Lemma* and *(nostalgia)* do, keeping viewers on their toes by engaging them in a sustained game of attention, anticipation and memory while also, at some level, using the very mechanics of cinema to attempt to visualise, or externalise, the mind's internal and invisible processes. While *(nostalgia)* does this at a ponderous and slow pace, *Zorns Lemma*, especially in its distinctive central part, bombards the viewer with a rapid-fire montage, a visually heterogeneous flow of images which is at once continuous *and* discontinuous – 'a controlled riot of colour and shape and semantic meaning', as Paul Arthur described it.[97] Structured around a twenty-four-letter alphabet, the montage proceeds through a fast, yet regular and rhythmic, alternation of one-second shots of imagery of words starting with the relevant letter, found in the urban environment.

Figure 2.1   *Zorns Lemma* (1970)

Figure 2.2   *Zorns Lemma* (1970)

In the course of forty minutes, this imagery, which, but for a few exceptions, is different at each run through the alphabet, is gradually, though not alphabetically, replaced by another set of images. These are on-going segments of human actions, such as peeling a citrus fruit or hand washing, animal behaviour and natural phenomena.

As the film unfolds, returning imagery is progressively substituted to the initial 'impossible onslaught of rapid-fire signs'. Viewers, then, come not only to *get* the film ('master it conceptually', as Arthur puts it) but also, because of the thought gymnastics that the film requires, to gain awareness of their own mental engagement with it.[98] Furthermore, this happens through a regular, pulsating structure of alphabet cycles whose intermittence of images and cuts arguably works to bring to the surface cinema's very mechanics.[99] As each alphabet cycle, marked by a black-screen pause of one second at each end, lasts twenty-four seconds, its duration seems to echo the number of frames (twenty-four for a second of film projected at standard sound speed) of which each of its shots is composed. It is as if the twenty-four-second cycles, with their cut to another image or shot at each second, were a sort of twenty-four-times enlargement of one second of film: film's very mechanics put under a time-magnifying lens to bring them above the threshold of perception. The editing cut, a sort of 'second order' of the cut in cinema, is used to enact and fictionalise, didactically, cinema's basic intermittence, the 'first order' of the cut constituted by the shutter's interruptions. Frampton was keen on attracting attention to this. When 'watching a film', he said, 'you believe you are watching a complete illusion of something real, but you're actually watching an illusion of only half what took place. The camera shutter was closed half of the time . . . And when you play that back, the shutter in the projector is also closed half of the time, so that half of the time you are sitting in total darkness'.[100] And, of course, the cinematic intermittence and discontinuity dovetails, as we have seen, with his understanding of mental activity itself as intermittent, made of 'stases' as well as 'kineses'. Through processes that, as P. Adams Sitney, citing the Russian formalist Victor Shklovsky put it, produce a defamiliarisation of perception, it is not only by deconstructing the dynamics between cinema and the viewer's mental activity, but also by unpacking and exposing the mechanics of cinema itself, that certain works came to use the medium to construct an 'analogue[s] of consciousness', as Annette Michelson put it with regard to Michael Snow's films, with a view to scrutinising or learning about its workings.[101] Such workings, as Frampton's position in particular makes manifest, are understood in terms of movement and flow, as with Jamesian or Bergsonian models of consciousness, but also as being constitutively intermittent and therefore heterogeneous.

But the alignment of cinema and mind that culminated with some modulations of structural film and apparatus theories of cinema in the 1970s, as well as the vocabulary of 'apparatus', 'machinery' and 'mechanism' routinely used in both quarters (with either pejorative or positive connotations) had begun to intensify before this moment. For, already in the early 1960s, both film critics and filmmakers, including Antonioni with his turn from 'externals' to 'internals', had started to refer to cinema and its machinery as a tool for the articulation of – to return to the expression Aristarco used for Antonioni's films – the 'psychic machinery itself'. And in 1962, Resnais similarly explained his *Last Year at Marienbad* as 'an attempt, still crude and primitive, to approach the complexity of thought and of its mechanisms'.[102] If statements such as these form a kind of precursor to the conviction expressed by experimental filmmakers and apparatus theorists in the early 1970s that cinema could provide not so much a representation or description of individual states of mind or emotions but a kind of formal model of the working mind itself, the emphasis, however, seems to be not so much on its functioning as on its *mal*functioning.

INSIDE OUT

If *Zorns Lemma* addresses 'consciousness' in general and abstract terms ('consciousness, period', as Frampton put it), Antonioni was interested in situating such consciousness historically, amidst the radical processes of social, economic and cultural transformation of the post-war period. Where Frampton's focus lay mostly in (re)producing a 'model', addressing how consciousness *functions*, Antonioni's was on how consciousness might have come to *malfunction* in response to these dramatic changes. Indeed, as he pointed out during his CSC talk, his chief aim in moving towards 'an internal form of filmmaking' had been to analyse the effects of 'history' on the psyche, to see 'what remained inside the individual'.[103] With its concentration on the neurotic Giuliana, *Il deserto rosso* is undoubtedly the culmination of Antonioni's efforts in such direction. In a reality stricken by modernity as if by a plague, and transfigured by progress 'to the point of becoming monstrous', 'the reality of our time' is portrayed, Antonioni explains, through Giuliana's eyes.[104] By adopting what Pasolini, as mentioned, termed the 'free indirect point-of-view' (the character's subjective view independent of his or her contingent, physical point-of-view), the film enacts her alienated subjectivity, exteriorising her psyche, unrolling it on the screen, so to speak.[105] Giuliana's neurosis is presented not so much as an isolated pathology but as an acute manifestation of the impact of radically changing socio-historical conditions on the modern subject in general, a subject who, Antonioni feels, is often too slow to 'adapt to the new "way" of life'.[106] Even though at a peak in her crisis Corrado consoles her by saying that 'we all have [your illness] a little', Giuliana is a limit case that becomes exemplary of the dramatic moment of reconfiguration of subjectivity that Antonioni felt to be lying 'behind industrial transformation', and of which the film makes itself at once symptom and diagnosis.[107]

As I considered at length in the previous chapter, *Il deserto rosso* was Antonioni's first colour film. Yet, as Briony Fer has put it, 'much of it looks as if colour has been drained out of it'.[108] The film's overall appearance is dull, almost faded (an effect achieved through lens filters and pro-filmic interventions), if interspersed with occasional vivid patches of reds, greens and blues. In addition, as I mentioned, *Il deserto rosso* unfolds at a more sustained, choppier and fragmentary, editing rhythm than any of his previous films. Talking about it after the initial release, Antonioni himself reflected that he had 'chosen very short shots', and related this decision to the use of colour film: '[p]erhaps it was colour that demanded this, insinuating this deep need to treat it in blots, as if they were pulsations penetrating confusedly into the character'.[109] This further contributes to the sense that the film articulates Giuliana's 'view', her subjective, and disturbed, experience of the world. Yet, by aligning the film's work of cutting with its treatment of colour as 'blots', the suggestion is also that Giuliana's interiority is rendered not only through the hue, the 'look', of colour in the film, but also through its dynamics. If the idea of colours as external stimuli sampled by – or, in fact, as Antonioni puts it, penetrating into – the subject intermittently, according to an on/off, on/off dynamic, is reminiscent of the syncopated functioning of consciousness described by Freud in 'A Note Upon the Mystic Writing-Pad', or, similarly, by Frampton, the working that Antonioni evokes is nevertheless less predictable, disorderly, irregular. Rather than a mechanism ticking over, it seems one on the verge of breaking down. The 'psychic machinery' that Antonioni's film models and enacts is one that misses beats and gets stuck: that of a subject who 'isn't able to get into gear' ['*non riesce a ingranare*'], as Giuliana's husband, Ugo, puts it by also using the example of a machine, the car.

The idea of malfunction is suggested at various moments in the film. One dramatic instance is in the scene after the party in the shack by the port. As the landscape fills with white fog obscuring visibility all but completely, Giuliana's mind also goes 'blank', and she confusedly drives her husband's car towards the sea end of the pier in what may be a second attempt at suicide. A particularly crucial example, however, occurs in the sequence dedicated to her most acute moments of crisis towards the end of the film. Disturbed by the fact that her son has feigned paralysis, Giuliana leaves her house to end up at the hotel where Corrado (her husband's school friend who has returned to Ravenna to recruit workers to take to Patagonia) is staying. Unlike Ugo, who is emotionally distant and cold, Corrado (himself at a moment of crisis in his life) has shown her some sympathy and understanding. In an increasingly distraught state, Giuliana rushes into the hotel's lobby. Here – similarly to the famous earlier scene in Ravenna's centre – everything, even a plant in a pot by the door, seems to be white.[110] Her confused state is evident from the way in which she is unable to provide either Corrado's surname or room number to the receptionist. She runs upstairs, down a stark white, futuristic-looking corridor, to which the interior of Corrado's room – wood panelled, carpeted and furnished in browns and reds – stands in stark contrast. As the two talk and eventually have sex, in what seems an opportunistic, if not problematic, attempt on Corrado's part to 'calm' her, Giuliana's crisis unfolds. The editing becomes increasingly fast, disconnected and disorientating as her discomfort and confusion, if not panic, reach their peak. The electronic, metallic noises (reminiscent of signal interferences) that pierce the room every now and then in brief bursts, and which Giuliana alone seems to hear, also underline her acutely disturbed state. In a film that presents Giuliana's perception of the world in what, as we saw, Pasolini called the 'free indirect subjective', colour, sound and editing all concur to articulate the state of a 'psychic machinery', to use Aristarco's expression, that has started to *mal*function.

From the initial shots alternating between Giuliana and Corrado at the start of the scene, through to the more confusing shots towards the end, when both spatial and temporal co-ordinates have become unclear, the flow of the sequence is continuously not simply interrupted but *dis*rupted by cuts. As it follows and embodies the crescendo of Giuliana's crisis, the scene is chopped up by drastic and sudden re-framings, obtained through jump cuts (and, to the same effect, some zip pans), which, in a different context, Slavoj Žižek has characterised as 'hystericizing' film.[111] Rather than moving towards them gradually, the camera skips to different corners of the room (the bare walls, the bed's red metal railing, a sofa by the window), and/or the actors' faces and bodies (often cropped, as in the views of Giuliana's writhing legs), generating an effect of both disconnection and collision. The 'shocks and collisions' of 'moving through traffic' that film 'established as a formal principle' according to Benjamin, are here internalised, in the sense of being brought into the enclosed space of the room, and put to the service of an externalisation of mental activity.[112] As the film shifts rapidly between enigmatic shots of Giuliana by the window alone then apparently back on the bed, fending off Corrado's embrace or, again, on a sofa by the window, with and then without Corrado, we realise that the disorientation engendered by these cuts is temporal as well as spatial. Indeed, in its use of cutting, this scene offers a micro-view of the stories without 'connective links', without 'logical narrative transitions', which Antonioni felt imperative to start telling in the 1960s.[113] The cuts, as Deleuze suggests, gain hold 'in themselves', as something *between* images, and which, though not exactly at the same level as in *Zorns Lemma*, replaces a logical and hypotactical organisation of shots with a more paratactical and serial arrangement.

But what it is interesting and crucial to underline is that, if Antonioni uses the dynamics of, and *between*, colour, sound and cutting to produce a cinematic enactment of Giuliana's psyche, the cinematic exteriorisation of interiority produced is concerned not with the appearance or look of such psyche but with its dynamics or behaviour, however malfunctioning. This may be 'the states of mind themselves', yet not represented or figured, but enacted *through* externals.

ACTING LIKE A BRAIN

If interest in the mind and its interiority is no doubt related to the institutionalisation and popularisation of disciplines including psychology, psychiatry, neurology and psychoanalysis in the second half of the twentieth century, the recurrent search for 'models' or 'analogues', as well as the insistent vocabulary of machinery and mechanism, drew inspiration from the then blooming discipline of cybernetics and its applications in the development of 'thinking machines' and 'artificial brains'. Cybernetics itself, a buzzword in the 1950s and 1960s, was not only routinely associated with physiological brains as well as machines but, in its own turn, had important links with psychiatry and the brain sciences.[114]

As the French Pierre de Latil, author of one of the first critical studies of the field, put it at the start of his 1953 *Thinking by Machine* (which Antonioni had in his library in the Italian translation of 1962): 'Cybernetics? The word suddenly has become fashionable . . . Every newspaper carries headlines about "mechanical brains", "thinking machines", "synthetic animals".[115] This was certainly so in Italy during the technology-driven modernising years of the economic miracle. Set aside sensations such as Cygan, a 2.5-metre-tall 'mechanical man' built by the engineer Piero Fiorito, and whose dancing performances toured within and beyond Italy, the country was at the forefront of research and application in the field of electronic calculators and 'artificial brains'.[116] Olivetti, the typewriter manufacturer, had embarked on research in electronics and was in strict competition with international firms such as IBM in the development of computers, launching its mainframe, transistorised, Elea 9003 in 1959.[117]

Even though Olivetti eventually ceded its electronics division to General Electric in 1964, a number of the company's subsequent generation of electronic calculators, the 'desktop' Programma 101, was even acquired by NASA for use in route calculations for the Apollo missions.[118] On a more experimental and philosophical front, Silvio Ceccato, director of the first

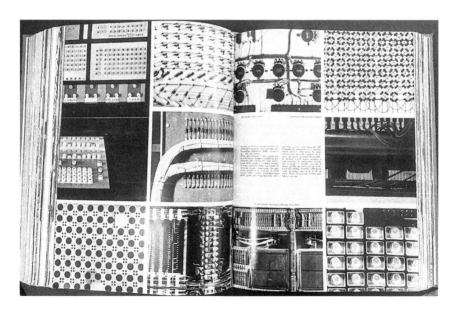

Figure 2.3   Photos of Olivetti Elea 9003, in *Domus* (August 1961)

Italian Centre for Cybernetics, at the University of Milan, had partnered with Leonardo Sinisgalli, the 'poet engineer' editor of the periodical *Civiltà delle macchine* (published by Finmecannica, the mechanical engineering arm of the state-owned Institute for Industrial Reconstruction) to build a 'mental machine'. This resulted in Adamo II, exhibited in Milan's Museum of Science and Technology on the occasion of a congress and exhibition on automation in 1956.

Figure 2.4 Silvio Ceccato with a fragment of the 'brain' of Adamo II, Milan, 1956

By the early 1960s, Ceccato had directed his research on electronic brains towards the development of a much-talked about automated multi-lingual translating machine and a 'mechanical chronicler', a device able 'to see' and describe what it saw.[119]

So, not only in newspapers and mass-consumption magazines, but also in the learned press, alongside the similarly new phenomenon of television, 'electronic brains' and cybernetics were the hottest topics of exposition and critical discussion. A case in point, alongside *Civiltà delle macchine* and the *Pirelli* magazine, is the *Almanacco letterario Bompiani*, which, even before turning to (audio-)visual mass media as the leading theme for the 1963 volume, focused on cybernetics in 1962. In addition to explanations of basic principles and concepts, the volume included an article by Ceccato on his artificial translator, an essay by Eco, whose *The Open Work* was crucially influenced by cybernetics, and a central art section curated by Bruno Munari, whose 'Programmed Art' exhibition would open in Olivetti's shop in Milan in May 1962.[120] Perhaps it was in part as a response to all this excitement about the automation of creative production that Giovanni (Marcello Mastroianni) in *La notte* describes writing as 'antiquated'. But if for Giovanni this 'solitary, artisanal' labour seemed non-subjectable to 'mechanization', by the late 1960s, according to Italo Calvino, the situation had changed. In an often-cited lecture titled 'Cybernetics and Ghosts' (first delivered and published in 1967) he pursued the idea of 'literary automata' – literature-writing machines. Meanwhile, Ceccato, who would regularly be invited onto television to illustrate the subject for the general public, published a book on 'cybernetics for everyone', *Cibernetica per tutti* (1968).[121]

The development and use of models and simulators of the mind – or rather, more empirically, of the *brain* – for exploratory and heuristic purposes was one of the central features of cybernetics. This was so in important respects because the discipline was premised on the possibility of a parallel, if not an affinity, between the living and the non-living, the mechanical and the biological. As Raymond Jones put it in the sci-fi novel *The Cybernetic Brains*, whose initial shorter version, published in 1950, was certainly one of the first platforms for the popularisation of Norbert Wiener's ideas, cybernetics 'pointed out . . . that the study of neural activity is the study of communications engineering'.[122] The discipline's guiding idea, as de Latil explained, was that the machine could function 'as a "model" of life', and enable, via artificial means, the study of 'phenomena which are impossible to investigate *in vivo*'.[123] While in the cultural imagination cybernetics has come to be mostly associated with robotics and the development of artificial intelligence – with, that is, an exploitation of knowledge about the living or the biological geared towards the improvement of the machine – at its emergence, the discipline, at least, was animated by a sense of reciprocity. In other words, the traffic of knowledge, as de Latil put it, could flow both ways: not only to 'improve our machines by imitating life processes', but also 'to understand life' better via an 'understanding of machines'.[124] This was markedly the case with the European, particularly British, articulations of cybernetics, which emerged out of the life and brain sciences and, as Andrew Pickering has demonstrated, psychiatry in particular.[125]

In fact, if it is indeed the American mathematician Norbert Wiener that coined and put the term into the public domain with his famous books *Cybernetics: Or Control and Communication in the Animal and the Machine* (1948), and *The Human Use of Human Beings: Cybernetics and Society* (1950), the discipline arguably shot to mass prominence thanks to the devices developed by two British medical scientists: the tortoises Elmer and Elsie (1949), built by (American-born) William Grey Walter, and the homeostat (1948) of William Ross Ashby, which became famous worldwide 'almost overnight'.[126] BBC radio aired a thirty-minute programme by Ashby called 'Imitating the Brain' in 1949, and both Ashby and Walter's 'thinking machines' featured prominently in national and international news media. Both Ashby and Walter came from a life-sciences and mental-health background. The former was a psychiatrist whose career was spent in mental institutions, and the latter a neurophysiologist who pioneered electro-encephalography, while both had been involved in the development and application of electroconvulsive treatment.[127] As well as contributions to robotics and artificial intelligence – as they are nowadays mostly seen – the homeostat and the tortoises 'could be understood as "brain science"', functioning as models of the physiological brain, both normal and pathological. Walter, as Pickering notes, drove the tortoises 'mad', for instance, by over-stimulating their light sensors, and then 'cured' them.[128] In this respect, it is interesting that, while Wiener lectured extensively in Italy as a visiting professor in the late 1950s and early 1960s, especially in the newly founded 'Cybernetics Section' of the Physics Institute of the University of Naples, this section was headed by a psychiatrist (Valentino Braitenberg) and that, from the early 1960s, the town hosted some of the first conferences dedicated to cybernetic medicine specifically. Relatedly, as we have seen, the other important Italian research centre for cybernetics was headed by Ceccato, whose background was philosophical rather than mathematical.[129]

If in Wiener's *Cybernetics* neurons or the brain are an analogy used to explain the machine, the first publications on the subject by Ashby and Walter, *Design for a Brain* (1952) and *The Living Brain* (1953) respectively, seem to reverse this focus.[130] The interest here appears to be on the externalisation of the workings of the physiological brain *through* the development of 'synthetic' electromechanical models, however basic to begin with.[131] 'For teachers and educationists throughout the ages', Walter writes in *The Living Brain*, 'the brain has been a Black Box'.[132] Indeed, as he saw it, although the brain had come 'to maturity in complete ignorance of its own existence', electromechanical models such as his tortoises, or Ashby's electromagnetic homeostat, were finally offering this crucial organ 'the first possible glimpses of itself'.[133] Yet, if cybernetics was offering the brain a 'mirror' that was bringing to a close 'the millennial period of its unconscious evolution' and inaugurating 'a new phase', as Walter triumphantly announces at the end of his book, such mirror is not to be intended literally.[134] Rather, as he explains, the breakthrough in such investigation consisted precisely in the construction of something imitative '*not in appearance but in behaviour*', that could be determined to bear analogous functions and properties – or, as Ashby also pointed out in a paper of 1962, to be understood to proceed by 'simulation'.[135] As de Latil was at pains to stress, 'the machine does not "think"': rather, 'using entirely different methods', it can 'imitate the functions in man we call "thought", without necessarily understanding any more about the nature of thought'.[136]

The objective of cybernetics was to simulate – to *enact* – mental processes rather than to figure the mind, to turn it into a picture, as it were. As Walter put it in *The Living Brain*, 'any discussion of mind except as a *function* . . . of brain' was beyond his concerns, and thus, if the word 'mind' should be used at all, it might rather be 'mentality', as a term that expresses something that happens or an operation, rather than an appearance, 'in the same class as velocity'.[137] In other words, as Pickering has explained, cyberneticians approached the brain not 'as a thinking machine' but as 'an *acting* machine', 'an immediately embodied organ' that was 'not representational but *performative*', and whose performances or behaviour were the 'object' of study.[138] Ceccato's recurrent emphasis is consonant with these intentions. In the presentation of Adamo II, he pointed out that one of the obstacles in the 'reproduction' of the human mind had been its understanding as 'a constellation of physical entities', but that such obstacles 'had been eliminated by addressing thought and its contents *as activities* instead'.[139] In the presentation of his mechanical translator in the 1962 *Almanacco letterario Bompiani*, Ceccato further explains that cybernetic activities in Italy have 'organised the study of the human mind so as to produce results both in the construction of artificial models and in the observation of the [physiological] brain'.[140] In the course of a 1961 television interview, his unit's project at Milan University's Cybernetics Centre is described in terms of its focus on the '*operational activities* of the brain', as a 'study of the human mind to become aware of the *way* in which man thinks and constitutes thought'.[141]

Antonioni was fascinated by all these developments, and it is telling that his interest in machines and mind, electronic and human brain – even, indeed,

Giuliana's pathological one – co-exists in *Il deserto rosso*. Earlier versions of the screenplay reveal not only that Giuliana's condition was to be addressed in more specific detail (including mention of her having received electroconvulsive therapy), but that the factory scene towards the beginning of the film was meant to feature more emphatically the presence of the electronic calculator being programmed by a young woman.[142] Certainly, Antonioni had gathered extensive notes on programming and programmers, describing, among other things, the working environments and practices at IBM's Rivoltella del Garda training centre (which opened in 1956), and in Milan, where production of a transistor-version of IBM's vacuum-tubes and punch-card electronic calculator had started in the mid-1950s.[143]

Furthermore, as the director excitedly reports when interviewed by Jean-Luc Godard after the film's release, he had been very impressed by Ceccato's machines, as well as by another synthetic brain – 'one of the most extraordinary discoveries in the world', as Antonioni puts it – shown to him a few months earlier by a scientist heading to a conference in Naples (presumably one of the cybernetic medicine ones).[144] 'I am still amazed', Antonioni explains:

> by a conversation I had with a professor of cybernetics at the University of Milan, Silvio Ceccato . . . He is amazing, he has invented a machine that is capable of seeing and describing what it sees, of driving a car and writing an article from any given aesthetic, ethical, or political point of view. It's not a television, but a true electronic brain . . . Six months ago another scholar came to visit me in Rome, Robert M. Stewart. He had invented a chemical brain and he was going to Naples to a congress on cybernetics to tell them about the invention, one of the most extraordinary discoveries in the world. It was in a tiny box, mounted on a load of tubes: there were cells, made up of gold and other substances, in a chemical solution. These cells have a life of their own and have certain reactions: if you walk into a room, they take on one shape, whereas if I walk in, they take on another, and so on. In that little box there were a few million cells, but from such basis you can actually reconstruct a human brain.[145]

Antonioni's fascinated account of these devices' capabilities, however detailed, is obviously hyperbolic, and resonates with imaginary descriptions abounding in contemporaneous science fiction – even though these descriptions themselves may in turn borrow from real-life experiments. The monumentally sized intelligent machine in Dino Buzzati's *Il grande ritratto* ('*The Great Portrait*') of 1960, for instance, was inspired by Ceccato's contraptions, and, bar the difference in size, its 'impressive filigree of metallic objects . . . connected by an inextricable tangle of wires' and emitting a 'barely perceptible crackling' or 'teeming with flashes of blues, greens, yellows, reds' in response to external stimulation, bears a core affinity with the chemical brain described by Antonioni.[146]

But, enthusiastic or fearful exaggeration apart, several things are worthy of note in Antonioni's account. While, in parts that I omitted from the passage above, the director apologises for only partially understanding the scientists' explanations despite their impressive avoidance of technical jargon, he seems to have absorbed well, and have deep sympathy for, some key cybernetic ideas. Like the cyberneticists, he is talking about these machines as exteriorisations of the brain not so much in terms of representations of the inside of the 'Black Box' but of externally manifested behaviours and activities: *enactments* rather than *picturings*. Antonioni understands that what is allegedly imitated and put on view, held up for scrutiny, is not the mind's appearance but its performance ('mentality' as an operation, a function of the brain, as Walter put it). From this perspective, unlike the contemporaneous Alfred Hitchcock's *Marnie* (1964) and Roman Polansky's *Repulsion* (1965), where the colour red and cracks in the wall respectively exteriorise their protagonists' disturbed states of mind through, and as, an image, in *Il deserto rosso*, Giuliana's mental state is not so much *figured* – turned into a picture – but, rather, dynamically *performed* through the visual (and aural) rhythm of the film itself.[147] It is not the red walls or the white-painted fruit in themselves, but their dynamic interrelation in the film's unfolding (and we have noted Antonioni's harnessing of editing to this effect) that 'exteriorise' her psyche. Antonioni's 1961 announcement of a focus on 'the states of mind themselves' seems to have become inflected by a different nuance.

Puzzlingly at first perhaps, Antonioni also calls into play television. 'It's not a television', Antonioni says of Ceccato's machine (the 'mechanical chronicler', it would seem) 'but a true electronic brain'. While, as we have seen, television might be associated with notions of exteriority in contemporaneous assessments, from a psychological viewpoint it would more readily be judged to act negatively on interiority than to function as a tool for its exteriorisation. But Antonioni's mention of television in the context of his discussion of cybernetics does indeed register a contemporaneous connection between the two.

Nowadays, it is the screen that, above all, provides a synecdoche for the computer and signifies it in the cultural imagination. Yet, like earlier 'cybernetic' devices such as the homeostat or Elmer and Elsie, Ceccato's Adamo II, for instance, had no screen, and made its 'thinking' visible through a series of light-bulbs fixed to its frame turning on or off. While by the time of Antonioni's interview with Godard, television's cathode-ray-tube (CRT) technology had come to be used for computer displays, this was still an era antecedent to the diffusion of so-called 'mini' and 'personal' computers. Computers are still a large – often room-sized – multi-part affair. Rather than a machine to pick up like one might a tool, they are an environment or 'electronic landscape' to enter, as the designer of Olivetti's sleek-looking Elea 9003, the artist-architect, Ettore Sottsass, put it in a mesmerised, and mesmerising, photographic presentation of it in *Domus* in 1961.[148] As presentations of mainframe computers in print and other media also concur to suggest, even when CRT displays are part of the apparatus, screens are not the *one* feature to which such machines would and could be synecdochically reduced. Olivetti's Elea 9003, IBM's 700/7000 series or its System/360 (introduced in the same year as *Il deserto rosso*'s release in 1964) were all still mainframe computers consisting of magnetic tape drives, punch-card functions, and large operator consoles with buttons, switches and panels with lights coming on and off enabling the 'monitoring' of operations.[149] In attunement with the emphasis of cybernetics on behaviour rather than appearance, what seems to be at stake in Antonioni's statement is not so much the look of television but its way of functioning.

Such way of functioning, one of whose crucial aspects is that visual information is captured and, after conversion into and transmission as an electromagnetic-wave signal, reproduced line-by-line, so to speak, via a raster-scanning process, recurs in cybernetics as an explanation of mental activity. If critiques of television, as we saw, were preoccupied by the medium's *action on* the mind, cybernetics rather thought that the brain *acted* like television, finding the medium a useful analogue of mental processes.[150] Walter, whose electroencephalogram sought to 'scan' brain activity, in turn described such activity as a 'scanning mechanism', 'the most familiar example' of which, as he wrote, 'is in television, where a space-pattern is most economically converted for transmission into a time-sequence of impulses by the scanning mechanism of the camera'.[151] In *Thinking by Machine*, referring to Walter and his electroencephalograms and neurophysiologists (and then cyberneticians) Warren McCulloch and Walter Pitts, who developed an artificial model of the neuron in 1943, de Latil is similarly enthused by the analogy between brain and television, and the affinity that the 'scanning operation of [its] electronic mechanisms' bears with 'the basic rhythm of the brain'.[152] Thus, cybernetics' emphasis on the processual functioning of television and its perceived affinity with the scanning activity of the brain offers yet another intermedial lens through which to consider Antonioni's pursuit of interiority; a lens which indeed shows us not the purity of his cinema, but its richly layered impurity as a marker of its enmeshment in the world.

Finally, and as a way of bringing this chapter to a close, it is important to note how Antonioni's perceptive understanding of cybernetics – and, indeed, the cybernetic understanding that he brings to *Il deserto rosso* and its exteriorisation of interiority – places emphasis on questions of adaptation and environment. For, indeed, if one of the premises of cybernetics was that the brain, and living organisms, could be seen to behave mechanistically, *like a machine*, the most attractive aspect of such living behaviour, was that, *unlike machines*, it was also adaptive, able to modify itself, in response to changes in the surrounding environment.[153] What was crucial in devices such as the homeostat and Elmer and Elsie – and what Antonioni singles out in his account of the 'chemical brain' in particular, which reacts to people entering the room – was that they were designed, and understood, to be not simply 'mechanical' but 'adaptive', 'to have the power *to adapt . . .* to changes which take place in [their] *environment*'.[154] As Ashby argued in the 1950s, 'there can't be a proper theory of the brain until there is a proper theory of the environment as well . . . the subject has been hampered by our not paying sufficiently serious attention to the environmental half of the process . . . the "psychology" of the environment will have to be given almost as much thought as the psychology of the nerve network itself'.[155] In fundamental respects, cybernetics, another of whose central concepts, as is well known, is 'feedback', sought to study the continuing interaction between a mechanism or system and its environment, the way in which changes in each affect and cause the other to adapt.[156]

In *Cinema II*, hinting at a cybernetic reading of Antonioni's cinema, Deleuze writes that the director's 'unrivalled method' has been that of pursuing 'the interior *through* behaviour'.[157] This makes Antonioni's cinema, as Deleuze goes on to explain, 'the perfect example of a double composition' – of a 'cinema of the body' and a 'cinema of the brain', as he calls it.[158] The cybernetic understanding that Antonioni reveals in his discussion with Godard informs, as I want to suggest, both his filmmaking of the 1960s more generally – when, as we have seen, he felt the need to focus on interiority, and make it manifest or externalise it in some way while being aware of its fundamental un-picturability – and *Il deserto rosso* more specifically. Together with television, the emerging discipline of cybernetics and its applications in electronics (for which, in turn, the very technology of television constituted a conceptual and sometimes material resource) were crucial features of the changing reality whose impact on the individual and 'transformation of . . . human psychology' Antonioni observed and sought to address in his 'modern' cinema.[159] In fact, not only this; for cybernetics additionally seemed to provide useful ideas or tools for thinking about the dynamics of such changes and transformations.

The interrelation of environment and adaptation is key. In his interview with Godard, as well as in other contemporaneous writings, Antonioni returns to these questions more than once. These cybernetic notions, I want to argue, are very important to Antonioni's thinking about modernity and the mind in *Il deserto rosso* and its focus on Giuliana's psyche in particular. The dynamics of adaptation to a changing environment Antonioni focuses on in his description of Stewart's cybernetic device is also at the core of his film, where Giuliana, as he explains to Godard, is, instead, unable to 'adapt' to her 'environment'. '[I]t's not her environment that causes her crisis', Antonioni underlines on different occasions. 'I have to say that the neurosis I sought to describe in *Red Desert* is above all a matter of adjusting. There are people who do adapt and others who can't manage', he tells Godard; 'if we learn to adapt ourselves to the new techniques of life, perhaps then we will find new solutions to our problems'.[160]

Furthermore, Antonioni's excitement about the scientists' devices points to a certain affinity that he might be detecting between the operations of (his) cinema and the artificial brains of cybernetics. If Antonioni, as we have seen, had sought to move towards 'the states of mind themselves' and away from 'strictly figurative' results at the same time, so cybernetics was in pursuit of an externalisation of the interiority of the mind – the 'black-box' quality of the brain – not in appearance but in behaviour, as enactment rather than figuration.[161] Not unlike other filmmakers, including, as we mentioned, Resnais or Frampton, Antonioni in this period seems to treat cinema as a means 'to reconstruct the human brain', not in a box, as with the chemical device that he describes, but on the screen. Just as cybernetics is not quite a picturing of the inside of the brain, but a simulation by means of a model based on performance, so Antonioni uses cinematic form to *enact* the psyche's very structure and dynamics. But unlike films such as *Zorns Lemma*, the 'psychic machinery' that *ll deserto rosso* at once enacts and constructs is a *mal*functioning one. It is not only a machinery, as Giuliana's husband Ugo puts it, that 'isn't able to mesh' or 'get into gear', but one that, from the cybernetic perspective that Antonioni outlines in his discussions of the film, lacks the important feature of adaptability in a rapidly changing environment. If the remarkable audio, visual and colour dynamics of the film enact Giuliana's mind – interiority *acted out*, so to speak – then their strangeness signals her inadaptability, the jarring encounter between her interiority and exteriority. While the end of the film does not make clear whether Giuliana's brain has managed 'to adapt', she herself points to such behaviour in the birds in response to her son's questioning: 'the birds have learnt' about the poisonous fumes from the chemical plant and 'do not fly near them anymore'.

NOTES

1. Sadoul, 'Puro come *La notte*', pp. 91–2.
2. Aristarco, 'Literary Cinema' (*Cinema nuovo*, January–February 1961), p. 162.

3. 'Antonioni, 'A Talk with Michelangelo Antonioni on His Work', p. 22.
4. Antonioni, 'A Talk', p. 45 (my emphasis). The English translation uses the term 'actor'. In the original Italian, Antonioni uses more often the term 'personaggio' [character], but does describe filming the 'attore' [actor] even after he or she thinks that the scene has ended.
5. Antonioni, 'Il deserto rosso', p. 253 cited.
6. Pasolini, 'The "Cinema of Poetry"', esp. pp. 178–9. Dalle Vacche, in *Cinema and Painting* (ch. 2) develops Pasolini's position in her discussion of Antonioni's strategy as 'visual ventriloquism'.
7. Andrew, 'The Stature of Objects in Antonioni's Films', p. 41.
8. Antonioni, 'A Talk', pp. 26 and 25.
9. Carpi, 'Il Film Letterario', pp. 48–9.
10. Ibid., (my emphasis).
11. Antonioni, 'A Talk', p. 26.
12. See Visalberghi, 'Industria culturale e società', data from the Ufficio Rilevazioni Estere di RAI-TV, p. 26 (where it is noted that in 1953 RAI only did experimental broadcasts, prior to the official launch in January 1954, at the end of which year the number of TV licences had risen to 80,000).
13. For discussions and historical surveys of television in Italy, see among others: Forgacs, 'Cultural Consumption, 1940s to 1990s'; Wagstaff, 'The Media'; Richieri, 'Television from Service to Business: European Tendencies and the Italian Case'.
14. See, for example, Marotti, 'La Televisione come fenomeno sociale'.
15. See, for example, Mannucci, *Lo spettatore senza libertà*.
16. Adorno, 'How to Look at Television', pp. 213 and 221–2 cited.
17. For example, Eco, *Apocalittici e integrati*, p. 333; or Marotti, 'La televisione come fenomeno sociale', p. 33. The danger of 'hypnosis' and 'addiction' seems to be more specifically related to television than cinema. The negative effects of cinema have tended more often to be described in terms of identification with, and reproduction of, actions or behaviour seen on the screen (e.g. violence, etc.).
18. Bellotto, *La television inutile* cited in Umberto Eco, 'Appuntamenti sulla televisione', p. 357. The English translation of Eco's book, *Apocalypse Postponed*, does not contain the chapter on television. This chapter elaborates material on television that Eco presented or published in the late 1950s and early 1960s, including the article 'Verso una civiltà della visione' in *Pirelli* magazine and the *Opera aperta* chapter 'Il caso e l'intreccio: stutture estetiche della ripresa diretta', which is included as 'Chance and Plot: Television and Aesthetics' in the book's English version, *The Open Work*.
19. Cohen-Séat, 'Civiltà dell'immagine', p. 139.
20. Bellotto, 'Il teleschermo nuovo focolare'.
21. Williams, *Television*, pp. 86ff.
22. McLuhan, *Understanding Media*, p. 332.
23. Morin, *L'Esprit du temps*, p. 9.
24. Adorno, 'How to Look at Television', p. 216.

25. Siegel, 'Identification of a Medium: *Identificazione di una donna* and the Rise of Commercial Television in Italy'.
26. Adorno, 'Transparencies on Film'.
27. Carpi, 'Il film letterario', p. 48.
28. Ibid., p. 49.
29. Ibid. More cautiously than Sadoul, Carpi writes of *La notte* that it only 'brushes against pure cinema at moments'.
30. Eco, *Apocalittici e integrati*, pp. 318–19.
31. Ibid.
32. Marotti, 'Tecnica ed estetica dell'espressione televisiva', p. 19.
33. See, for example, Feuer, 'The Concept of Live Television: Ontology as Ideology' and Doane, 'Information, Crisis, Catastrophe'.
34. Eco, *The Open Work*, p. 116. The English translation (which I have used here) adapts quite freely the Italian original, but the essence of the point is maintained. For a comparison see Eco, *Opera aperta*, pp. 201ff.
35. As is well documented, the shooting of *L'avventura* was fraught. Money ran out during production, and actors and crew remained stranded on Lisca Bianca as the weather worsened. For more details see Nowell-Smith, *L'avventura* and Chiaretti, *L'avventura*.
36. Eco, *The Open Work*, p. 116.
37. Carpi, 'Il film letterario', p. 48.
38. Eco, *Opera aperta*, p. 201. *The Open Work*, p. 116.
39. Kael, 'Are Movies Going to Pieces? (originally in *The Atlantic Monthly*, December 1964), p. 351.
40. Metz, *Film Language*, p. 185.
41. Kael, 'Are Movies Going to Pieces?', p. 344.
42. Williams, *Television*, p. 86.
43. Ibid., p. 89.
44 44. Ibid.
45. Henning, *Photography: The Unfettered Image*, p. 139, and 'Image Flow'.
46. Henning, *Photography*, p. 139.
47. Williams, *Television*, pp. 92, 88 and 87.
48. Cavell, 'The Fact of Television', p. 86 (my emphasis).
49. Williams, *Television*, p. 77.
50. Ellis, *Visible Fictions*, p. 160 (my emphasis).
51. Eco, *Apocalittici e integrati*, p. 320.
52. Benjamin, 'The Work of Art', p. 171.
53. Eco, *Apocalittici e integrati*, pp. 318 and 321.
54. Cavell, 'The Fact of Television', p. 85.
55. Ibid., p. 89.
56. Ibid.
57. Ibid.
58. Ibid.
59. Ibid.

60. Ibid., pp. 89, 90.
61. Eco, *Opera aperta*, p. 200.
62. Ibid.
63. Bolter and Grusin, *Remediation*.
64. Antonioni, 'A propos of eroticism', p. 159.
65. Eco, *The Open Work*, p. 116; *Opera aperta*, p. 201.
66. Antonioni, 'Il mondo è fuori dalla finestra', pp. 160, 158.
67. Tassone, 'Conversazione', p. 214.
68. Frampton, 'The Withering Away of the State of the Art', p. 265.
69. Cuccu, *La visione come problema*, p. 77.
70. Resnais and Robbe-Grillet, 'Last Words on *Last Year*', p. 171.
71 Leutrat, *L'année dernière à Marienbad*, p. 33. Leutrat reports an anecdote by Sylvie Baudrot, the film's script-supervisor: 'In *Marienbad*, for example, there was a very long scene in which Delphine Seyrig and Albertazzi walk side by side down a corridor. We shot in three different corridors . . . We'd put potted plants so that the continuity between the potted plants might disguise the passage from one section of corridor to another, but Resnais didn't want to hide the fact that three different corridors were involved.' Baudrot's statement appears in Thomas, *L'Atelier d'Alain Resnais*, p. 157.
72. Cuccu, *La visione come problema*, p. 77.
73. Antonioni, 'A Talk', p. 202.
74. Robbe-Grillet, 'Time and Description', p. 151.
75. Badiou, 'The False Movement of Cinema', p. 78.
76. Deleuze, *Cinema II*, p. 213.
77. Ibid., pp. 213, 214.
78. Ibid., p. 277.
79. Ibid., p. 213.
80. Ibid., p. xii.
81. Antonioni cited in Di Carlo, *Il primo Antonioni*, p. 12, from Bernardini, *Michelangelo Antonioni da Gente del Po a Blow-Up*, p. 27. The quote (in Italian) reads: 'Una signora andava a trovare una donna di malaffare che la ricattava a causa di certe lettere in suo possesso. La macchina da presa seguiva in panoramica la signora che si avvicinava alla donna di malaffare. La trovata era che signora e donna erano interpretate dalla stessa attrice. Eppure il movimento della macchina non era interrotto. L'inquadratura era unica. Nessuno riusciva a capire come avessi fatto. In realtà l'interruzione c'era, ma era assolutamente inavvertibile.'
82. Marcus, *Italian Film in the Light of Neorealism*, p. 202.
83. Eco, *Apocalittici e integrati*, p. 320.
84. James, *The Principles of Psychology* vol. 1, pp. 538–9.
85. Bergson, *Time and Free Will*.
86. Cf: Freud's crucial notion of *Nachträglichkeit* (which Strachey translates as 'deferred action' and Jean Laplanche proposes to re-translate as 'afterwardsness') at work as condensation and displacement in screen memories, repression and trauma.

Freud, 'Screen Memories' and 'Remembering, Repeating and Working-Through'. See also Laplanche, *Essays on Otherness*, in particular 'Note on Afterwardsness'.

87. Freud, 'Beyond the Pleasure Principle', p. 299.

88. Freud, 'A Note Upon the "Mystic Writing-Pad"', p. 433.

89. Laplanche, 'Psychoanalysis, Time and Translation', p. 164.

90. See, for example, Baudry, 'Ideological Effects of the Basic Cinematographic Apparatus'; Metz, 'The Imaginary Signifier'. See also Comolli, 'Machines of the Visible', which likens the visible (i.e. shooting, projection, etc.) and invisible (i.e. chemical baths, editing, etc.) processes of the cinema to the conscious and unconscious activities of the mind. For a comprehensive study of 1960s and 1970s apparatus theories, see Rodowick, *The Crisis of Political Modernism*. Of course, the association between cinema and the mind dates back to the emergence of the medium itself, which coincides with the development of systematised scientific or medical attitudes to the study of mental activity including neurology, experimental psychology, psychiatry and psychoanalysis. One of the first treatises on cinema, Münstenberg, *The Photoplay*, is written by a psychologist who argues that as well as 'influenc[ing] the mind of the spectator', the cinema also contributed to the visualisation of mental activities (p. 44).

91. Kuntzel, 'A Note Upon the Filmic Apparatus', p. 267 cited. Freud refused to sanction G. W. Pabst's *Secrets of the Soul* (1926), objecting with Karl Abraham, who acted as a consultant for the film: 'I don't believe that satisfactory plastic representation of our abstractions is at all possible'. Freud, 'Letter to Abraham, 9 June 1925', p. 80. For a discussion of Freud's objection to cinema and of how, however, his recourse to the idea of the 'apparatus' influenced theorists in the 1970s, see Marcus, 'Introduction: Histories, Representations, Autobiographics in *The Interpretation of Dreams*', esp. pp. 33–43.

92. Frampton, 'Incisions in History/Segments of Eternity', p. 44 cited.

93. Field, 'Interview with Hollis Frampton', p. 53.

94. Frampton, 'The Withering Away of the State of the Art', p. 164.

95. Field, 'Interview with Hollis Frampton', p. 66 (my emphasis). Contemporary literature on experimental filmmaking certainly tended to highlight and lever on this metaphorics as opposed to other aspects. See, for example, the exhibition catalogue: Singer, *A History of American Avant-Garde Cinema*. See also Turvey, Foster, Iles, et al., 'Round Table: The Projected Image in Contemporary Art', in which Turvey suggests that Sitney's and Michelson's reading of 1960s and 1970s avant-garde cinema 'in terms of the use of film as a metaphor for the mind' could, *mutatis mutandis*, apply to many artists, such as Douglas Gordon, working with the moving image in the late 1990s and early 2000s (p. 84).

96. Frampton, 'The Withering Away of the State of the Art', p. 264.

97. Arthur, *A Line of Sight*, pp. 52, 54. For discussions of the film as a whole see, among others, James, *Allegories of Cinema*, pp. 254–60; Weiss, 'Frampton's Lemma, Zorn's Dilemma'; and Melissa Ragona, 'Hidden Noise', esp. pp. 104–9 for a discussion of Frampton's use of the alphabet and conceptual mathematics.

98. Ibid., p. 54.

99. As Frampton discussed in interviews, there are in fact irregularities (whether deliberate or unintentional) in this regular structure, with missing frames or frames in
excess here and there. Gidal, 'Interview with Hollis Frampton' (London, 24 May
1972), p. 97.

100. Field, 'Interview with Hollis Frampton', p. 66.

101. Sitney, 'Structural Film', p. 335; Michelson, 'Towards Snow', p. 29.

102. Resnais, 'Trying to Understand My Own Film', p. 160.

103. Antonioni, 'A Talk', p. 199.

104. Maurin, '*Red Desert*', p. 285 (I have slightly adapted the English translation, see
Maurin, '*Il deserto rosso*', p. 253).

105. Pasolini, 'The "Cinema of Poetry"', pp. 178–9.

106. Maurin, '*Red Desert*', p. 284.

107. Ibid., p. 252. See also the talk at the CSC, where Antonioni comments on
our psychology and morality as lagging behind material change: Antonioni, 'A
Talk', p. 209.

108. Fer, *The Infinite Line*, p. 170.

109. Maurin, '*Red Desert*', p. 283.

110. As Forgacs notes in his very informative commentary to the BFI DVD of *Red
Desert*, the paint appears 'grey' as an effect of the blue filters that the director of
photography Carlo di Palma used on the camera lens. Famously, the sequence
dedicated to the fable Giuliana tells her son – shot on the island of Budelli, off
the north-east of Sardinia – was the only one for which there were no 'interventions' with filters or paint on the pro-filmic.

111. Zizek, *Looking Awry*, p. 96.

112. Benjamin, 'On Some Motifs in Baudelaire', p. 171.

113. Antonioni, 'A Talk', p. 202.

114. On psychiatry and psychoanalysis in Italy, see David, *La psicoanalisi nella cultura italiana* and Foot, *The Man Who Closed the Asylums*. For a discussion of
Antonioni's interest in psychiatry and antipsychiatry, see Eugeni, 'La modernità a disagio. Michelangelo Antonioni e la cultura psichiatrica italiana'. On
cybernetics, in particular with regard to its relation to brain sciences and
psychiatry and its use of models, I am indebted in particular to Pickering,
The Cybernetic Brain, and de Latil's 1950 book *Thinking by Machine*. See also
Riskin, *The Restless Clock*, ch. 9.

115. De Latil, *Thinking by Machine*, p. 3.

116. Russell, *Robots*, pp. 84–5.

117. For an informative account of the story of Elea 9000 series, see the documentary by Rao and Contadini, in collaboration with Archivio Storico Olivetti,
Olivetti Elea 9003.

118. Associazione Archivio Storico Olivetti, 'Alle origini del personal computer:
l'Olivetti Programma 101'; Whittle, 'NASA Johnson Space Center Oral
History Project', p. 23.

119. See Forleo, *La cibernetica italiana della mente nella civiltà delle macchine*, pp. 51–9;
Enrico Maretti, 'Adamo II'. On Ceccato's life and career more broadly, see also

Ceccato, *Un tecnico fra i filosofi* and *Il perfetto filosofo*; and Lopez, *Il sogno delle tre faraone*. For a report in English on the mechanical translator, see Ceccato, *Linguistic Analysis and Programming for Mechanical Translation*.

120. See Morando, *Almanacco Letterario Bompiani 1962*. For Ceccato's 'cronista meccanico [mechanical chronicler], see Lopez, *Il sogno delle tre faraone*, pp. 50–2. For a review in *Corriere della sera* of the presentation in Lambrate outside Milan, see Nascimbeni, 'Il cronista meccanico'.

121. Calvino, 'Cybernetics and Ghosts', delivered under the title 'Cibernetica e fanstasmi' in various Italian towns (Turin, Milan, Genoa, Rome and Bari) for the Italian Cultural Association, which also published it as part of its conference proceedings in 1967–8; Ceccato, *Cibernetica per tutti*. Ceccato's 'lessons' for RAI were published as Ceccato, *La mente vista da un cibernetico*. For an in-depth study of cybernetic ideas in Italian literature, see Antonello, *Il menage a quattro*, pp. 169–242.

122. Jones, *The Cybernetic Brains*, p. 19.

123. De Latil, *Thinking by Machine*, p. 13.

124. De Latil, *Thinking by Machine*, p. 17.

125. Pickering, *The Cybernetic Brain*, p. 69.

126. Holland and Husbands, 'Pioneers of Cybernetics', p. 88 cited. Walter had a summer house in Italy, in Bordighera on the Ligurian Riviera and, as de Latil explains in *Thinking by Machine*, it is there that he 'met' the tortoises (p. 23). Wiener, *Cybernetics: Or Control and Communication in the Animal and Machine* (1948) was translated into Italian as *La cibernetica* in 1953. Wiener's *The Human Use of Human Beings*, also appeared in Italian in 1953, as *Introduzione alla cibernetica*.

127. Pickering, *The Cybernetic Brain*, esp. chapters 2 and 4. See also de Latil, p. 208.

128. Pickering, *The Cybernetic Brain*, p. 5.

129. Montagnini, 'Quando Wiener era di casa a Napoli'. See also *Proceedings of the International Congress on Cybernetic Medicine* (Naples) and Parin and Bayevskiy, *Introduction to medical cybernetics*.

130. Yet in *Cybernetics*, ch. VII, Wiener himself discusses neurology and psychopathology, noting that 'computing machines . . . may suggest new and valid approaches to psychopathology, and even to psychiatrists' (p. 168).

131. Ashby, *Design for a Brain*. The details of the homeostat had been presented by Ashby in a paper by the same title 'Design for a Brain', published in 1948 in *Electronic Engineering*.

132. Walter, *The Living Brain*, p. 179.

133. Ibid.

134. Ibid.

135. Ibid., p. 177 (my emphasis). That such imitation could also be generative and informative, as Walter explains, was a crucial point. See also Ashby, 'Simulation of a Brain' (1962), and de Latil's early emphasis on this in *Thinking by Machine*, for example, p. 222. For further discussion see, among others, Asaro, 'From Mechanisms of Adaptation to Intelligence Amplifiers: The Philosophy of W. Ross Ashby'.

136. Walter, *The Living Brain*, p. 224. An important background for this is Alan Turing's famous 1950 essay 'Computing Machinery and Intelligence', in which, conversely, he suggests that if a machine exhibits the same behaviour and performs the same tasks as a thinking person or intelligent being, then that machine can be said to be thinking, to display intelligence.
137. Walter, *The Living Brain*, p. 180.
138. Pickering, *The Cybernetic Brain*, p. 6.
139. 'La riproduzione della mente umana si presentava . . . ostacolata . . . da una descrizione che ne faceva una costellazione di enti concepiti sul tipo delle cose fisiche, ma affatto sprovvisti delle caratteristiche di queste . . . Questo ostacolo e' stato eliminato quando il pensiero ed i suoi contenuti sono stati visti invece come attività', in Maretti, 'Adamo II'. See also Ceccato, 'A Model of the Mind'.
140. Ceccato, 'La storia di un modello meccanico dell'uomo che traduce', p. 124. See also Ceccato, 'Da cibernetica a filosofia'.
141. Silvio Ceccato interviewed in *Arti e scienze. Cronache d'attualità*, RAI, March 1961 (my emphasis), <https://www.youtube.com/watch?v=SIyJqmWMBTg> (last accessed November 2019).
142. *Il deserto rosso*, screenplay, BA16, fasc b2, Michelangelo Antonioni Archive, Ferrara.
143. 'Appunti generici sui programmatori IBM', 8D, fasc. 150 a-c, Michelangelo Antonioni Archive, Ferrara. For a history of computing, see Ceruzzi, *Computing*, esp. pp. 54–80.
144. Godard, 'The Night, the Eclipse, the Dawn', p. 291.
145. Ibid., pp. 290–1.
146. Buzzati, *Il grande ritratto*, pp. 116–17.
147. For an interesting take on filmic pace and rhythm, see Bíro, *Turbulence and Flow in Film*.
148. Sottsass, 'Paesaggio elettronico', p. 39.
149. See Ceruzzi, pp. 54–64.
150. See de Latil, *Thinking by Machine*, p. 13; Pickering, *The Cybernetic Brain*, p. 46–7.
151. Walter, *The Living Brain*, p. 108. See also pp. 144ff., where Walter describes the 'alpha rhythm' that he detected and associated with visual perception in particular. As Pickering discusses, Walter was also a friend of the experimental psychologist Kenneth Craik, who, in *The Nature of Explanation* (1943), also thought about cerebral activity via analogies with television.
152. De Latil, *Thinking by Machine*, p. 13.
153. See Ashby, *Design for a Brain*, p. 1; and, for example, Pickering, *The Cybernetic Brain*, pp. 5ff.
154. De Latil, *Thinking by Machine*, p. 23.
155. Ashby, 'Homeostasis'; Pickering, *The Cybernetic Brain*, p. 105.
156. Ashby, *Design for a Brain*, p. 35.
157. Deleuze, *Cinema II*, p. 189. In footnote 20 (p. 317) Deleuze mentions the passage about the artificial brains in the interview with Godard.

158. Ibid., p. 205.
159. Maurin, '*Red Desert*', p. 284.
160. Godard, 'The Night, the Eclipse, the Dawn', pp. 289, 288 and 290. See also, Maurin, '*Red Desert*', especially pp. 284–5.
161. Antonioni, 'A Talk', pp. 23, 25.

CHAPTER 3

(Quietly) Noisy Images: Sonic Landscapes, Audiotape and 'the New Musicality'

There is a background noise, incessant, hollow, dull. It's the traffic of the city. Then, another noise, less unbroken: the wind. It comes in gusts, but even during the pauses, one can hear it blow further away, against the skyscrapers. Then the other noises. Intermittent, a very brief and faint siren. Two short toots on a horn. A receding dull rumble, which suddenly gets closer, but is immediately struck out by an abrupt, dry, irritated gust.

It's six o'clock in the morning . . .

Another roar couples with the first, eclipses it. A muted blast, far-off. Surging up as if from nowhere, the wind comes back, swells and seems to expand more and more, but at a point, unexpectedly, stops. Again, a hint of a tram. No, it's not a tram, at last it becomes clear: it's a car. This other . . . it could be a motorbike, but too soon it turns into another indistinguishable noise. A truck, another truck accelerating. Two or three cars passing: the roads around Central Park bend going uphill. A series of car roars, petering away quickly. A moment of absolute void, which is almost frightening. A big lorry, extremely close, as if we were on the second floor, while we are at the thirty-seventh. But it drops immediately. A screech: impossible to say what it is. A ship siren, protracted, hoarse. Apparently there is no wind anymore. The siren continues. The background noise, below the siren. A bell toll: it sounds wrong, as if it hadn't come out well, clumsy. Maybe it's not a bell, but a blow struck on iron. Another one. Enraged intrusion of a car engine speeding up, very brief. The siren continues in the distance. It's emerging, just now, something like the echo of that metallic knock. But it must be something else. A very noisy lorry, seemingly driving up towards the window. But it's an aeroplane. All the noises now intensify: the horns, the siren even, then descend little by little. It's almost silence. But no: another roar, and then again, louder, the siren. Irritating yet suggestive: it makes one feel the horizon.

It's quarter past six.[1]

Dated 'New York, April 1961', this account – a textual 'image' of urban noise in some respects – continues over several more paragraphs and across a few pages, its detailed chronicle punctuated here and there by the terse statement of the time breaking, as well as structuring, the text into chunks. Covering a period of about three hours in the morning, the texts conveys the modern sonority of the quintessentially twentieth-century city: the rumble of rush-hour traffic resounding up to a building's high floors, the roar of the aeroplanes in the sky. Michelangelo Antonioni was in the United States for the American premiere of *L'avventura* (1960), and this was his first experience of New York city.

It may be a little surprising that a director routinely seen to be driven by visual concerns above all, extolled for his ability to look and as a 'poet of images', should be the author of such a focused and meticulous account of sounds.[2] As Seymour Chatman among others has argued, Antonioni is felt to be a director that works 'primarily in images'. Whatever it is that the director's films are about, 'it is not spelled out in dialogue or connoted by mood music. It is always depicted, never pronounced. It occurs in visual details'.[3] Yet, if this extended sonic diary points to an often-ignored keen ear and aural attentiveness on Antonioni's part, it *also* coincides with a new parsimony of sounds in his films with which such aural attentiveness may even, at first, seem to be at odds. For, dated to less than a year after *L'avventura* and just a few months after the Italian release of *La notte* (1961), this diary of sounds is aligned with a conspicuous move towards greater quietness in the soundtracks, as dialogue becomes sparser and music (especially extra-diegetic) is drastically reduced – or even, by *L'eclisse* (1962) and *Il deserto rosso/Red Desert* (1964), all but eliminated.[4] 'What I reject', Antonioni declared after *Il deserto rosso* as an explanation for such drastic reductions, 'is this refusal to let silence have its place, this need to fill alleged voids'.[5] Indeed, in one of his sketches for possible films, Antonioni had hypothesised bucking this trend by giving 'silence', as the 'negative dimension of speech', centre stage in a story about a husband and wife at the end of their marriage that would show 'not their conversation but their silences'.[6] In many ways, this is more than partly realised in *L'avventura*, *La notte* and *L'eclisse*, whose memorable opening scene offers the nearly wordless exchanges – or, as Antonioni put it in the sketch 'Silence', the 'silent words' – between a couple in the aftermath of their breakup.[7] Indeed, in this respect, as Frank Tomasulo has put it, 'in contrast to, say, talkathon Hollywood movies or the films of Eric Rohmer, Antonioni's cinema is replete with silence'.[8]

Together with the widely debated narrative and visual shifts through which Antonioni's films of this period are enlisted among the crucial initiators of modern cinema, this reduction or parsimony at soundtrack level – manifested by an economy of dialogue and a declared scepticism towards 'music', especially in the early 1960s – tends to be seen as one aspect of the director's (modernist) pursuit of cinematic purity. If Antonioni's 'minimalist audio field' is 'modernist', as Tomasulo suggests by referring to *Blow-Up* in particular, it is also the case that cinematic purity is most often aligned with visual attributes above all, and therefore the very reduction of the 'audio field' might be seen as an effort to reach this goal. Tomasulo quotes Antonioni himself in this respect, who, interviewed about *Blow-Up*, went on to say that 'one could tell a story by images alone, without words, as pure as poetry'.[9]

Yet, even though these soundtrack changes may at first appear as a form of retreat from sound, if not, more radically, a pursuit of silence, the sonic attentiveness manifest in the New York morning diary begins to suggest a different interpretation. As a poetic take on urban sounds – and, indeed, as a textual writing of sounds – the New York text instantiates what Giuseppe D'Amato has called 'the phonographic attitude of the director towards the world'.[10] Subsequently published under a title that identifies it overtly as a 'soundtrack' for a potential film, Antonioni's text points to how his increasing reticence towards *certain* sounds is counterbalanced by an interest in *other* sounds. These are sounds that may be described as environmental – or simply 'in the air' and, even, in the category of noise – and that Valentina (Monica Vitti) in *La notte*, anticipating Richard Murray Schafer's introduction of the term 'soundscape' in the late 1960s, calls 'sonic landscape'.[11]

So, if films such as *La notte*, *L'eclisse* and *Il deserto rosso* become quieter in some respects, by abating dialogue and traditionally extra-diegetic film music, they are also noisier, more overtly attuned to a different category of sounds: the urban and industrial sounds of the 'booming' and modern(ising) Italy of the economic miracle. The scene around and inside the chemical plant in Ravenna's industrial port in *Il deserto rosso* and Lidia (Jeanne Moreau)'s famous stroll in Milan in *La notte* are compelling examples of Antonioni's attention to such 'soundscapes'. If in the former the noise of industry forcibly covers the voices of the characters at points, in the latter, as Lidia wanders from the city centre to its outskirts, it is a generally more subtle, but persistent and subsistent metropolitan sonic background that is brought into the foreground – literally and metaphorically amplified in the absence of musical soundtrack and all but total elimination of dialogue. From this perspective, the seemingly quieter films heralded by *L'avventura* are in fact precisely the product of an *increased* attentiveness to sonority and aurality.

This increased attentiveness coincides with a crucial moment of reconfiguration and expansion of sonority and aurality themselves, not only in the broader context of socio-economic modernisation but, more specifically, in the wake of important developments in sound recording technologies, including improvements in electroacoustic microphony and the diffusion of portable audiotape recorders. If *Il deserto rosso* testifies to audiotape's facilitation of the documentary capture of *found* sounds, it also points to the technology's crucial role in the creation of *artificial* or *synthetic* sounds: the prominent inclusion of the 'noise' of industry on the one hand co-exists, on the other, with the use of electronic sound compositions by Vittorio Gelmetti. *La fabbrica illuminata* [*The Illuminated Factory*], an experimental composition by Luigi Nono whose premiere, at the Venice Biennale's Music section, coincided with that of *Il deserto rosso* at the city's Film Festival in September 1964, is based on an analogous co-existence. Produced at RAI Studio di Fonologia Musicale in Milan, *La fabbrica illuminata* used audiotape for collecting the sounds of the factory and its workers (the Italsider steelworks complex in Genoa, another key centre of Italy's post-war industrial boom), and as the material support for their electronic manipulation and the production of new sounds.

The thematic and aesthetic resonance and temporal co-incidence between Antonioni's film and Nono's music composition is not incidental. Rather, it points to another, slightly counter-intuitive, twist in the director's abatement of music in favour of environmental sonority. For, in fact, it is particularly music or, more precisely, particular kinds of music, such as the experimental practices of the *musique concrète* movement, John Cage and the Milan's Studio di Fonologia, which help to illuminate the change of tack. Even though accompanied by a belligerent stance against the 'rancid quality' (as he put it) of music in film in interviews of the time, its drastic decrease signals, counter-intuitively, Antonioni's participation in contemporaneous debates and practices in the field of music itself, as magnetic tape crucially fostered not only the inclusion of non-traditionally musical sounds – from prosaic and worldly noises to synthetic or artificial sounds – but also a new conception and awareness of 'silence'.[12]

By mapping the cultural context for the seemingly greater silence of Antonioni's films of the 1960s, this chapter seeks to suggest that their images – remade through rich and layered intermedial exchanges rather than 'purified' – become in fact (quietly) noisier in two interrelated ways. In addition to being 'noisy' by being more open and attuned to environmental sonority and prosaic sounds, they are 'noisy' in the sense of being intermedially 'impure', in sustained dialogue, somewhat paradoxically, with the very art form which they seemingly avoid or reject – music – albeit in some of its most experimental, if not transgressive, manifestations.

DOWN WITH MUSIC

Shortly before beginning to shoot *L'avventura* in the late summer of 1959, Antonioni told a critic from the French journal *Positif* that, despite loving music, he 'detest[ed]' it 'in a film'.[13] He expanded on his objection in subsequent elaborations. 'I feel something old-fashioned, rancid in it', he observed in an interview before the turbulent premiere of *L'avventura* at Cannes in May 1960: 'often it serves merely to put the spectator to sleep'.[14] 'The use of music in films', he declared on another occasion later that year, 'no longer has any right to exist'.[15] 'It's the idea of "setting images to music", as if it were a question of an opera libretto, that I don't like', he further explained in 1965 after the release of *Il deserto rosso*, before condemning the 'refusal to let silence have its place', the 'need to fill supposed voids'.[16]

Antonioni's project at the turn of the 1960s begins to come clearly into view through these comments. *L'avventura* inaugurates a process of progressive – measurable – diminution in the overall use of music, as its modality, quantity and volume are substantially changed.[17] Indeed, as D'Amato has demonstrated, where in *Le amiche* (1955) the amount of music nears half the duration of the entire film (that is, 43 out of 90 minutes), in *L'avventura* it is down to just over 20 per cent of the film (or 30 out of 140 minutes) and in *Il deserto rosso*, to less than 10 per cent of it (16 out of 120 minutes).[18] Moreover, while in the films up to *Il grido* (1957) the musical soundtrack had tended to be constituted of more conventionally melodic mood pieces, with *L'avventura* and *La notte* the music that does remain becomes more minimal in character – and, from the latter film in particular, it tends to be integrated diegetically into the narrative.

While, with the exception of some shorts, from the lyrical documentary *Nettezza urbana* (1948) onwards, the musical scores for Antonioni's films had been composed by Giovanni Fusco; *L'avventura* marks a change in this collaboration.[19] On the one hand, Fusco's pieces themselves become more rarefied and economical, as the number and range of instruments used are gradually reduced, up to the unaccompanied singing voice of Cecilia Fusco, the composer's daughter, in *Il deserto rosso*. For *L'avventura*, as Geoffrey Nowell-Smith reports, Antonioni told Fusco that he 'would like a tiny orchestra: a clarinet, a saxophone, and something sounding like a drum-kit', in a style that should be jazz as 'the classical Greeks might have written a jazz score, if jazz had existed in those days'.[20] (In the end, Antonioni discarded about half of the short, mainly woodwind pieces that Fusco provided, reducing the extra-diegetic music to just over 20 minutes.) On the other hand, Antonioni introduces new sounds and music by other composers – which, unlike Fusco's music up to *L'avventura* – tend to be integrated, diegetically, into the 'story world' of the film. Notably, this new music includes the jazz of Giorgio Gaslini's quartet in *La notte* which, with the exception of the electronic sounds in the opening credits sequence (Antonioni's first use of such sounds), provides the totality of the music in the film, as the live (in the film diegesis) accompaniment to both the night club and the grand party that the protagonists attend, and the sparse, cutting-edge electronic compositions by Gelmetti in *Il deserto rosso*. Indeed, even Cecilia

Fusco's solo singing in this latter film is diegetic: part of the story within the story Giuliana (Monica Vitta) tells her son, in which the rocks are like flesh and have a voice. This is a trend that continues well into the 1970s. If there is hardly any music – and no extra diegetic music at all – in *The Passenger* (1975), there is considerably more in *Blow-Up* and *Zabriskie Point* (1970). But, even here, the music of Herbie Hancock and The Yardbirds in the one, and by Jerry Garcia of The Grateful Dead and Pink Floyd in the other, tends to be integrated diegetically. In the famous love-in in Death Valley and the explosive finale of *Zabriskie Point*, rather than simply accompanying the film's images, the music takes over the images – in what can be seen as pioneering forms of the music video. At the same time, however, not unlike in the embedded fable in *Il deserto rosso*, the music remains part of the diegetic world as a 'soundtrack' to Daria's fantasies.

The gradual cutting out of music, or preference for including music which is part of the sonic environment of the film's story, on a par with other sound effects or characters' dialogue, is profoundly connected to the attention to environmental sonority manifested by the New York text quoted at the start of this chapter. Yet, the relationship between music elimination and attunement to environmental sonority is not as straightforwardly antithetical as it may at first seem.

In the course of explaining to the *Positif* interviewer in 1959 his dislike for music in film, Antonioni then wistfully concluded that if producers allowed him, he would use '*only* a soundtrack of noises' in his films.[21] But this desire for a 'soundtrack of noises' does not envision a replacement of music as abstract sounds 'external' to the images, for a direct, 'documentary' capture of concrete sounds and noises naturally linked to the images in their spatial and temporal coincidence with them. It is worth quoting more extensively from the aforementioned interview before the premiere of *L'avventura*:

> I give enormous importance to the soundtrack ... And when I say 'soundtrack', I allude to natural sounds, to noises, rather than music. [For the scenes in the Aeolian Islands] I got the sound engineers to record a huge quantity of sound effects: every possible type of sea, from smooth to choppy to very rough, the rumble of the waves as they break against the rocks, and so on. I had at my disposal about a hundred reels of magnetic tape, just for the sound effects. Then I selected those that now constitute the soundtrack of the film. To me, this is the music that best fits the images. It's rare for music to really fuse with the images, generally it is used to stupefy the spectator, to obfuscate his sharpness of vision ... The ideal would be to compose, exclusively with noises, a beautiful soundtrack, and to appoint an orchestra director to conduct it ... Even though, perhaps, in the end the only one able to conduct it would be the director himself.[22]

In the face of practical and technical limitations, as well as opposition from producers unwilling to back a film entirely without music, endeavours such as the one to obtain recordings of the sea that Antonioni describes above would have started to work towards his aspiration to do away with 'musical commentary' and its 'rancid' quality in favour of a valorisation of what Béla Balázs called a film's 'acoustic environment'.[23] Yet, not only does Antonioni's reference to sound 'effects' and processes of 'selection' preclude an understanding of the cinematic soundtrack – and soundscape – as simply *found* and directly *captured* on tape, but his evocation of such soundscape occurs *through* musical terms.

This 'beautiful soundtrack' of noises is composed, like music, it *is* music: 'the music that best fits the images'. Even though Antonioni concludes that perhaps the best conductor for such a soundtrack would not be an orchestra but a film director, what comes into relief here is the fact that the juxtaposition between music and noise which – and *on* which – these reflections may at first seem to draw is significantly blurred.[24] Indeed, rather than advocating the replacement of music with ordinary sounds and noises, Antonioni is rather thinking within a broadened understanding of sonority in which the distinction between musical and non-musical sounds has loosened considerably. It is such loosening of the opposition between music and noise, rather than, as it may at first seem, the very idea of a steadfast opposition between them, that bears on Antonioni's subtly 'noisy' images of the early 1960s. To consider it further, we need to turn to one of the major catalysts for such effect: audiotape.

AUDIOTAPE

Developed from prototypes employed by the German military during World War II, magnetic audiotape technology started to become available for professional use from the early 1950s.[25] Often described as 'revolutionary' in its impact, audiotape radically transformed sound and its experience.[26] Not only at professional level in the fields of music, cinema radio and television broadcasting, but also in everyday and lay use, audiotape facilitated sound reproduction by marrying high-fidelity – thanks to improvements in electrical microphony and amplification – with unparalleled lightness, flexibility and cheapness. In addition to extreme ease of capture, magnetic tape introduced a range of features unavailable with earlier sound recording technologies: instant playback, the option of erasure and re-use and, gradually, of stereo and multi-track recording, as well as portability. Even more than a decade after its initial commercialisation, audiotape's basic features still offered 'something at which we may just marvel', as the (arguably not-unbiased) author of a user's manual published by Philips after its launch of the compact cassette in 1963, put it. 'There is still a trace of the magical', the manual's author continued, in what the tape recorder 'enables us to do – record speech, music, or any sound at all, for that matter, and hear the same sound again whenever we wish to (even *immediately* after recording, if desired) simply *by pressing a push-button*'.[27]

In music – of whatever kind – the '*immediately . . . simply by pressing a push-button*' enabled performers and singers to record their own compositions, at the same time as audiotape's other basic features fostered the utilisation of the technology not simply as a tool for reproduction and playback, but also for production and experimentation, leading, by the mid-1960s, to the practice of 'studio recording' as a new default or standard over the live performance. In profound ways, audiotape sealed the activity of *making* records (or recordings) rather than *recording* music. This spanned both commercial enterprises, including, perhaps most notably, the Abbey Road recording studios made famous by the Beatles, and the research initiatives that flourished under the aegis of national broadcasters or university centres, such as the Groupe de recherche de Musique Concrète of the Radiodiffusion-Télévision Française in Paris founded by Pierre Schaeffer in 1951, the Studio for Electronic Music at Westdeutscher Rundfunk in Cologne founded by Karlheinz Stockhausen in 1953, and the Studio di fonologia musicale of RAI Radiotelevisione Italiana in Milan founded by Luciano Berio in 1955.[28] Indeed, where electronic-music pioneer Berio had stopped short of hoping for 'the burning of old concert venues', even while contemplating their 'incongruity' for the new music, classical pianist Glenn Gould famously went all the way.[29] He declared the concert 'dead' in 1966, championing magnetic recording at once for its reproducibility (whose potential for the democratisation of music enthused him) and its productive function – that is, the unprecedented possibilities it opened up for assembling a 'perfect' rendition of a classical composition through the selection of fragments from takes performed in the studio.[30] If this optimised rendition could never exist as a 'live' performance, the productive possibilities of audiotape's reproductive capability were exploited even further in commercial pop, rock and experimental music. Features including multi-track recording and mixing, playing backwards, accelerating or slowing down standard running speed, and splicing randomly, often complemented by the employment of electronic devices – from oscillators to synthesisers – for the generation of the very sounds to be recorded and modified, fostered the rise of what Brian Eno came later to describe as 'the studio as a compositional tool'.[31]

Alongside the suppleness that audiotape brought to studio – and generally indoor – recording and production, it also, with the development of portable equipment, greatly facilitated outdoor sound recording, fostering crucial changes in a range of different activities, from field anthropology and ethnomusicology to location or 'direct' sound recording in film production.[32] The Nagra professional portable recorder, launched as early as 1951 in Switzerland by the Polish émigré Stefan Kudelski, quickly became a standard in the film industry, transforming Hollywood production and fostering independent filmmaking in the early 1960s thanks to the perfecting of a system for lip-synchronisation of audio recordings with moving images.[33] While only experimental or documentary movements – such as direct cinema and *cinéma verité*, one of whose funding documents, Jean Rouch and Edgar Morin's *Chronique d'un Été* [*Chronicle of a Summer*] (1961), is centered around the motif of the audiotaped interview to passersby – pursued the opportunity of direct sound with most intensity, magnetic tape nevertheless greatly facilitated cinema soundtrack production more generally. This was the case even in Italy, where the post-synchronisation of sound and voice dubbing, instituted during fascism for censorship reasons, continued to remain the norm well into the late 1970s, despite protestations from many directors, including Antonioni, who had in fact been sceptical about sound post-synchronisation and dubbing since his days as a film critic under fascism.[34] In 1967, he was one the signatories of the 'Manifesto di Amalfi', against the 'systematic abuse of dubbing' and 'the use of stock sound-effects' which compromised 'the very possibility of an Italian sound cinema'.[35] Even though post-synchronisation remained a distinctive stylistic feature of the country's post-war art cinema (think, for instance, of Federico Fellini's deliberately very loose matching of voices to lip movements), tape recorders nevertheless made the capture of location sounds – even as a material that could be manipulated and worked on in the studio – a possibility that, however partially, could be actively pursued.[36]

ENTERTAINING TAPE'S NOVELTIES: IMMEDIACY AND MEDIATION

It is in this context of technological novelty that Antonioni employed audio-tape to obtain some 'location' sounds of the sea and wind for the soundtrack of *L'avventura* (at which point, moreover, the portable synch-sound systems of the mid-1960s were still somewhat in the future). And, indeed, it is as a novelty that Antonioni overtly features the tape recorder in *La notte*, not unlike Felllini had done just the year before in *La dolce vita* (1960). In both films, the magnetic recording apparatus is presented as a device which can itself constitute a form of entertainment, since, as the author of the Philips manual to which I referred above was to put it a few years later, its features were still a source of 'marvel', if not something with 'a trace of the magical'.[37]

Figure 3.1   The tape recorder in Steiner's flat, *La dolce vita* (1960)

In *La dolce vita*, the tape recorder is introduced by surprising the guests at the *soirée* of the intellectual and socialite Steiner with a recording of their own ongoing conversation, of which they are, at a point, given to hear a brief snippet that occurred only instants before.

This is immediately followed, in an almost didactic fashion, by a demonstration of the device's function as a tool that facilitates the capture of the 'natural' sounds of the world, as Steiner's guests are entertained with a montage of just such recordings (a stormy sea, wind, chirping birds). In *La notte* too, Valentina, during the grand party organised by her father at their villa in the outskirts of Milan, exhibits a tape recorder to entertain her 'guest', Giovanni, who has split off from his wife and the rest of the revellers. After dragging it over from a corner of her room, she proceeds to play him a recording of her own voice, in a scene in which her charmed guest is thus shown to be fascinated not only by Valentina herself, but also by her 'acousmatic' (as Pierre Schaeffer would put it) voice on the reel of tape and its lyrical account of outdoors sounds.[38]

I will return to this account's resonance with, and departure from, Antonioni's New York morning diary, but for the moment I want to draw attention to the way in which the salient properties of the new technology are played out: demonstrated and engaged in their novelty and potential as sources of entertainment at both narrative and metanarrative level.

By presenting lay uses of the tape recorder – employed, in both cases, to 'hunt down' ordinary, prosaic sonority – what is brought into relief perhaps above all is magnetic tape's crucial contribution to the democratisation of sound recording, which increased exponentially as the decade progressed, and non-professional users became able to afford a portable, battery-operated system with which to play, but also – crucially – inscribe, music and any

Figure 3.2a   Valentina with the tape recorder in *La notte* (1961)

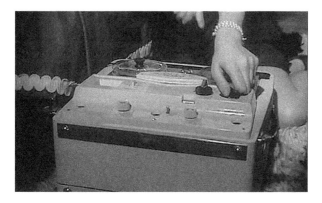

Figure 3.2b   Valentina with the tape recorder in *La notte* (1961)

other sounds, including noises and their own voice.[39] Such opportunity was truly innovative because, while phonographic prototypes (such as Thomas Alva Edison's of 1877) had been intended to incorporate recording and play-back functions in a single device, the bulk of commercial machines had been listening devices only.[40] After nearly a century from the invention of sound recording, the re-joining of these functions in tape recorders was addition-ally giving the technology, according to the author of our manual, 'a clear advantage over photography, still or otherwise', where, except for the costly Polaroid system, developing and printing processes would force a temporal separation between shooting and seeing the results.[41]

This re-joining of recording and playback functions is at the core of mag-netic tape's staging in both Antonioni's and Fellini's films. As the impromptu recording of the guests' conversation in *La dolce vita* shows, audiotape affords

spontaneity, bringing instantaneity to sound recording and enabling the capture of the voices of nature and inanimate things, as well as of people. All of
these can be recorded, instantly replayed and even, as Valentina, caught by a
whim of dissatisfaction, demonstrates in *La notte*, just as easily and immediately
erased. Furthermore, such 'magical' qualities of the technology are brought into
relief with respect to the ability to capture the users' own voice. While recording
one's own voice before magnetic tape had not been impossible, the procedure
had generally been limited to specialised commercial services (such as those
offering the cutting of brief aural messages on shellac discs for special occasions) or devices for office use (such as the Dictaphone memorably featured in
Double Indemnity in 1944).[42] Overall, not many people had been able to hear
their voice, as the slogan of one such service put it, 'as others hear it', for, as
Michael Chanan observes by quoting an often-cited phrase by André Malraux:
'you hear other people's voices with your ears, your own with your throat'.[43] Yet,
as tape recorders started to become common household devices in the course
of the 1960s, people became acquainted with their 'deboned' voice, as Douglas
Kahn calls it – an effect which, captured as novelty in *La notte* and *La dolce vita*,
Antonioni will richly exploit in *The Passenger*, when the 'deboned' voice of one
of the characters returns on the scene after his death.[44]

But as well as capturing the sense of wonder and possibility that the novel
technology generated in the early years of its diffusion, *La notte*'s staging
of audiotape, not unlike *La dolce vita*, makes manifest the mediatedness of
audiotaped sound *through* a demonstration of its immediacy. If Valentina's
monologue resonates with Antonioni's text on the sounds of a Manhattan
morning, this is so also because, in both cases, a 'sonic landscape' is evoked
and represented, but *without* resorting to an actual recording of the sonic
landscape as such. While this may seem obvious in the case of Antonioni's
written text, it is stranger in the case of Valentina's tape recording. Why produce a recorded verbal account of the sounds around her rather than taking
her tape recorder outdoors and capture the sounds themselves (as is the case
with the recording of 'nature' in *La dolce vita*)? Hearing Valentina's recorded
voice describe what she heard brings into relief the delay between the sonic
events at issue and their narrated inscription. Her voice is itself a level of
mediation which contributes to draw attention to the mediation of audiotape
and the *made*-ness of the recording, even in the unprecedented spontaneity,
instantaneousness and ostensible directness of sound capture, preservation
and erasure that the technology afforded. The non-coincidence between the
sounds and their translation into language which Valentina's approach underlines points to how magnetic tape contributed not only to the *re*production
of a found soundscape, but also to the very *production* of soundscape. In
other words, complicating somewhat the reception of magnetic tape's novelty

in terms of directness and immediacy, the indirectness of Valentina's mono-logue *about* soundscape helps to bring into relief how audiotape is not a 'non-medium', a transparent technology whose mediating function is erased by the instantaneity and spontaneity of use that it affords.[45]

In this respect, and considered in light of the New York text, this scene, while brief, has an important meta-diegetic function as a reflection on sound, and sound in film, on Antonioni's part.[46] As Valentina combines descriptions of sounds with reflections on sonority and aurality, the formative role of the technology is – indirectly but profoundly – further brought into relief by the very content of her recorded speech:

> Today, from the living room, I heard snatches of a dialogue of a film shown on television. 'Follow that car!', 'Some more whiskey?', 'If I were you, Jim, I wouldn't do it.' After this line, the howling of a dog: sustained, sincere, perfect. It rose and then fizzled out, its sound tracing a trajectory of pain into the air. Then, at first, I thought I'd heard an airplane, but it was silence. And I was very happy about it. The park is full of silence made of noises. If you press your ear against the tree, and stay like this for a while, eventually you hear a noise. Maybe it depends on us, but I prefer to think that's the tree. Then, in that silence, all of a sudden, some strange bangs, disturbing the sonic landscape around me. I didn't want to hear them. I shut the window but the noise persisted, driving me mad. I wouldn't want to hear useless sounds, I'd like to be able to select them throughout the day, and to select voices and words. Oh, so many words I'd rather not listen to, but you can't avoid them, you're subjected to them and can only try to endure them, the way you ride the waves you're exposed to when you float in the sea.[47]

Even as Valentina is talking about an unavoidable 'immersion' in sound, Antonioni is forcing some reflective distance from such immersion – and, as viewers, from our absorption by cinema's audiovisual flow – through the very display of the tape recorder. From the perspective of the historical moment she inhabits, the sounds Valentina pricks up her ears to are new and modern – television, the Americanisation of Italian life alluded to by the film dialogue, an aeroplane perhaps – but already ordinary enough to have become background. This is so to the point that silence and the roar of an aeroplane may be hard to tell apart. Additionally, her subtle attentiveness to the 'sonic landscape' around her also speaks of the new forms of sonority and conditions of aurality fostered by the availability of electroacoustics and magnetic tape themselves, which crucially enabled attunement to ordinary sounds and prosaic noises. As contemporaneous promotional material such as the 'manual for the non-technical amateur' that we considered brings into relief, this is a technology whose very novelty and marvel were deeply entangled with ordinariness. Cheap and re-usable (unlike film in point-and-shoot cameras), audiotape made ordinary the very capture of the ordinary.

Furthermore, if the twentieth century was, as Aldous Huxley had put it in 1944, 'The Age of Noise', the development of such a high-fidelity, mobile and plastic recording technology as audiotape was set to make a significant contribution not only to the awareness of the century's noise but to its noises themselves, expanding the range of the audible and putting new sounds in circulation.[48] Marvelling at its revelatory qualities, in 1955 the filmmaker Jean Epstein noted that audio recording, thanks to sound isolation and amplification, had the ability to make us hear 'the voice – which exists – of a passing cloud, a rejoicing house, grass growing'.[49] If Epstein's hyperbolic praise of audio-recording's potential for disclosure of previously unnoticed or inaudible sounds evokes an 'aural' equivalent of Walter Benjamin's famous notion of an 'optical unconscious', then Valentina's claim to being able to hear the noises of silence in the park and the sound of a tree suggests – as Benjamin did – that the new technological conditions might have started to affect, and transform, human perception itself.[50]

Not unlike Antonioni in New York, Valentina displays a sensibility (if not a sensitivity) informed by the existence of such technologies: an enhanced aware-ness and discrimination of sounds whose perception may have been trained on the model of the higher receptiveness of the machine. Just as, as is well known, Antonioni was excited by the possibility of machine vision and the ability of the camera to capture what might be unavailable to the naked eye, so he was enthused by the possibility of machine hearing. Just as he praised visual technologies and conjectured that perhaps, on exposure, 'film stock reg-isters everything . . . and only our technological backwardness prevents us from revealing all that is [imprinted] on the film frame', he also enthused that 'most professional microphones are much more sensitive than the human ear . . . and a great many unexpected noises and sounds' might therefore come to be captured on a recording.[51] Yet, in this instance, and to an even greater degree than Antonioni in his hotel room, we could perhaps even imagine Valentina as having somewhat internalised, and partially replaced, the recording machine itself (as, in *Il deserto rosso*, Giuliana, who hears sounds that others do not seem to perceive, will also appear to have done, to pathological extremes). The tape recorder's function is at once denied and redoubled by Valentina's approach to it, as she seems to substitute for it perceptually on the one hand, while commit-ting her conscious elaboration of data to the tape on the other. Flaunting a tape-recorder-like receptiveness both in her ability to isolate and amplify sounds and in her inability to be selective, Valentina indirectly broaches audiotape's trans-formation of the very domains of aurality and sonority. What is summoned is also a sense of audiotape's role in the production and making of sound, not only through capture and preservation, but also by putting new sonic entities into the world and by affecting human sensibility to, and perception of, them.[52]

As the co-existence, in Valentina's monologue, of excitement about 'sounding' silence and discomfort at her powerlessness to shut out what disturbs her suggests, the line between enthusiasm and anxiety is a fine one – and one whose blurred demarcation is perhaps reflected in Antonioni's ambivalent attitude to the cognisance of sound's 'incessant' presence in the New York text. If, at a time when sound technologies and media were still in their infancy, the futurist Luigi Russolo had nothing but excitement for 'noise', by the 1960s the worry is also about noise pollution and the possibility that, as Schafer explained in *The New Soundscape*, noise may find our ears without us searching for it. This does indeed seem to be the case for both Antonioni – from a 'thirty-seventh floor over Central Park' (as the title of his Manhattan sound diary points out) – and Valentina in *La notte*. No need, then, for them to 'cross a large modern capital with our ears more sensitive than our eyes' in active search for noise, as Russolo had incited his readers to do several decades earlier.[53] In a world already too noisy, Schafer wrote in 1969, 'the prevention of sound may well be as important as its production'.[54] The mass diffusion of broadcasting and recording media meant, as Schafer put it, that 'modern life [had] been ventriloquized', with all sorts of sounds 'torn from their natural sockets and given an amplified and independent existence', constantly available 'in our cars, in the streets, in our public buildings, anywhere and everywhere'.[55] From this perspective, the 'world sound diary' that Schafer encouraged his readers and their pupils to keep in *The New Soundscape*, whose subtitle reads *A Handbook for the Modern Music Teacher*, is at once a kind of music made of environmental sounds and noises and a form of monitoring of the very sounds and noises that constitute environmental sonority. If Schafer himself, bidding 'farewell' to the 'slumbering piano', practised this ambivalent form through his World Soundscape Project in Vancouver from the late 1960s, Antonioni and Valentina's poetic, and slightly anxious, accounts of urban sonority a few years earlier can be seen as manifestations of a similar endeavour.[56]

For indeed, what brings them together is also the way in which the world's noises, via audiotape, could be channelled or recycled against a 'rancid' music and towards a 'new musicality'.

'THE NEW MUSICALITY'

> Today, for the first time we have composers who even our fathers would not hesitate to define 'anti-musical'. Naturally, the opinion of our fathers does not interest us in the least.
>
> Luciano Berio, c. 1956[57]

> I used noises. They had not been intellectualized; the ear could hear them
> directly and didn't have to go through any abstraction about them.
>
> John Cage, 1959[58]

Paradoxically, Antonioni's ostensible turn *away* from music in the early 1960s
is also, at the same time, precisely a manifestation of his participation in contemporaneous debates and practices in the field of music, at a moment of
radical redefinition and expansion of the very category.[59] Certainly, the push
for an opening out of the category towards traditionally non-musical others –
including, indeed, the sounds and noises of 'the world' – can be traced back
to early-twentieth-century avant-gardes, including Futurism and Dada. But,
as one reading of the first epigram above suggests, even those very 'fathers'
might not have hesitated to define as 'anti-musical' what Berio – pointing to
Cage in particular, whom he will invite to RAI's Studio di Fonolgia in 1958 –
introduced as 'the new musicality' in the course of his essay. It is in the context
of this experimental ferment, for which innovations in sound technology and
recording, such as audiotape, provided an important catalyst, and to which
broadcast mass media, such as radio and television, gave increased visibility,
that Antonioni's own kind of 'anti-musical' rhetoric and sonic change of tack
in the early 1960s can best be understood.

In an attempt to rejuvenate music, Russolo, and others inspired by him,
including Edgar Varèse and George Antheil, had turned to the sounds of the
modern environment – 'the noises of trams, of automobile engines, of carriages
and brawling crowds' – in the earlier decades of the last century.[60] Where Russolo built a range of *intonarumori* [noise-tuning] devices to imitate syntheti-
cally such noises and sounds in musical performances (such as *Awakening of a
City*, 1913), Varèse and Antheil prescribed the direct use of worldly objects in
some of their compositions (such as a siren in the former's *Amériques*, 1921,
and an aeroplane propeller in the latter's *Ballet mécanique*, 1924), seeking to
recuperate prosaic noise as music, and to transform both in the process. The
development of radio, cinema sound and electroacoustic technology in the
course of the 1920s and 1930s further galvanised attempts to reform music
through extra-musical sounds. But the critical point in these endeavours was
reached in the 1950s. For, indeed, as it transformed the means and processes
for making music, audiotape contributed to a radical elasticisation of the
boundaries of music itself, precipitating a redefinition of the category in much
more expanded terms. As Cage enthusiastically diagnosed in the early years of
the diffusion of the technology, music could not be – and was not to be – the
same after 'tape came into being', since the new medium was 'revealing to us
that musical action . . . can occur at any point . . . in total sound-space' or, as
Schafer put it, it offered up 'the universe' as 'your orchestra'.[61]

The French *musique concrète* movement occupies an important place in the project of 'expanding' music to the noise of the world with the help of technology. Initiated by Schaeffer and Pierre Henry in the late 1940s, and then supported and housed by the French radio service in Paris from 1951, the movement yielded influence not only on Italian experimental music – informing some of the ideas of Berio and Bruno Maderna at the Studio di Fonologia, especially the inaugural work *Ritratto di Città* (*Portrait of a City*, 1954) – but also, as Di Carlo noted in 1964, on Antonioni himself.[62] Even though, before being able to switch to audiotape, Schaeffer made do with phonographic and disc equipment, with works such as *Cinq Études de bruits* (*Five Studies on Noises*, 1948), he employed recording technology to create a musical composition out of environmental sounds – indeed, noises – rather than orthodox instruments. Ordinary worldly sounds, such as those of the railway in the *Étude aux chemin de fer* (*Railroad Study*), one of the 'five' studies, could be freed from their original source and turned into absolute, yet materially concrete and manipulable, 'sound objects'.[63] Not unlike Russolo with the *intonarumori* or Varèse with the siren, however, Schaeffer still worked within a definition of music as a circumscribed category *within* the wider realm of sound. His objective was not the direct transferal of common noises into music *as themselves*: rather than making music noise, Schaeffer sought to make noise music, using recording technology to transfigure mundane sounds, metamorphosing them from their 'concrete' state in worldly sonority into musical 'abstractions'.[64] Schaeffer himself, who later openly rejected all his earlier experimentations, was ambivalent about the achievement of his *Railroad Study*, for he thought that, while technologically manipulated (e.g. slowed down, interrupted, repeated) the train sounds still retained their 'drama', that is, were still too recognisable to be considered 'sound objects' in themselves.[65]

While for Schaeffer non-manipulated prosaic sounds were still *too* prosaic to count as music, Cage approached the question from a different perspective. In contrast to the position of the *musique concrète* composer, Cage, whose work Berio saw as a 'catalysing element' in the break with the music of 'our fathers' he both described and called for in 'The New Musicality' (1956), found noises appealing precisely because one '*didn't* have to go through any abstraction about them'.[66] While including himself in the context of what he saw as the tendency, running throughout the twentieth century, 'to use noises, anything that produced sound, as a musical instrument', Cage endeavoured to reframe the project from the more radical perspective of the assimilation and alignment of music to sound – *any* sound.[67] 'Organization of sound', he suggested, might be a 'more meaningful term' than 'music'.[68] And, indeed, while his campaign for a widening of the category to include not only 'any and all sounds that can be heard' but 'the entire field of sound' had begun as early as 1937, it is in the course of the 1950s that the invitation achieved critical prominence (when, not incidentally, several of his talks first saw publication).[69] Berio among others, who, as mentioned, invited Cage to a residency at the Studio di Fonologia in the autumn of 1958, and published his 'Lecture on Nothing' (1949) in the Studio's journal *Incontri musicali* in 1959, articulated a similarly radically expanded conception of music in 'The New Musicality', welcoming the emergence of a new 'musical order', charac-terised by 'unlimited sonic possibilities' in which any and all sounds can be 'included' – freed from the notions of 'playing' as well as of 'instruments'.[70]

In Cage's view, however, both the move towards a much more expan-sive category of music as sound and the greater receptiveness to such invita-tion in the second half of the century were not his own particular merit, but a by-product of the particular historical moment. Turning to noise and understanding music as all sound had simply been the result of, as he put it, 'opening my ears to what was in the air'.[71] The implication of this opening of ears is twofold, since it meant not only following the direction in which the artistic wind blew, and taking the earlier avant-gardes' recourse to noise and prosaic sounds to extreme – or even, indeed, different – conclusions. It also meant, more literally, tuning into 'the air' around him and acknowledging the increasing role that auditive – and audio-visual – technologies and mass media played in transforming the century's sonority and aurality, not only by putting new sounds into the air, but by revealing existing yet previously neglected or unperceivable ones. In other words, as he later concisely put it, music had been transformed primarily not by artists and musicians like him-self, but by 'the media we are involved in'.[72]

For indeed, as Cage insisted, the transformation and expansion of the cate-gory of music, whereby, as he explained in 1957, it had become so 'free-ranging' that, among other things, its doors had swung open 'to the sounds that happen to be in the environment', was in 'striking coincidence' with the diffusion of 'the technical means' for utilising them so easily.[73] From this perspective, the noises of everyday objects, the sounds big and small that Cage tuned in to, were not only those of his historical moment; they were also – as I also suggested that Antonioni's Manhattan text and Valentina's monologue in *La notte* prompt us to realise – those which the very technologies of the historical moment attuned him to, providing the means for their pursuit and revelation.

In this respect, one of the principal reasons for the importance of auditive technology, in Cage's understanding, resided not so much in the fact that it put new sounds in what may otherwise be 'silence' but, rather, in the contri-bution to the realisation that silence itself was a fallacy. Just as the technologi-cal abatement of external sounds provided by the anechoic chamber, as Cage explained via the famous anecdote to which he himself would often return, made audible to him the internal sounds of his own body ('the nervous system in operation', 'the blood in circulation'), so the enhanced amplification and isolation of sounds afforded by electroacoustics and audiotape contributed to reveal the fundamental continuity of sound – the base-line sonority of silence itself – in a world made of matter in a state of constant movement and vibration.[74] While the magnetic tape recorder of the 1950s could not perhaps yet be the 'suitable technology' with which, in the 1970s, Cage suggested to an interlocutor that he could 'listen to [an] ashtray' and 'its inner life', it could nevertheless complement the anechoic chamber in its disclosure of silence's constitutive sonority – as *La notte* perhaps suggests that tape indirectly contributed to, by fostering Valentina's enhanced receptivity to the park's 'silence full of noises'.[75] 'The magnetic plate of tape', as Cage argued in 1958, had 'handed to us' a whole new range of sounds, 'in any combination and any continuity issuing from any point in space in any transformation'.[76] According to Cage, these developments meant that 'musical activities', or what we have seen he had suggested it would be better to call 'organization of sound', could consist of nothing other than 'discovering and acting upon these new ... resources' with these new technologies themselves.[77] Among these technologies, Cage was excited by magnetic tape in particular not only because 'the sound materials available now through [it] are virtually unlimited', but also because, as he suggested to an audience of creative filmmakers in 1956, '[a]nything' could be done with it'.[78] Thanks to its plasticity, even past music could be recycled as 'material' to be cut up and spliced elsewhere – and this, according to Cage's irreverent provocation, was 'the best thing that could have happened to it'.[79] Cage himself turned to audiotape for several of his works in the 1950s. In *Williams Mix* (1952) and *Fontana Mix* (1958) – this latter one of the pieces that he produced during his residency at the Studio di Fonologia – audiotape features both as a means of gathering sounds and as raw material from which instantiations of the final work may be produced, via minute cutting and splicing determined, not without paradox, by chance-led methods and graphic patterns.[80] As the 'music for tape recorders' premiered at the Museum of Modern Art in New York in October 1952, by which Berio was also enthused, had contributed to show, audiotape technology had come to be 'used not simply to record performances of music' but indeed, from tape collages to synthetic electronic sounds, 'to make a new music that was possible only because of it'.[81] This is encapsulated in *Williams Mix* and *Fontana Mix*, where the library of tape-recorded sounds which provides the source from which the collages may (the scores are not prescriptive in this respect) be stochastically assembled includes sonic categories such as 'city sounds', 'electronic sounds' and 'small sounds requiring amplification' which were greatly facilitated – if not, indeed, made possible – by the diffusion of audiotape itself.[82]

SCREEN WALKS: CAGE AND ANTONIONI

> Art needs to remain an outlet for those who do not make financial gains from it, for those who do not want power, for those who prefer to hide in the woods to pick mushrooms in the right season.
>
> Michelangelo Antonioni[83]

Premiered in Rome on 5 January 1959, the cacophonic collage of *Fontana Mix* showed how magnetic tape could not only capture noise but, literally, help to make it. Played *simultaneously* with Cathy Berberian's live solo voice performing another new piece by Cage, *Aria* (1958), the concert felt probably 'anti-musical' enough to please Berio (Berberian's husband) in his sense of rebellion towards the music of 'our fathers'. Certainly, the classical concert's venue, the Accademia Filarmonica Romana, contributed to provide evidence of how dramatically the boundaries between the traditionally antonymic categories of music and noise had blurred.

In fact, during his residency at the Studio di Fonologia, Cage was also welcomed at an even more unusual venue for an experimental musician: the television quiz show *Lascia o raddoppia* [*Double or Nothing*]. This is a venue, as we shall see, which compellingly helps to bring into relief the two interconnected phenomena that I have been pursuing in this chapter. At a broader level, it points to the deep entanglement between the avant-gardes and auditive – and, indeed, audio-visual – technologies and mass media in this period of profound redefinition of, and intense dialogue across, music and the visual arts. More narrowly, it illuminates the strong resonance between Cage's very vocal and visible 'anti-musical' pursuit of noises and Antonioni's equally prominent 'anti-musical' rhetoric and pursuit of what I have called (quietly) 'noisy images' – images open to prosaic sounds as well as to intermedial exchanges with other art forms.

Cage participated to the popular quiz on Italy's then only television channel, by RAI, for five consecutive weeks in early 1959.[84] Like the Studio, set up after Maderna and Berio's successful pitch to RAI's executives for a research facility dedicated to experimentation in electronic music as well as, more prosaically, the provision of soundtracks and sound effects for radio and television programmes (even possibly *Lascia o raddoppia* itself, if required), the quiz show had been running since 1955.[85] Hosted by Mike Bongiorno (whose 'fame' and 'idolaz[ation] by millions of people', which continued well into the new millennium, Umberto Eco felt compelled to analyse as early as 1961), *Lascia o raddoppia* was broadcast live from Milan's Fiera, not far from the Studio di Fonologia.[86] While Cage was interrogated on mushrooms rather than music, his status as a musician of a very experimental kind was frequently underlined, and joked about, by both the host and the press in news features on his televisual appearance. In addition to being able to exploit his mycological knowledge for the jackpot prize (of five million lire), Cage was given the opportunity to perform some of his compositions. As well as presenting the older *Amores* (1943), he premiered *Water Walk* (1959) and *Sounds of Venice* (1959), which, like *Fontana Mix*, he produced during the residency at Berio's Studio.[87]

Despite the chuckles and winks that the performances provoked (on the last week, Bongiorno, as one paper reported, invited the American composer to come back to Italy soon, but preferably without his music), there is something remarkable about Cage's presence at *Lascia o raddoppia*.[88] Obviously, one cannot claim that this marked the moment when experimental music went 'mainstream', or when Cage's, and others', radical proposals for a redefinition of music as any and all sounds came to be accepted as 'ordinary'. Nevertheless, Cage's appearance on Italian television compellingly crystallises the American composer's cultural significance and yield; which, as we have seen, he attributed to an opening 'to what was in the air' and 'the media we are involved in', and for both of which television represents a fitting shorthand. At the same time as it provides a snapshot of Cage's involvement with the RAI-funded experimental studio, it is also emblematic, and foretelling, of the intense traffic and interdependence between avant-garde and mass media, music and the visual arts, the aural and the visual fostered by the similar initiatives that flourished in the 1950s and 1960s, from groups such as those of Schaeffer and Stockhausen, supported by French and German national radio and television broadcasters respectively, to the legendary *9 Evenings: Theatre and Engineering* (1966) and the 'Experiments in Art and Technology' (1967–70) led by Billy Klüver and Robert Rauschenberg, among others, under the sponsorship of Bell Telephone Laboratories in the United States.[89] Cage's push for a radical opening out of music – which, as we shall see, crucially opened music out into the visual – provided significant momentum for an opening out of the visual arts too, and cross-contamination between disciplines if not, as Dick Higgins was to put it in his 1966 essay 'Intermedia', between 'the general area of art media and those of life media'.[90] After all, this was the moment that saw the emergence of aurally-inclined 'painting' (e.g. Rauschenberg's *Broadcast*, 1959, which incorporated a radio receiver) and 'sculpture' (e.g. Robert Morris's *Box with the Sound of its Own Making*, 1961), as well as of those mixed or 'combined' forms *par excellence* such as the happening and performance.[91] Furthermore, as scholars including Roland

Barthes and Marshall McLuhan began, in different ways, to consider at the time, such exchanges may even in turn perhaps be manifestations of a broader re-organisation of the hierarchy of the senses and rebalancing of the cultural primacy of visuality towards the auditory.[92]

One of the few photographs documenting Cage's appearance on the programme shows him surrounded by the 'stuff' needed for *Water Walk* and *Sounds of Venice*.[93] A grand piano (used for *Amores*) is in the background, while in the foreground, just to the edge of the stage, a heterogeneous barricade of objects has been laid out: a small tub in the middle separates two pairs

Di John Cage, più che la micologia, è nota la passione per la musica « concreta », quella che dal passaggio di un treno o da un volo di campane trae una sinfonia. Per la rubrica « Rumori quotidiani » John Cage ha messo su un complesso formato da un pianoforte, due radio, un frullatore, un innaffiatoio, un fischio, un gong, un bollitore

Figure 3.3   John Cage at *Lascia o raddoppia*, February 1959 (from *Radiocorriere TV*, 15–21 Feb 1959)

of small tables pushed next to each other, on which lie radios, a glass decanter, possibly a rattle, an electric blender and a pressure cooker. A watering can and, partially hidden by the tub, a gong, are also visible on the floor. Though not visible in this photograph, both *Water Walk* and *Sounds of Venice* also include a magnetic tape recorder, loaded with recordings of ordinary sounds and noises that Cage had collected for *Fontana Mix* as well as, for the latter piece, in Venice itself.[94] While no footage of these televised performances at RAI seems to have been preserved, Cage also presented *Water Walk* in January of the following year, 1960, on CBS's TV show *I've got a Secret*. The available recording shows Cage, the sole performer, moving around the space to 'play' the objects laid out around him: turning on the tape recorder and radios, getting the pressure cooker to hiss, crushing the ice cubes in the mixer, watering flowers, squeezing a rubber duck, spraying seltzer water from a syphon, and so on.[95] The overall effect is that of a strange equilibrium: Cage's timed and well-rehearsed actions seem to just manage to contain – organise? – the sounds of the objects being played, even as the objects themselves seem on the verge of playing up.

It is tempting to link Eco's analysis of Bongiorno and his television quizzes as manifestations of the ordinariness on which television thrives to Cage's cacophonic orchestration of 'quotidian noises', as the news features called them, in *Water Walk* and *Sounds of Venice*.[96] The selected objects are prosaic household items. The water theme, in the functions that these objects perform, and in the aquatic dimension of Venice's soundscape, also reinforces the sense of banality: as Cage explained, such theme was chosen because, while it was useful to have something 'to concentrate on', 'the world is made up of water'.[97]

Even though he was based in Rome, Antonioni is very likely to have been acquainted with the circle and activities of the Studio di Fonologia since its inception. He certainly was by the time he started work on *La notte* in Milan in 1960, also as Eco, who worked for RAI at the time and was actively involved with the Studio, features as an extra in the film.[98] Equally, Antonioni is unlikely to have needed *Lascia o raddoppia* to become acquainted with Cage's work and ideas, even though his reference to artists as mushroom pickers in the epigraph at the beginning of this section is evocative of Cage and the mycological expertise that he showcased on the programme. Yet, the resonance between Cage's absorption by aquatic sounds and tapes in works which flaunt music's move towards prosaic sonority, and Antonioni's concomitant 'anti-musical' rhetoric *and* new receptiveness to noise and environmental sounds is hard to ignore. The contemplation of Cage on Italian television in the early months of 1959, as an unusual conductor of household items, including radios and tape recorders, dovetails almost perfectly with the aspiration that Antonioni articulated of producing 'only a soundtrack of noises' in the summer of that year, as production for *L'avventura* got under-way and the director set out to capture tape recordings of the Sicilian sea to produce a montage for 'the sound effects'.

In fact, I want to suggest that, with *Water Walk* and *Sounds of Venice*, Cage performed a compelling instance of such 'soundtrack of noises', and one whose affinity with Antonioni's approach is richer and more complex than may at first appear. Above all, these are works which, devised for televi-sion, pointedly embrace the visual – in parallel, if differently, to how the score for *Fontana Mix* moves away from traditional musical notation and edges towards graphic images. Indeed, *Water Walk* and *Sounds of Venice* take fur-ther that 'mov[ing] towards theater from music' to which Cage had aspired from at least the earlier 1950s, with works such as *Water Music* (1952), the famous *4'33"*, and the *Untitled Event* at Black Mountain College of the same year, where the sounds – or lack thereof – of the 'musical' performance are overtly complemented by 'actions that were interesting *to see*'.[99] If for Schaef-fer one of the cultural consequences of the diffusion of sound recording, and audiotape especially, was an increase in the practice and status of 'pure listen-ing' (listening to sounds as recordings, and therefore in abstraction of their original source or cause), for Cage such experience prompted 'the reflection that a human being isn't just ears but also has eyes'.[100] And so, as he walks through the space and negotiates the array of objects needed for *Water Walk* and *Sounds of Venice*, Cage looks more like a Foley artist than a traditional musician, but – significantly – a Foley artist who, unlike in the cinema, is here on view, laying bare the tricks of the trade, so to speak.

Showing quite literally what Cage may refer to as 'organization of sounds', these performances on, and for, television also, as their titles suggest, conjure soundscapes: the 'sounds of Venice', a 'water walk'. Yet, not only are such soundscapes, rather than *re*produced, artificially *produced* – through the use of techniques and technologies, including radio and audiotape, as well as noisy objects such as a pressure cooker and a squeezable rubber duck – but they are *shown to be produced*. The production process is made visible, quite literally, as the sources of the sounds (or sound effects) are revealed, and the made-ness of the soundscape is *played out* at the same time as this is played or performed. While both *Sounds of Venice* and *Water Walk* use audiotape, the sound is not a naturalistic, 'captured' soundscape, as may be that which one's ears would 'capture' during a walk through Venice or a landscape with water features. While such soundscapes may be evoked, in the piece they are produced: the 'walk', in other words, is Cage's own through his stage and props as he per-forms and makes the sounds. In this context, tape recordings and radios are additional objects and sources of sounds, whose random playing adds to the cacophony of the pieces, and underlines Cage's interest in 'tuning in' to what was 'in the air' and the role of 'the media we're involved in' as shaping factors in the transformation of aurality, sonority and the very definition of music.

The resonance and temporal coincidence between Cage's performances of his soundtracks of noises for the small screen and Antonioni's desire to orchestrate them for his cinema is noteworthy. At this moment of sonic change of tack in his films, and when Cage himself was very much in the air in Italy, Antonioni too was 'tuning in to what was in the air'. And, for him too, seeking to replace an old musicality for a new one, performative screen walks offered a convenient route for an organised soundtrack of environmental or prosaic noises.

Possibly the first, most memorable and longest of such performative screen walks is Lidia's in *La notte* (although other, shorter, examples include Vittoria and friends' nocturnal exit in EUR to find Marta's dog in *L'eclisse*, and Thomas's stroll in the park in *Blow-Up*). In an extended sequence which, while intercut with shots of her husband waiting for her in their flat, lasts for about twenty minutes, Lidia starts her walk through Milan's centre during the lunch rush hour and, thanks to a taxi ride, ends up in Sesto San Giovanni in the city's periphery, from where she finally leaves before nightfall as her husband has reached her there. In this music-less sequence, in which dialogue is stripped to a minimum, emphasis is on the sounds of the urban environment through which Lidia moves. From its incessant, but perhaps sometimes also unnoticed, murmur to its most obviously loud and disruptive noises, this sequence brings into relief what J. G. Ballard described as 'the cacophonic *musique concrète* of civilization' in one of his short science-fiction stories of the time in which avant-garde music and audiotape are disguised elements of a dystopian allegory of a world without 'traditional' music.[101] The sounds themselves, modulated spatially and temporally as Lidia moves through different zones of the city, and from noon till dusk, tell a story – a story of the urban organisation of both time and space in the city. The car roars and horns of rush-hour traffic are replaced by relative quietness after a factory siren announces the end of the morning shift, and Lidia moves away from the centre. Not unlike in Antonioni's New York text, certain sounds stand out, almost amplified: church bells, a toddler crying, an aeroplane. The soundscape changes again in the periphery, and as evening approaches, youth firing rockets and leisurely voices stand out more clearly – it is even possible to catch snippets of conversation – and mellow music can be heard from a radio in a bar kiosk.

If Lidia's walk connects this sequences to a range of avant-garde music practices across the twentieth century for which the urban walk provided *the* privileged tool for tuning in to 'soundscape', then indeed, one of the key

aspects of such connection is that capture and making, reproduction and production, immediacy and mediation are inextricably linked in such pursuits.
Not unlike the soundscapes that Cage crafted for – and on – the screen during his appearance at *Lascia o raddoppia*, so the sonic landscape of *La notte*'s
sequence is mediated and made, as well as cinematically organised. While
also using sounds captured on location as in Cage's pieces, this soundscape
is not merely found but, rather, the result of a process of selective amplification and abatement, sound editing and sound production. If Cage shows the
tricks, matching 'the boot with its creaking', as Sergei Eisenstein would put
it, Antonioni orchestrates a subtle de-naturalisation of sounds that resonates
with the 'contrapunctual' montage of visual and aural, moving away from
'consonance', championed by the Soviet avant-garde filmmaker.[102] This is the
case, among others, of the roar of the aeroplane that Lidia hears, whose sound
is too loud and 'too close' to have been a location sound, or the unnaturally
resounding footsteps throughout much of the sequence, which, both when
Lidia walks on gravel or her husband is seen waiting for her on the balcony
of their high-rise flat, are offered as sound 'close-ups' which do not match
the kind of sounds the visual image offered would logically require. Another
famous instance of this de-naturalisation is the iconic sequence in *Blow-Up* in
which the photographer studies the enlarged snapshots of an ostensibly flirt-
ing couple that he surreptitiously took earlier in the day. As he observes the
prints, pinned up around his studio, the sounds of his surroundings fade out,
and the sounds – or 'silence' – of the park (the rustling leaves, the chirping
birds) suddenly return to accompany these images.

While sometimes talking of a desire for 'natural sounds' Antonioni tends
to counteract any sense of immediacy that technological developments
brought to the reproduction and production of sound by also foregrounding
its *mediation* and *made-ness*.[103] This is perhaps the crux of his dialogue with
the musical avant-garde of the period. Not unlike Cage's harnessing of visuality in his music performances and scores, Antonioni uses cinema to make
the mediated-ness of recorded sound, and its construction with the image,
visible – if in an often subtle and 'quiet' way. As improvements to sound
technology seemed to pave the way for the reproduction of an aural dimension that may match in seeming accuracy and detail that of the visual image
and immerse us further into a cinematic 'reality', it seems that, while working *within* such possibilities, Antonioni also worked *with* the mediation of
sound to bring it into relief and trouble our absorption by the audiovisual
flow. In important respects, Antonioni's strategies resonate with the way in
which the Argentinian director Lucrecia Martel recently spoke of sound as
the 'third dimension' of cinema. Using the metaphor of a swimming pool
to describe sound as that dimension which may be – and is often – used to

make the cinematic experience more realistic, more immersive, Martel said that film sound is also at the same time that which enables the foregrounding of the very mediation and constructedness of cinema, if sound itself is used to upset the referentiality of the image, to call into question its 'reality'.[104] It is in this sense that Antonioni, in an actual or virtual dialogue with Cage and other avant-garde musicians, uses sound as an avenue for what I have suggested we could call 'critical intermediality'.

NOTES

1. Text by Antonioni in Di Carlo, *Michelangelo Antonioni*, footnote 11, pp. 29–31, initially untitled and described as 'notes found in an unpublished notebook written after completing *La notte*'. The text has since then been published in English as Antonioni, 'From a Thirty-Seventh Floor over Central Park: Soundtrack for a Film in New York'. I have discussed this passage and some of the ideas considered in this chapter in 'Some Reflections on Antonioni, Sound and the Silence of *La notte*'.
2. See, for example, Païni, *Lo sguardo di Michelangelo*, which in turn refers to Antonioni's last short film, *Lo sguardo di Michelangelo* (2004); Arrowsmith, *Antonioni: The Poet of Images*; Tassone, *I film di Michelangelo Antonioni. Un poeta della visione*.
3. Chatman, *Antonioni, or the Surface of the World*, p. 66.
4. *Blow-up* (1966) and then *Zabriskie Point* (1970), while continuing this trend in part, also introduce especially commissioned music not by cinema composers, but commercial rock and pop musicians such as Herbert Hancock, the Yardbirds, the Grateful Dead and Pink Floyd. See, for example, Boschi, '"La musica ache meglio si adatta alle immagini": suoni e rumori nel cinema di Antonioni'; D'Amato, 'Antonioni: la poetica dei materiali'.
5. Billard, 'An Interview with Michelangelo Antonioni' (originally in *Cinéma* 65, November 1965), p. 146.
6. Antonioni, 'Silence', p. 23.
7. Ibid.
8. Tomasulo, '"The Sounds of Silence": Modernist Acting in Michelangelo Antonioni's *Blow-Up*', p. 111.
9. Ibid., p. 120, quoting Antonioni in Wyndham, 'Antonioni's London', p. 13.
10. D'Amato, 'Antonioni: la poetica dei materiali', p. 154.
11. Balázs, *Theory of the Film*, p. 197; Schafer, *The New Soundscape*.
12. Labarthe, 'A Conversation with Michelangelo Antonioni', p. 139.
13. Anon., 'Questions à Antonioni', p. 10. A trained violinist, Antonioni had a keen interest in music, manifested, among other things, by a discographic collection of more than 1,400 items (holdings can be consulted via the online inventory of his archive, Michelangelo Antonioni Archive, Ferrara).
14. Labarthe, 'A Conversation', p. 139.
15. Maurin, '*L'avventura*' (interview with Antonioni, first in *Humanité dimanche*, September 1960), p. 272.

16. Billard, 'An interview', p. 146 cited.
17. D'Amato, 'Antonioni: la poetica dei materiali', offers an in-depth discussion, and a very helpful diagram (p. 181), of Antonioni's progressive reduction of music in the first half of the 1960s.
18. Ibid.
19. For more on Fusco's collaboration with Antonioni, see Calabretto, 'Giovanni Fusco musicista per il cinema di Antonioni'.
20. Antonioni quoted in Nowell-Smith, *L'avventura*, p. 27.
21. See Anon., 'Questions à Antonioni', p. 10 (my emphasis).
22. Labarthe, 'All'origine del cinema c'è una scelta' (originally in *Cahiers du cinema*, October 1960) p. 127. Curiously, this passage is omitted from the English version of the interview from which I have quoted above, so this is my translation from the Italian.
23. Balász, *Theory of the Film*, p. 197.
24. Labarthe, 'All' origine', p. 127.
25. For histories of magnetic tape technology, see, for example, Chanan, *Repeated Takes*, esp. pp. 116–50. and Millard, *America on Record*, esp. pp. 285–327.
26. Cox and Warner, *Audio Culture*, p. 113.
27. Nijsen, *The Tape Recorder*, 'Introduction', not numbered (my emphasis).
28. For an overview, see, for example, Griffiths, *Modern Music*.
29. Berio, 'Agli amici degli "Incontri musicali"' (originally in *Incontri musicali*, 1958), pp. 14–15.
30. Gould, 'The Prospects of Recording'.
31. Eno, 'The Recording Studio as Compositional Tool' (initially a lecture at the New Music Festival, New York, in 1979). See also Berio, 'Note sulla musica elettronica' (first in *Ricordiana*, 1957), and 'Commenti al rock' (first in *Nuova Rivista Musicale Italiana*, 1967). For broader accounts, see also, for example, Millard, *America on Record*, esp. pp. 295–304.
32. Ethnomusicology received a boost in Italy precisely in the mid to late 1950s, when, in the wake of major projects by Alan Lomax and Diego Carpitelli, it emerged as an academic discipline. See Casadei, 'Milan's Studio di Fonologia: Voice Politics in the City, 1955–8', esp. p. 423.
33. For an overview of sound reproduction in cinema, see, for example, Monaco's technical section in his classic *How to Read a Film*, pp. 98–103. Independent filmmaking was buoyed by the launch of improved soundproofed, professional-standard models 16 mm cameras (e.g. Bolex, Éclair) in the 1960s which could be rigged with Nagra portable audio-equipment. See Nowell-Smith, *Making Waves*, pp. 85–6 and MacDonald and Cousin, *Imagining Reality*, pp. 249ff. Vitello, 'Stefan Kudelski, Polish Inventor of Recorder that Changed Hollywood'. By the early 1970s, Nagra had even developed a miniature recorder which actors could carry around in their pockets and which, as its featuring in Francis Ford Coppola's Watergate-inspired *The Conversation* (1974) also shows, found further applications in secret intelligence and surveillance.

34. Indeed, as a critic, Antonioni had initiated a debate and reflection on dubbing in the 1940s. See, for example, 'Vita impossibile del signore Clark Costa' (originally in *Cinema* 105, 10 November 1940) and 'Conclusioni sul doppiato' (originally in *Cinema* 116, 25 April 1941). For a discussion of this, see Sisto, *Film Sound in Italy*, esp. pp. 11–15.

35. First published in the periodical *Filmcritica* in February 1968 and, in English, in *Sight and Sound* later in the same year, the 'Amalfi Manifesto', produced on the occasion of a symposium on film sound in Amalfi, was also signed by Pier Paolo Pasolini, Federico Fellini, Bernardo Bertolocci, Francesco Rosi, Marcho Bellocchio, Gillo Pontecorvo and Paolo and Vittorio Taviani, among others. Now in McKenzie, *Film Manifestos and Global Cinema Cultures*, p. 572.

36. On loose synchronisation in Italian art cinema, see, for example, Chion, *The Voice in the Cinema*, esp. pp. 129ff.

37. Nijsen, *The Tape Recorder*, 'Introduction', n.p.

38. Schaeffer, *Traité des objets musicaux*, pp. 91–102. Schafer in *The New Soundscape*, describes sound recording's separation of sounds from their original source as a form of 'ventriloquism', p. 44.

39. Nijsen, *The Tape Recorder*, 'Introduction'.

40. Sterne, *The Audible Past*, offers a remarkable study of sound reproduction in the nineteenth century. See also Kittler, *Gramophone, Film, Typewriter* and Gelatt, *The Fabulous Phonograph 1877–1977*.

41. Nijsen, *The Tape Recorder*, 'Introduction'. Indeed, when magnetic videotape was launched only a year or so later, 'immediacy' would be one of its most celebrated attributes. See Kaizen, 'Live on Tape: Video, Liveness and the Immediate'.

42. See, for example, *Listen: 140 Years of Recorded Sound*, exhibition, British Library, London, 6 October 2017 to 11 March 2018.

43. Kodisk slogan, 1930s, exhibited at *Listen: 140 Years of Recorded Sound*. Chanan, *Repeated Takes*, p. 137. The quote is from Malraux, *La Corde et les souris*, pp. 614–15, but the same idea also appears in *Les Voix du silence*.

44. Kahn, *Noise, Water, Meat*, p. 7.

45. See Kaizen, 'Live on Tape: Video, Liveness and the Immediate'.

46. At the aural level, this strategy resonates with what in *Cinema and Painting* Dalle Vacche, following Pasolini's notion of the 'free indirect subjective', describes as 'visual ventriloquism', a way for the director to 'speaks through the actor's body' (p. 48). See Pasolini, in 'The "Cinema of Poetry"', esp. pp. 178–9.

47. Here and subsequent transcription and translation from the film's dialogue are mine.

48. Huxley, *The Perennial Philosophy*, p. 218. For the futurist Luigi Russolo, noise was a product of the nineteenth century, and 'the invention of machines'. See Russolo, 'The Art of Noises: Futurist Manifesto', p. 23.

49. Epstein, 'The Counterpoint of Sound', p. 363.

50. Benjamin, 'A Small History of Photography', p. 243; and 'The Work of Art in the Age of Mechanical Reproduction', p. 216.

51. Billard, 'An Interview with Michelangelo Antonioni', p. 145. Antonioni, 'Preface to Six Films', p. 63.

52. On the unselectivity of recording machines Kittler, following Edison, writes that 'the phonograph . . . does not hear as do ears that have been trained immediately to filter voices, words, and sounds out of noise; it registers acoustic events as such'. Kittler, *Gramophone, Film, Typewriter*, p. 23.

53. Russolo, 'The Art of Noises', p. 26.

54. Schafer, *The New Soundscape*, esp. 'Introduction' and p. 57 (cited). Gelmetti, among others, articulated similar concerns in 'Musica-Verità?'.

55. Schafer, *The New Soundscape*, p. 44.

56. Schafer's 'World Soundscape Project' was a research initiative that he led at Simon Fraser University in Vancouver from the late 1960s, see <https://www.sfu.ca/~truax/wsp.html> (last accessed November 2019).

57. Berio, 'La nuova musicalità' (c. 1956, previously unpublished), p. 8.

58. Cage, 'Lecture on Nothing' (first delivered in 1949), p. 137.

59. See in particular Kahn, *Noise, Water, Meat*, pp. 45–67 and Thompson, *The Soundscape of Modernity*, pp. 115–68, for compelling, yet different, accounts.

60. Russolo, 'The Art of Noises', p. 25.

61. Cage, 'Experimental Music' (talk first delivered at the National Music Teachers Association Convention in Chicago, 1957; first printed for retrospective at Town Hall, New York City, in 1958), pp. 11 and 9. Schafer, *The New Soundscape*, p. 62.

62. For a discussion of the Studio di Fonologia's early partial affinity with *musique concrète*, see Casadei, 'Milan's Studio di Fonologia', esp. pp. 411ff. and De Benedictis, 'Opera prima: Ritratto di città e gli esordi della musica elettroacustica in Italia'. For Antonioni and *musique concrète*, see Di Carlo, 'Antonioni', esp. pp. 28ff.

63. See Schaeffer, *In Search of a Concrete Music*, p. 14. Griffiths, *Modern Music*, pp. 31–2.

64. Schaeffer, *In Search of a Concrete Music*, p. 25.

65. Schaeffer, *In Search of a Concrete Music*, pp. 14–15. See also Kahn, *Noise, Water, Meat*, pp. 110–12.

66. Berio, 'La nuova musicalità', pp. 9 and 8; Cage, 'Lecture on Nothing', p. 137 (my emphasis).

67. Kostelanetz, *Conversing with Cage*, p. 165.

68. Cage 'Credo: The Future of Music' (talk first delivered in 1937 at the Seattle Arts Society; text printed for retrospective at Town Hall, New York City, in 1958), p. 3.

69. Interviewed by Kostelanetz in 1968, Cage explained how in Europe he had been taken as a 'clown' on his tour in 1954, but then, when he returned in 1958 'there was a marked change', 'we were taken quite seriously, for the most part'. Cage in Kostelanetz, *Conversing with Cage*, p. 17.

70. See Berio, 'La nuova musicalità', p. 9 cited; and Berio, 'Prospettive nella muisca. Richerche e attività dello Studio di Fonologia Musicale di Radio Milano' (first published in *Elettronica* and *The Score* in 1956), p. 183.

71. Kostelanetz, *Conversing with Cage*, p. 165.

72. Kostelanetz, *John Cage*, p. 15.
73. Cage, 'Experimental Music', p. 8.
74. Cage 'Experimental Music', p. 8. Cage would often return to his experience in the anechoic chamber. See Kahn's discussion in *Noise, Water, Meat*, esp. pp. 194–9.
75. Cage in *For the Birds*, pp. 220–1, cited in Kahn, *Noise, Water, Meat*, p. 196.
76. Cage, 'Erik Satie', p. 77.
77. Ibid.
78. Cage, 'On Film' (first delivered as a talk at the Creative Film Foundation, New York City, 1956), p. 115.
79. Ibid.
80. Cage described *Fontana Mix* as an 'indeterminate tape', different each time it is performed. Cage, 'Letter to Peter Yates – 28 December 1959', in *The Selected Letters of John Cage*, ed. Laura Kuhn (Middletown: Wesleyan University Press, 2016), pp. 210–13; p. 212 cited.
81. Cage, 'Experimental Music', pp. 8–9. Berio, who had just arrived in the United States with a scholarship, wrote an essay on the the Museum of Modern Art performance, through which he was introduced to Vladimir Ussachevksy and the 'music for tape recorders' collaboration between Columbia-Princeton University. See 'Musica per *Tape Recorder*' (first published in *Il Diapason*, 1953).
82. See Cage, 'Williams Mix', p. 109; Cage, *Fontana Mix* (premiered in Milan in November in 1958) score published in New York in 1960.
83. Michelangelo Antonioni, unpublished typewritten note (n.d.), Michelangelo Antonioni Archive, Ferrara, fasc. 209 a-b.
84. For an accurate reconstruction, see Pocci, '*Lascia o raddoppia*'.
85. See Berio, 'Prospettive nella muisca'. For histories of the Studio di Fonologia see, in English, Casadei, 'Milan's Studio di Fonologia' and Novati, 'The Archive of the "Studio di Fonologia di Milano della Rai"'; in Italian: Rizzardi and De Benedictis, *Nuova musica alla radio*, including De Benedictis, 'Opera prima: Ritratto di città'. See also Scaldaferri, *Musica nel laboratorio elettroacustico*; De Benedictis, *Radiodramma e arte radiofonica*.
86. Eco, 'The Phenomenology of Mike Bongiorno', p. 158. For more on *Lascia o raddoppia* see RAI's online archive, <http://www.teche.rai.it/2015/11/26-novembre-1955-prima-puntata-di-lascia-o-raddoppia/> (last accessed November 2019). For discussions of Italian television broadcasting and the popularity of *Lascia o raddoppia*, see Forgacs, *Italian Culture in the Industrial Era 1880–1980*, esp. pp. 24 and 126.
87. Kostelanetz, *Conversing with Cage*, pp. 113–14; Cage, *The Selected Letters*, esp. pp. 196–200.
88. Bertocci, 'Il profeta e il burattino'. (Cage says that while he is leaving, his music will stay, and Bongiorno says the opposite would be better.)
89. See Klüver, Martin and Rose, *Pavilion: Experiments in Art and Technology*. Hultén and Königsberg, *9 Evenings: Theater and Engineering*; Morris and Bardiot, *9 Evenings Reconsidered*.
90. Higgins, 'Intermedia' (first in *Something Else Newsletter* 1, 1966), p. 49.

91. Ibid.

92. See, for example, McLuhan, *The Gutenberg Galaxy*, esp. pp. 24–31; McLuhan and Powers, *The Global Village*, esp. pp. 37–46; Barthes (with Roland Havas) 'Listening'.

93. In *Radiocorriere-TV*, 15–21 February 1959. See also *Stampa sera*, 6–7 February 1959, p. 6.

94. Cage, 'To John Cage Sr and Lucretia Cage – 6 February 1959', in Cage, *The Selected Letters*, p. 199.

95. See <http://johncage.org/pp/John-Cage-Work-Detail.cfm?work_ID=242> (last accessed November 2019).

96. Eco links television to ordinariness and argues that Bongiorno's fame is due to the fact that he encapsulates 'television's ideal' of 'the absolutely average person' (p. 157), he is 'superman . . . reduced to everyman' (p. 158).

97. Kostelanetz, *Conversing with Cage*, p. 113.

98. Eco, who worked at RAI in the late 1950s, collaborated with Berio on *Thema (Omaggio a Joyce)* (1958–9), produced while Cage was in residence at the Studio, and contributed regularly to the Studio's journal, *Incontri musicali*. The first essay in which he introduced his famous concept of the 'open work' – whose affinity with experimental music and Cage's pursuit of 'indeterminacy' is well documented, and which he will use to think about Antonioni's films too – appeared there, in the same issue in which Cage's 'Lecture on Nothing' was first published. See Eco, 'L'opera in movimento e la coscienza dell'epoca'. See also, Eco, *Opera aperta*, pp. v–xxiii.

99. Kostelanetz, *Conversing with Cage*, p. 113 (my emphasis).

100. Ibid. See also Schaeffer, *Traité des objets musicaux*, p. 93, and pp. 91–102 on the 'acousmatic', the availability of sounds more broadly.

101. Ballard, 'The Sound-Sweep', p. 62.

102. Eisenstein, 'Synchronization of the Senses', p. 70. Eisenstein, Pudovkin and Alexandrov argued for a 'contrapunctual' use of sound in 'A Statement' (1928), trans. Jay Leida, in Elisabeth Weis and John Belton (eds), *Film Sound: Theory and Practice* (New York: Columbia University Press, 1985), pp. 83–5.

103. Labarthe, 'All' inizio del cinema', p. 127; see also, for example, Billard, 'An Interview', p. 145.

104. Lucrecia Martel, in conversation at the Institute of Contemporary Arts, London, 20 May 2018.

CHAPTER 4

The 'Image-World' and the Reality of Photography

[M]odern man feeds on images.
Roger Munier, *Contre l'image* (1963)[1]

Chung Kuo, Cina/Chung Kuo, China, the documentary that Antonioni shot in China in 1972 for RAI (Italy's national radio and television broadcaster) starts with a series of medium and close-up shots of people's faces. As the opening credits end, the camera gradually zooms out to reveal more of the scene and an off-screen voice starts to 'locate' the images. We are in Beijing's Tiananmen Square, and the faces we have just seen in close-up, in framings evocative of both street photography and photographic portraiture, are shown to belong to people waiting in queues to have their pictures taken in front of the Tiananmen Gate – with its portrait of Mao Zedong between placards commemorating the People's Republic – by a number of photographers standing under large white-canvas umbrellas.

The manifest justification for this scene, as the commentary explains, is to start a documentary about China with the country's *chung kuo* – its historical and cultural 'core' across the centuries. However, the decision to begin this way also suggests another motivation. Antonioni's images of China are introduced with the Chinese *themselves* engaged in the activity of taking and posing for images. In so doing, attention is reflexively focused on questions of image production and circulation, as well as on the *kind* of images that both photography and cinema are. The scene invokes a resonance and technological affinity between the two, perhaps even suggesting that the former is the ontological kernel of the latter, or that the two are close relatives in a family of media (including television, for which Antonioni's documentary, though shot on 16 mm film cameras, was produced) which constitute the 'core' of modern image culture, whose images are largely technologically produced and, in turn, are themselves reproducible.

Figure 4.1a   *Chung Kuo, China* (1972)

Figure 4.1b   *Chung Kuo, China* (1972)

Figure 4.1c   *Chung Kuo, China* (1972)

Arguably, even in this day of mobile phones and selfie sticks, variations of the photographic services portrayed in this scene still survive in some theme parks and other attractions, where it may be possible to buy a photo of oneself mid-air on a rollercoaster ride. Yet, to Western audiences in the early 1970s, queuing to be photographed might have already seemed outmoded, a ritual premised on a relative scarcity of cameras and photographic images in stark contrast with the proliferation of both these types of object in late-capitalist consumer cultures.

Susan Sontag addressed photographic growth in her book *On Photography* (1977), which collects and develops essays that she had written for the *New York Review of Books* since the early 1970s. 'There seems no way', Sontag writes in the last chapter, 'of limiting the proliferation of photographic images'.[2] '[T]he unlimited production and consumption of images' seems to be a requirement of capitalism itself, wherein, often as commodities, images both stimulate and partake of the larger economic cycles of production and consumption.[3] Not unlike other media critics and scholars, from Vilém Flusser and Pierre Sorlin with their inclusive categories of, respectively, 'technical' and 'analogue' images to, more recently, Michelle Henning, who sees photography as radically hybrid and adaptive from its inception, Sontag understands the medium to provide the basis for several variations of its 'core' technological principles. These variations include forms ranging from holography to infrared, cinema to television and video.[4] Through these manifold manifestations, photography is considered (albeit implicitly) as both a medium and a form of (mass) media which has come to provide, as Sontag puts it, the 'spectacle' and the 'surveillance' required by a capitalist society.[5]

Photographic proliferation had already caused anxiety earlier in the century. Siegfried Kracauer, among others, had talked of a 'blizzard of photographs' in the 1920s, thinking of their presence in the illustrated press in particular.[6] But it was from the 1950s, in the wake of the diffusion of television as another route through which photography's principles – if not sometimes also photography's actual images – could be modulated and circulated, that the idea of a parallel world of images, a veritable 'image-world', as Sontag calls it, began to take hold. In his 1952 book *Art and Technics*, Lewis Mumford had expressed concern at the 'ever-rising flood of images' and, in tones that in some way anticipate Baudrillardian simulation, at the 'ghost world' through which such images were replacing 'the multidimensional world of reality'.[7] Furthermore, from the late 1950s, satellites and space-exploration programmes started to make available images *of* the world itself. In this context, *Blue Marble*, the famous first image of the *whole* Earth which the crew of the Apollo 17 Mission took on the same year as Antonioni's China documentary, may be seen to endow with a literal meaning Martin Heidegger's earlier claim that 'the fundamental event of the modern age is the conquest of the world as picture'.[8] In the 'image-world', even the world itself becomes an image. In so much as it allows us to 'accumulate, store' and 'appropriate the thing photographed . . . [t]he most grandiose result of the photographic enterprise', as Sontag writes in the first chapter of her book (from an essay first published in 1973), 'is to give us the sense that we can hold the whole world in our heads – as anthology of images'.[9]

Interestingly, as she outlines photography's exponential growth and accumulation of an 'image-world', Sontag draws at length on *Chung Kuo, China*, including the 'queue for photographs' with which the film starts. While Sontag sees a strict nexus between consumer capitalism and image proliferation, the reflections which Antonioni's film occasions are not aimed at drawing a contrast between their rarity in a communist country and their overload in western consumer societies. Rather, her intent is to point to differences in aesthetics and modalities of production and circulation within a baseline of increasing diffusion whose reach is *global*. Despite cultural specificities and more or less overt forms of political censorship which, as she explains, tend to make photography formal and formulaic, Sontag notes that photography abounds in communist China too. Not unlike Antonioni, who surveys domestic interiors adorned with portraits of leaders and loved ones, and captures people taking snapshots of themselves at landmark locations such as the Great Wall and in the Forbidden City, so Sontag, drawing on her own recent first-hand experience of the country, confirms that people both own photographs (including 'mass-produced photographic iconography of revered leaders, revolutionary kitsch, and cultural treasures') *and* take pictures, not unlike 'the sort of snapshots taken here [in the west] at family gatherings and on trips'.[10] And indeed, by the early 1970s, as the photographer and writer Gisèle Freund noted in *Photography and Society* (1974), in addition to having and taking photographs, the Chinese were rapidly developing their camera-manufacture sector and undercutting Japanese competition (which, in turn, by the 1960s, had outdone the lead that German production had in the 1930s).[11]

As we watch people queuing up to be photographed in *Chung Kuo, China*, the emphasis is not on the rarity or exceptionality of the activity. There are many people queuing, and many queues, yet everyone seems to wait without particular excitement or boredom.[12] Both the unhurried movements of the camera and the voice-over, which remarks that this is not a special day of marches, speeches or parades but, rather, 'a day like any others', concur to characterise the occurrence as unremarkable. If there is something of the ritual, this is, as Sontag puts it, of an 'elementary' kind – perhaps even a banal one.[13] But while suggesting that photography proliferates – and it is a global phenomenon – this scene also addresses photography as something broader than a category of images. No actual photographs are shown in this scene *about* photography, which is here captured as a number of 'doings' (even waiting is). Photography begins to come to the fore not as a term referring to a specific type of image but as a multiform techno-cultural activity, something, as the philosopher Jean-Marie Schaeffer wrote in *L'image précaire* (1987), that is arguably better grasped 'at the level of its social circulation', 'as the result of a techne [and] a doing', than in terms of an elusive and ever-changing 'ontology'.[14]

It may seem strange to start a chapter on Antonioni and photography with this scene from a film that, as a documentary for television and because of its political vicissitudes, is neither among the most representative or better known of his oeuvre. Why not *Blow-Up* (1966), which is not merely *the* film by Antonioni on photography but also, arguably, one of the best-known and most cited films on photography more generally? This chapter will consider *Blow-Up*, which does indeed arguably constitute Antonioni's richest and most significant reflection on photography and the image in the late twentieth century. Yet, as the scene from *Chung Kuo, China* helps to bring into relief, the ensuing discussion seeks to do so by showing that *Blow-Up* is not the result of a one-off, occasional engagement with photography on Antonioni's part but rather of a consistent interest in photography across his cinema, which is recurrently and overtly addressed. Adopting this broader scope reveals such interest to reside not so much in a specific ontology of the medium but rather in the way in which photography constitutes a founding instance of what Flusser calls the 'technical images' of (mass) culture. Not unlike Sontag and others, Antonioni was very aware of the pervasive proliferation of such images – even if he reacted to it less anxiously and defensively than the author of the essay *Contre l'image* in this chapter's opening epigraph. If photography's pervasiveness affects Antonioni's cinema too, his cinema in turn demonstrates a commitment to addressing such proliferation and engaging in a (self-)critique of the role of the image. The 'queuing for photographs' shown at the start of *Chung Kuo, China* helps to reveal the different focus that I want to pursue in the discussion that follows. I want to suggest that, rather than a narrow interest in the 'reality' *in* the photograph – an interest, that is, in the evidentiary or documentary capacity of the photographic image in its presumed ability to 'capture' and reproduce reality – Antonioni's films, including *Blow-Up*, articulate a broader reflection on the reality *of* photography. By this I mean photography's multiform and adaptive material existence as both medium and mass media, technology and socio-cultural form: the material – if *differently* material – facts of the production, circulation and consumption of photographs. Surveying Antonioni's films, what emerges is an ongoing curiosity in photography's *how*: not only the technological but also the social reality of its proliferation, pervasiveness and adaptability in twentieth-century culture.

Coincidentally, the 'queuing for photographs' which Antonioni captured in China in 1972 had a western (and Italian) counterpart in that same year. At the Venice Biennale, punters would, at busy times, have to queue up to make use of the photo booth which the artist and photographer Franco Vaccari had installed as his contribution to the thirty-sixth edition of the exhibition, by the theme 'Opera o comportamento? [Work or Behaviour?]'.

A message on the wall invited viewers to obtain the characteristic strip of four passport-size photographs of themselves to pin around the room before leaving. While Vaccari drew on photography's capacity to seize the real, to provide 'evidence', by asking viewers to 'leave a trace of their passage' through the exhibition via the photo-booth images, this was not the primary rationale of the work. Writing about it a couple of years later for a book by the art critic Lea Vergine, Vaccari explained: 'I use photography as action and not as contemplation and this entails a negation of optical space in favour of the space of relations.'[15] With a statement that arguably pits him against the regime of opticality upheld by modernist critics such as Clement Greenberg (see Chapter 1), Vaccari seems to suggest that the main intent of his recourse

Figure 4.2 Franco Vaccari, *Esposizione in tempo reale 4, XXXVII, Venice Biennale*, 1972

to photography in the Biennale work, and in his practice more widely, is not that of creating images – or 'optical spaces' – for viewers to contemplate, but rather of drawing attention to the material conditions and activities – the 'space of relations' – through which photography is made, both as a techno-logical and a discursive product. Vaccari's explanation offers a concise way of framing the kind of attention that I want to suggest Antonioni pays to photography. Antonioni's engagement with photography manifests another articulation of his 'aesthetics of impurity', where intermedial dialogue with other arts and media functions as both a formative and a critical tool, directed outwards, towards an understanding of the contemporaneous visual regime, and inwards, in the service of a reflexivity about his main medium, cinema.

BLOW-UP: REALITY CHECK

It is not difficult to see how considerations of Antonioni and photography have tended to focus on both *Blow-Up* and photography's status as a reproduc-tion of reality. Narratively and aesthetically, photography is central to the film. Not only, through the actions of its photographer protagonist, does photogra-phy as an activity permeate the film, but the snapshots of a lovers' tryst that he chances to take in the park constitute a central diegetic and formal motif, on which hang both the murder-mystery plot and the visually arresting sequence in which the photographs are filmed at length by the movie camera as the intrigued photographer enlarges them and scrutinises them in his studio.

Figure 4.3 Thomas with the enlargements of the photos in *Blow-Up* (1966)

Over the decades since the film's initial release, this complex and conspicuous narrative and aesthetic staging of photography has generated a voluminous literature, and a variety of responses. It has been seen as a philosophical allegory on the nature of reality and our purchase on it; as a more or less conscious exploration of the specific ontology of the photographic image and the structures of seeing and knowing encapsulated within it; as a vicarious meditation on cinema itself – and, often, as all of the above together. In all of these interpretations, it is photography's relation to the reality reproduced in its images, however problematic or problematised such relation is seen to be in the film, which is a crucial focus.

As is well known, the film revolves around Thomas (as he is called in the script), a successful and somewhat disenchanted fashion photographer in the 'swinging' London of the 1960s, whom Antonioni styled on real-life contemporaries such as David Bailey, Terence Donovan and Brian Duffy.[16] As well as doing fashion shoots, including the famous one with the real-life model Veruschka, Thomas is working on a photobook – a project whose focus on urban degradation and deprivation stands in stark contrast to the glamorous subjects of his other work. It is possibly while out in search of inspiring photo opportunities for this project that he chances upon a couple in a park who attracts his attention, and whose seemingly romantic encounter he captures with a series of furtive, acrobatically taken, snapshots. When the woman notices his presence, her great distress at having been photographed further fuels Thomas's interest in this apparently banal situation. Ignoring her pleas to hand over the roll of film – she will even, somewhat mysteriously, track him down at his studio to try and recover it in exchange for sexual favours – Thomas finally manages to develop the exposures. He then sets out to examine them by printing a selection of enlargements, and enlargements of enlargements, which he arranges as a sequence along the walls. After further magnification of portions of two of the images, he eventually believes that he can discern a gunman and a corpse. The 'objectivity' of this conclusion is not *quite* confirmed in the film, as not only is the final blow-up with the victim's body extremely grainy and almost abstract, but the fact of the murder itself is left unresolved as the story unfolds. When Thomas returns to the spot in the park at night, without his camera, the body seems to be there, yet, when he goes back again in the morning – this time with his camera – there is nothing there (anymore). Meanwhile, his studio has been raided and all the negatives and prints taken from it, except for the last, very grainy enlargement. In the final sequence of the film, Thomas sees again a dressed-up group of protesters, the same ones that he bumps into at the beginning of the film. They are miming a game of tennis, but when Thomas joins in, and throws back to them the imaginary ball they have lost, the ball can actually be heard bouncing back and forth from one racket to the other. Though unseen and, one would think, imaginary, the ball is in fact, it seems, surprisingly 'real'.

Such a plot obviously encourages speculation on both reality as such and reality *in* photography. And indeed, as I have already noted, whether they consider it an existential allegory on the nature of reality and appearance, or a more specific analysis of the ontology of photography and, by extension (in view of their shared material base) of cinema (or, in fact, as is often the case, as a mixture of the above) – most scholarly accounts of *Blow-Up* have called upon the notion of photography as a record of the real.[17] This is an understanding which is variously articulated from the emergence of photography itself, as with William Henry Fox Talbot's presentation of his invention as a 'pencil *of* nature'.[18] Especially with respect to photography's historical analogue incarnation, it is pinned in particular to the set of photo-chemical reactions through which the image is generated as a physical trace on a material support (metal plate, paper, celluloid film). Implicitly referring to these processes, André Bazin famously wrote of photography in terms of imprint or 'death mask': an 'automatic' image largely made *by* – as well as, in a sense, *made of* – the very object being depicted, through the modifications that its reflection and deflection of light causes onto the reactive halides on the emulsion.[19] Although Bazin does not use the term, this has come to be commonly referred to as the 'indexicality' of photography, after C. S. Peirce's late-nineteenth-century classification of the 'index' type of sign as a sign that signifies through direct connection with its referent.[20] It is by implicitly drawing on this understanding of photography that, for instance, Seymour Chatman has remarked that '[p]hotographs are, of course, by definition visual records of the actual', while the Russian semiotician Jurij Lotman has suggested not only that '[w]ith respect to reality, photography functions as a reproduction', but that the still photographs specifically function in *Blow-Up* as something 'equivalent to reality itself'.[21] Finally, Amelia Jones, insisting specifically on the 'indexical' and 'analogue' character of photography in its pre-digital life, has recently summarised *Blow-Up* as being 'about chasing down the truth with the photographic apparatus, and within the photographic image'.[22]

However, as the film plot itself almost makes inevitable, most accounts, including the examples above, have also reflected on the ways in which *Blow-Up* complicates or throws into question the reality ostensibly captured by photography. Thus, in the discussion cited above, Chatman argues that the film also shows how photography's 'visual records' are liable to being used 'fictional[ly]'.[23] Crucially, Thomas makes such fictional use not only of his fashion work but also of the photos within which he wants to discover fact, evidence – for, as others have noted, the photographer's examination of these pictures builds a story out of them. It is as much a construction as a reconstruction of the event, a 'narrativis[ation]' or 'entexting' which builds upon and, at the same time, departs from their value as records.[24] Lotman has also pointed to the way in which, as well as drawing attention to the 'textuality' of a series of pictures, *Blow-Up* highlights how even a single photograph is always already a text, an interpretation. As the episode in the park is offered twice in the film, first, as shot in colour by the movie camera, and then, through Thomas's black and white enlargements, *Blow-Up* allows reflection – or, itself, reflects – on how even an individual photographic image constitutes a take *on* reality rather than simply a take *of* it. For, as Lotman has explained, while we are returned to the park episode by the photographs, that episode, interpreted by Thomas's compositional choices, is also substantially different from the film sequence seen earlier – Lotman highlights in particular its being more in 'close-up' and 'differently arranged', as 'the edges of the photograph have cut off the entire surrounding landscape, focusing only on the two human figures'.[25] If all of this relativises the status of photography as reality by showing it to be a complex representation, a mediation through – at least – eye, camera, film stock and specific format and display of the final image, the film is also seen to challenge this status more radically, by highlighting the medium's inherent opacity and indeterminacy. As critics have often noted, the motif of the progressive enlargements draws attention to how photography may ultimately obscure or even 'lose' the real, rather than help its capture and disclosure. As image yields to grain, the reality *in* photography 'disappear[s] into a general atomic welter',[26] delivering not 'truth' but 'the *diffusion* of truth into surface'[27] – a 'failure' of photography which, in Jones's somewhat schematic reading, is further representative of the 'failure' of a (modernist) model of seeing and knowing the world.[28]

But whether the 'disappearance' or 'diffusion' of the real in the photograph is symbolic of our relation to the world – and even, as Jones suggests, of the point of rupture of a specific epistemic and aesthetic regime – or not, what remains, and is in fact brought into the foreground in this pulverisation, is precisely the material surface of the photograph. Indeed, what, more generally, the concentration on *Blow-Up* as a critique of photography's purchase on the real fails to point out is that what is thrown into relief in this very process is the reality *of* photography itself – or *at least*, from our historical standpoint, the reality of photography in its pre-digital incarnation. Just as the real in the photographs is problematised and even obscured, the materials and procedures essential to the realisation and experience of photographs (certainly those that were essential to photography before digitality) are brought to light. Antonioni himself had in fact underlined this when, commenting on the short story by Julio Cortázar on which the film is based, he said that he: 'was not so much interested in the events as in the technical aspects of photography. I discarded the plot and wrote a new one in which the equipment itself assumed a different weight and significance.'[29] Perhaps it is even possible to see *Blow-Up* as less preoccupied with photography as the reproduction of reality than with the reality of photography as reproduction *as such*. Or, to put it slightly differently, *Blow-Up* may be more concerned with the 'how' than with the 'what' of photography, more concerned, that is, with the conditions and processes through which photographs are (or were) generated and circulated than with photographic content and its nature. In fact, this interest in photography's 'how' – an interest, moreover, which resurfaces in different ways across a number of Antonioni's films, from *L'amorosa menzogna/Lies of Love* (1949), *Cronaca di un amore/Chronicle of a Love Affair* (1950) and *I vinti/ The Vanquished* (1952) to *L'eclisse* (1962) and *Identificazione di una donna/Identification of a Woman* (1982) – may even turn out to be an answer for 'what' photography (still) is.

PRODUCTION, REPRODUCTION

Certainly, the 'image-world' (or, as an earlier title puts it, the 'photography unlimited') that Sontag described in her 1977 essay had started to accumulate with the invention of photography itself from the late 1830s. Yet, if photography had started to become a mass medium soon after the development of methods for fixing and reproducing the image in the second half of the nineteenth century, its diffusion reached new peaks in the second half of the twentieth century. Developments in camera and printing technologies, coupled with increased affluence during the economic boom of the 1950s and 1960s, further fostered the taking and consuming of pictures. At the same time, the emergence of forms of professionalisation of photographic practice and its study promoted critical debate on the medium and its function among other mass media and, indeed, as Freund put it in *Photography and Society*, as the very 'starting point of the mass media'.[30] In an increasingly global market, cameras were being made at considerably lower costs and in far greater numbers than in previous decades as, pioneered by Canon in 1959, their production gradually turned from high-skilled manufacture to line assembly.[31] In the same period, 35 mm roll film (first popularised in the mid-1920s through the Leica camera) finally overtook plates and film packs as the format of choice in professional photography. Its suppleness and compactness met the practical needs of the burgeoning field of photojournalism, from reportages from war zones such as Korea and Vietnam to more frivolous lifestyle or fashion features.[32] An indication of the 'advantages' of this transition can be gained by comparing the photo shoots in *Blow-Up* with the ones represented in a famous Hollywood musical of a decade earlier, *Funny Face* (Stanley Donen, 1956). While Thomas, in Antonioni's film, is all contortions and acrobatics thanks to his compact roll-film camera, in the earlier film, both photographer and model are rather constrained (and restrained) by the use of the plate camera.[33] Small-format roll film for non-professional use, too, gained in popularity thanks to the development of easy-load, slot-in cartridges, developed for use in simple cameras such as the Kodak Instamatic (launched in 1963 and, in an even slimmer 'Pocket' version, in 1972). Overall, increased automation of camera functions across the spectrum – from automatic exposure in inexpensive family machines to through-the-lens metering in high-quality models – made picture taking a much easier and faster activity. One of the reasons for the immediate popularity of the Nikon F camera – the camera Thomas sports in *Blow-Up* – when it was launched in the late 1950s, was the introduction of an optional film-winding motor drive which enabled the shooting of several pictures per second.

Considered as a whole, these new ranges of equipment contributed to what photographers Martin Parr and Gerry Badger have recently described as 'the great photographic "boom"' of the 1960s and 1970s.[34] In addition to the flourishing of professional photography, cheaper cameras and consumer buoyancy encouraged the expansion of family and amateur markets. Freund's aforementioned 1974 *Photography and Society* and Pierre Bourdieu's earlier *Un art moyen: essai sur les usages sociaux de la photographie* (1965) paid pioneering attention to photography in the context of material culture and as a vernacular social practice. From a distinctly sociological angle, Bourdieu argued for the need to analyse not only 'the need for photographs', but 'the need *to take* photographs'.[35] Even before these efforts, Italo Calvino – with whom Antonioni had hoped to collaborate on the script for *Blow-Up*[36] – had captured some of the flavour of photography's technological and social boom with characteristic incisiveness in one of his short stories, 'The Adventure of a Photographer' (1955).[37] This traces the protagonist's journey from bewildered scepticism to complete obsession with the medium as a 'hobby': in addition to continuously updating to the 'most advanced equipment' and installing a dark room, he will at one point have 'to snap at least one picture a minute'.[38] Such relentless making of 'private images' unfolds against the backdrop of photography's public proliferation in daily life via, and as, mass media – what the story evocatively describes as 'the creased background of massacres and coronations'.[39] Indeed, as Antonino realises at a point, 'photographing photographs was the only course he had left, or rather, the true course he had obscurely sought all this time'.[40]

As Calvino's story also comes to suggest, professional and vernacular, family snapshot and art photography, material medium and mass media would often be inextricably connected given that, prior to the full institutionalisation of photographic training in art schools and colleges (a process which began in the 1960s), many professionals were self-taught and often, not unlike Thomas aspires to do in *Blow-Up*, would combine photography 'for a living' with other less commercially oriented but, possibly, conceptually freer ventures. This was largely the case with Don McCullin, the famous British photojournalist – renowned for his hard-hitting coverage of the Vietnam war and deprived areas of London's East End – whom Antonioni commissioned to take the stills for the park sequence, and some of whose photographs also appear in Thomas's photobook project.[41]

In the context of radical cultural and aesthetic upheavals broached in the preceding chapters, art too became an important and lively locus of photographic production. Of course, the question of whether photography was an art had been debated from the late nineteenth century, while its entitlement to artistic status on its own merit, rather than by striving to imitate established arts, particularly painting, had been battled for with particular intensity by (modernist) photographers and critics in the first half of the twentieth century. In this context, John Szarkowski's landmark 1964 exhibition *The Photographer's Eye* at New York's Museum of Modern Art (MoMA) encapsulates the zenith and nadir of such efforts. Building on another influential exhibition at MoMA, Beaumont Newhall's *Photography 1839–1937*, in 1937, the show consolidated photography's status *as* art by establishing the medium's 'specific' material and aesthetic qualities (which Szarkowski found in framing and the inescapable tie to the 'the fact of things', among others).[42] Yet it did so by radically displaying artist and vernacular photographs alongside each other, as both equally part of what it called the 'unending stream' of photography, whose images, it insisted, were '*taken*' rather than '*made*'.[43] In its very ambivalence, then, this demonstrates how the final coronation of photography as art happened precisely at the moment when a large number of artists turned to photography, as well other media of technological reproduction and reproducibility, such as film and video, in order to mount a *critique* of art and its institutions.[44] Indeed, many artists often dispensed with making *altogether* new images, resorting instead to culling them from the vast, rapidly growing 'image-world' repertoire of mass media, recycling them into something else, like Stan VanDerBeek, John Baldessari and Mimmo Rotella did through various photo-collage practices (VanDerBeek made stop-motion films with them, too, such as *À la mode*, 1957 and *Science Friction*, 1959) or, more famously perhaps, like Andy Warhol and Robert Rauschenberg with screen-prints and combines.[45]

The recycling and repurposing of pop-oriented practices brings into relief how increases in photographic production were profoundly connected to increases in their reproduction. The photographic 'image-world' that Sontag saw to be proliferating in the 1970s was constituted in great part through the *re*production of photographs via other media. Print media above all constituted the mode in which a great, if not the greatest, number of photographs would be experienced and 'consumed' at the time; these are the 'inky shadows' and 'creased backgrounds of massacres and coronations' evoked by Calvino. Even the first inventors of photography, such as Talbot, had worked hard at developing methods of photographic reproduction in print, which they saw as part and parcel of the rationale of the invention itself.[46] The half-tone process, in use since the 1880s, and photogravure, whose industrialisation in the 1920s enabled the high-volume, high-quality ink reproductions that fostered the emergence of mass-consumption illustrated magazines in the first half of the twentieth century, effected a kind of 'second birth' of photography. Indeed, mass-printing methods such as rotogravure (as photogravure is called when a rotary press is used) constitute, as Patrick Maynard argued, a 'most important *re*invention of photography . . . without which even "the photograph" today would have a diminished historical significance'.[47] In Italy, the rotogravure process was so associated with the reproduction and consumption of photographs that the word for it in Italian, '*rotocalco*', had since the 1930s become the generic name for a cheap, heavily-illustrated periodical publication.[48]

As with camera technologies, the introduction of more sophisticated automation in the second half of the twentieth century significantly increased the quality, quantity and cost-effectiveness of photographic illustrations in print media. Continual improvements to photomechanical gravure printing, which saw tests with electronic engraving as early as the late 1940s, facilitated the inclusion of more and more numerous photographic illustrations in high print-run newspapers and magazines as well as, from the 1950s, full-colour reproductions – thus increasing the circulation of photographs in mass-consumption publications while also generating demand for further photographic production.[49] In this context, the Italian illustrated-press sector boomed in the first two decades after the war. Alongside other *rotocalchi* launched under fascism but revamped in the decade after the war, such as *Oggi* (first issued in 1938, but relaunched in 1945), *Grazia* and *Annabella* (both from 1938–9), a horde of new titles emerged, including *Epoca* (published by Mondadori from 1950), *Le ore* (from 1953), *L'espresso* (from 1955), *Gente* (from 1957) and *Amica* (from 1962), with circulations in some cases as high as nearly one million copies.[50]

An even more densely illustrated type of *rotocalco* had also emerged from the late 1940s: the photonovel, or *fotoromanzo*, magazine.[51] Published in dedicated weeklies with titles such as *Grand hotel* (from 1946) and *Bolero film* (from 1947), photonovels were effectively photographic (and often romantic) versions of the comic-strip cartoon, sequentially arranged and generally accompanied by speech bubbles. Antonioni himself had explored its popularity and specific format in the short documentary *L'amorosa menzogna* and his script for Federico Fellini's *Lo sceicco bianco/The White Sheik* (1952). As the narrator in *L'amorosa menzogna* aptly describes them, photonovels were 'a kind of pocket cinema': stories *in photographs* which, unlike the movies, one could hold in one's hand.[52]

Improvements in photomechanical reproduction unsurprisingly also affected books, from luxury items such as coffee-table volumes and exhibition catalogues, to educational publications (in Italy, Fabbri Editore specialised in serialised encyclopaedias to be gradually assembled from individual issues available from newsagents) and low-budget artist books. Indeed, it is at this time that a growing number of photographers and artists started to see the latter as tools suited to their aesthetics and politics, as well as their wallets, since technological improvements made it possible to self-publish illustrated books of sufficient quality at relatively low cost. For some artists, such as the American Ed Ruscha, who is widely acknowledged to have launched the novel format of the artist book with a prolific series of (self-produced) publications including *Twenty Six Gasoline Stations* (1962) and *Some Los Angeles Apartments* (1965) in the course of the 1960s, the photobook was a potentially democratic, multiple and unpretentious object with which to attack prevailing notions of art. For a number of journalists and photographers – not unlike, as *Blow-Up* suggests, Thomas himself – it constituted a way of articulating their vision more freely or fully than they might otherwise be able to do in the restricted or, even, controlled, context of reportages for the press – an extreme example here being the clandestinely produced exposure of apartheid in *House of Bondage* (1967), by the black South African photojournalist Ernest Cole.[53]

Intense critical debates on photography flourished in the context of this boom in photographic production, reproduction and circulation. This work reconnected with the pre-war interventions of critical theorists including Walter Benjamin, whose essays started to be translated from German in the course of the 1960s. Indeed, Benjamin's famous 1936 essay 'The Work of Art in the Age of Mechanical Reproduction' first appeared in Italian in 1966, the year of *Blow-Up*'s release, and in English in 1969. Photography started to be included in emerging studies on media and technology, as in Mumford's *Art and Technics* (1952) or Marshall McLuhan's famous *Understanding Media* (1964), and, as in the work by Sontag, Bourdieu and Freund or, indeed, Roland Barthes, who had started to reflect on photography as mass medium with *Mythologies* from the mid-1950s, made the principal subject of enquiry.[54] Crucial contributions to this range of critical and theoretical reflections were provided by 'conceptually' oriented artists and photographers such as

Hollis Frampton in the United States with his essays for *Artforum*, and Vaccari in Italy, whose volume of critical essays *Fotografia e inconscio tecnologico* [*Photography and the Technological Unconscious*] was published by photographer Luigi Ghirri's own publishing venture Punto e Virgola in 1979.[55]

Worth singling out here is Ugo Mulas, who had launched Veruschka's career when he discovered her in Florence in the late 1950s. Having risen to prominence as a photographer of art and artists by the time of *Blow-Up*, and contributed to the fame of pop art with his book *New York: The New Art Scene* (1967), Mulas turned to theorising photography in the late 1960s.[56] Between 1969 and 1972, he did so largely by unpacking and deconstructing the apparatus of photography through photography *itself*, producing a series of images and critical texts that he called *Verifiche* [*Verifications*]. This, as he explained, was 'a sort of analysis of photography' (more precisely, of the 'operazione fotografica', as he put it), to determine and assess the 'constitutive elements' of a medium he had used (or indeed, as his use of the term 'operation' suggests, *performed*) for years out of habit, as a mere means to an end.[57] Out of thirteen *Verifiche*, two tackle 'enlargement'. In a suggestively Thomas-like procedure, the fifth *Verifica* addresses enlarging from the negative, blowing-up a portion of it onto prints several metres wide, so that the image gives way to the silver grains of photographic emulsion.

That the range of developments outlined above form a significant context for Antonioni's engagement with photography – and, as Mulas's *Verifiche* indicate, a context to which Antonioni's cinema itself in turn actively contributed in certain ways – should be obvious enough. Indeed, it is surprising that they are generally and largely ignored, even in discussions of *Blow-Up*, possibly one of the most written-about films 'about' photography in cinema history, for they constitute the very premise of its story. Thomas would be simply unimaginable without the innovations in photographic production and photomechanical reproduction which his successful occupation as a fashion photojournalist, and as a budding 'serious' photographer of a documentary kind, both depends on and, conversely, stimulates. Yet, just as the focus on *Blow-Up* as 'the' film by Antonioni about photography has worked to obscure the recurrence of an engagement with the medium in his cinema more broadly, so the particular angle of such discussions has tended to draw attention away from how Antonioni's interest is focused on the complex and pervasive realities *of* photography as mass image in twentieth-century culture.

IDENTIFYING PHOTOGRAPHY

A brief exploration of Antonioni's engagement with photography across his cinema, from the pioneering effort to explore the *fotoromanzo* phenomenon in *L'amorosa menzogna* to the riot of photographic images in *Identificazione di una donna*, can help us see *Blow-Up* in a different light.[58]

L'amorosa menzogna is an important early indicator of Antonioni's approach to the material reality of photography as both medium and media, specific technology and socio-cultural apparatus of mass communication.[59] In the course of ten minutes, this short film outlines the steps of the *fotoromanzo*'s production, circulation and consumption, addressing its technological and socio-cultural dimensions, as well as their inextricability. The existence of a referent beyond the image, as the film suggests, is important to the *fotoromanzo*'s success, which is indeed partly measured through the fan culture of real-life actors (the 'stars' of the page of cinema's poorer sibling) that the medium, unlike drawn comics, enables. But the 'reality' captured by the *fotoromanzo* image is but an aspect of the broader techno-cultural reality of the phenomenon – its technologies of production and 'sociologies' of consumption – which the short film explores. Antonioni takes us through the photo shoot, in which the actors typically need to 'pose', rather than 'act', for the still camera, the darkroom, the 'post production' process (where speech bubbles and champagne flutes missing from a scene due to the low production costs are added manually with a pen) and their final destination and circulation on, and as, pages in a magazine. The film lingers in particular on how stacks of copies are sorted and distributed to newsagents' kiosks by vans, and bought and read by (mostly, though not exclusively, female) readers.

Through its focus on a fundamental manifestation, or 'culture', of photography, that of its circulation via print media, this film already outlines three aspects of the medium to which Antonioni will go on to pay recurrent attention in his cinema. The first aspect concerns the fact that, as we could put it following critics including Kracauer, Mumford and Sontag, photography proliferates: indeed, it multiplies. As the example of the photonovel shows, the experience of photography is an experience routinely 'in the plural': rarely does one take, encounter or 'consume' a single photograph. For, as Benjamin noted in his famous 'Work of Art' essay, photography is above all a technology of reproduction. In addition to its reproductive capacities *vis à vis* a phys- ical referent, photography is *itself* reproducible. That is, beyond what Erika Balsom has recently referred to as '*referential reproducibility*' – the ability to give us, largely through mechanical if not automated processes, a more or less recognisable visual likeness or 'copy' of whatever stands in front of the lens, or on top of photosensitive paper — photography (and film) are characterised by '*circulatory reproducibility*'.[60] Bar exceptions such as daguerrotypes or Polaroids, photographs are reproducible in high numbers by printing copies from their negatives (and, in today's digital condition of photography, by clicking on a file), as well as, as we noted earlier, by being reproduced in even higher quantities in print media (or, today, their screen replacements or equivalents).

Attention to such circulatory reproducibility recurs – and is crucial – in Antonioni's films. It features prominently in *I vinti*, especially in the French and English episodes, as well as in the prologue – even though the latter's particularly bleak view and moralising stance, linking newspaper and magazine images of violence and crime to the corruption of youth, is likely to have been the product of producers' preventative censorship measures to try and ensure distribution for this particularly troubled film, rather than of Antonioni's own stance.[61] Focus on what Balsom calls 'circulatory reproducibility' returns in *Identificazione di una donna*, in which, from brochures to magazines to life-size cut-outs in shop windows, photomechanically reproduced photographs abound and recur. Indeed, one of the key occupations of the male protagonist, Niccolò, is gathering a selection of photographs of women (from Louise Brooks to other less famous and iconic ones), culled from newspapers and magazines, attentively clipped to a board which becomes more and more crowded as the film unfolds.

Figure 4.4a   *Identificazione di una donna* (1982)

Figure 4.4b   *Identificazione di una donna* (1982)

look up

The cumulative effect of the growing presence of these reproduced photographs resonates with Sontag's suggestion that photography has contributed to the creation of an 'image-world', in which the real world is redoubled. Just as Sontag did in her essay, so the materiality of the photographic world shoots to attention in *Identificazione*, particularly as images are repeatedly shown being torn or cut out of magazines – acts which, like the life-size cut-outs in the window, turn images into obviously physical *objects*. Despite the fact that the protagonist's central quest for 'the woman' seems to dissolve into a welter of images on a wall, the film does not quite suggest, as Mumford or Baudrillard might, that reality is replaced by its image, its simulacrum. Rather, the point seems to be not so much that media images are the only reality, but that photography and other media are 'real': material not only at the level of the technologies they entail but also at the level of the socio-cultural relations they generate, foster and depend on.

In addition to those in Niccolò's collection, another photographic image plays an important role in *Identificazione*. This is a portrait of his lover Mavi, which the viewer first sees on the wall of her room as the movie camera zooms and lingers on it. Towards the end of the film, the picture reappears: it has ended up in *Time* magazine.

Figure 4.5a *Identificazione di una donna* (1982)

Figure 4.5b *Identificazione di una donna* (1982)

As the formulation '*circulatory reproducibility*' points to, this first aspect of photography is strictly connected to a second which comes vividly into view through this passage from wall to page, private to public: that of its mobility. While the photographic image may be still from an aesthetic point of view, it circulates and passes hands in a range of ways. It does so not only as a public form, as in its print reproduction, but also as a private and family form, since, as Flusser noted, 'there is no need of any complicated technical apparatus' to begin to distribute photographs: they are 'loose leaves which can be passed from hand to hand'.[62] As such 'loose leaves', photographs may be passed down through generations or turn up in unexpected or 'wrong' hands, as Antonioni arrestingly shows in *Cronaca di un amore*, his *noir*-ish first full-length feature film. Just after the credits, the film's opening sequence presents us with close-ups of a series of photographic prints of the main female character, Paola (played by Lucia Bosé).

These are being thrown one on top of the other to form a loose pile on a desk, while the off-screen voice of a private detective goes through a synthetic account of Paola's life. Photography's multiplicity, its plural existence and proliferation are evoked, as is its mobility. The detective, who has been hired by the woman's husband, explains that the husband became suspicious

Figure 4.6 *Cronaca di un amore* (1950)

of his wife and her past once these photographs of her youth 'ended up in his hands'. And, of course, in this scene, these private family photographs are now literally in a different pair of hands yet again: those of the investigator and his assistant, who use them as aids in their operations of surveillance and control. The photographic mobility addressed in these films also points to Vaccari's emphasis on photography's 'space of relations' mentioned at the beginning of the chapter. As object (be this a paper print, a reproduction on the page or even a digital file) or activity, photography is part of social relations and indeed, even more strongly, it sustains, provokes or engenders them.

Finally, the third aspect of photography addressed by *L'amorosa menzogna* – and, in a different way, *Cronaca di un amore* and *Identificazione* – concerns a slightly different sense of relationality. Photography is not only explored as a technological, material form that takes shape from a web of socio-cultural relations which it itself contributes to engender and sustain, but also in relation to other media. In *L'amorosa menzogna*, photography stands not only in relation to print media but also, as we have seen, to cinema – of which the *fotoromanzo* is the poorer 'pocket' form. More subtly, photography's relation to cinema is also arguably invoked in *Cronaca di un amore*'s opening sequence, whose use of photographs has a further extra-diegetic function beyond its overt diegetic one. Not unlike in *Blow-Up*'s central scene of photographic display, film is here positioned in relation to photography somewhat reflexively. The series of prints piling up on the table does, in a way, what a good part of the film will also do, as the detective sets off to investigate Paola's past and reconstruct the 'story' of her life. Only that the film will do so in an expanded, less synthetic and more exhaustive form which will, crucially, fill in the gaps 'between' these still images. Or again, in *Identificazione di una donna*, a film that, as Michael Loren Siegel has argued, is covertly about television and its key contribution to 'image and media saturation' in the late twentieth century, the recurrent presence of photographic imagery suggests that Antonioni perceived and addressed affinities between all of these media – photography, television, cinema – as part of a hybrid family of mass, technical images.[63]

TYPES OF PLURALITY

Awareness of Antonioni's recurrent engagement with photography makes *Blow-Up*'s reflection on the medium not less but more significant, the result (and not the final one) of a sustained enquiry into the 'technical image'. What distinguishes *Blow-Up* is that, as it explores photography's experiential abundance and phenomenological multiplicity in the second half of the twentieth century, it also comes to reflect on photography's constitutive plurality. As it addresses the sheer numerical proliferation of photographs, their quantitative multiplication, that is, *Blow-Up* also proposes a qualitative understanding of photography's plurality. In this sense, plurality refers to the intrinsic and structural (even if latent or potential) lack of singularity that characterises photography as a technology of reproduction – indeed, as a reproductive process by which, as Maynard argues, even things other than photographs themselves (e.g. text) become reproducible.[64]

As in the other films that I have considered, in *Blow-Up* photography is consistently associated with multiplicity – if not, indeed, multiplication. It is introduced (towards the beginning of the film itself) precisely through an evocation of numerical abundance, if not excess. Hinted at by the handful of film rolls that Thomas hands over to one assistant for development just before the fashion shoot with Veruschka, this exuberance is then also more directly suggested by the erotically charged encounter with his model, as the sheer quantity of images being taken is signalled by the increasingly rapid succession of camera clicks. This abundance is further thematised shortly after, as the focus shifts from photographing to actual photographs when Thomas surveys the contact prints from the rolls that his assistant has just developed. The characteristic numerousness of these proof images – actual-size positives of negatives, usually in uncut strips of five or six frames, aligned one next to the other on a sheet – is here enhanced by the high number of rolls shot by Thomas, which causes the proofs to extend over several sheets. Their quantity is further emphasised by the movie camera itself, which allows us to identify them as photographic images while leaving their individual contents indistinct by not focusing on them for long or from close enough. When, later in the film, we are shown enlargements of some of these shots, and are allowed to see that they are pictures of guests in a dosshouse that Thomas plans to include in his photobook, diegesis and aesthetics again put stress on the 'many-ness' of these, and other, photographs. While Thomas mentions to Ron, his agent or co-author, that he will select 'three or four' images from this particular batch, as they flick through the portfolio for the project (framed in close up by Antonioni's camera), the viewer is made aware of the already large series of pictures that these latter shots will augment. Furthermore, as they converse about what to put at the close of the book, even 'the end' is imagined by Thomas not as one photograph but as a cluster of photographs: the ones of the couple he has just taken in the park (which, having yet to discover anything in them, he describes as 'very peaceful, very still'). Their plurality (in all its complexity) will be visualised subtly and at length in the later, central scene in which Thomas enlarges and prints a selection of these images and physically groups them as a sequence surrounding him along three sides of his living room.

All of these instances of photographic abundance throughout the film outline what I described above as the experiential plurality of photography:

the fact, simply put, that photography is habitually experienced in the plural. Technological and cultural developments have conspired to make the production and consumption of photographs activities entailing more than one photograph if not, indeed, *many* photographs. In fact, to the extent that the film evokes this experiential plurality of photography, it also in turn makes plurality (vicariously, via cinema) an experience for the viewer who – from the rapid glimpses of the contact sheets to the more ponderous analysis of the park photographs, and from the photo shoot to the dark room – is called upon to engage with a plurality of photographic procedures and images. Precisely because this experiential plurality is shown to start from the very processes through which photographs are taken and made, a deeper, more fundamental, sense of photography's plurality also emerges.

In other words, *Blow-Up* emphasises the plurality constitutive of photography as such. Sontag summoned a sense of this plurality in *On Photography*. Not unlike the way in which – as I aim to suggest here – *Blow-Up* itself tackles photography, the essays collected in the book are as much an engagement with the historical reality (the 'boom', as we discussed) of photography from the 1960s onwards, as they are a philosophical contemplation of it. As she grapples with photography's pervasive proliferation in 'The Image-World', arguing that the sheer quantity of photographic imagery in the western world is not only a copy *of* the world but, also, a material world in itself, she eventually suggests that even *'one* photograph' – should we chance to come across it – *'implies* that there will be others'.[65] In a nutshell, it is this sense of photography's constitutive plurality that *Blow-Up* itself not only reflects and analyses, but also – as we shall see – amplifies and, literally, deepens, articulating it both 'horizontally' and 'vertically'.

But let me unpack Sontag's expression a little. Her characterisation both describes *and* interprets the photograph as a complexly repeatable entity. First, it points to the fact that the photograph – as a class or type of object – is repeatable because it is generated through a series of largely automatic technological procedures. While this is true of the photograph obtained through early processes such as daguerreotypy, such repeatability is not only greatly facilitated and encouraged but, also, made more immediately evident, if not 'obvious', by the range and sophistication of automation introduced from the late 1950s. In this respect, a photograph *implies* that there will be others because the virtuality of photography is already plural. Even before a picture is actually taken, repeatability and plurality are inscribed in the conditions of its making, which not only make it possible to generate more than one picture but that – as with the ease of shooting provided by roll film or the Instamatic, for instance – are often *conducive* to the addition of one photograph after another ('you must photograph as much as you can', as Calvino puts it in his short story).[66] Second, an individual and specific photograph is repeatable because it is reproducible. In addition to invoking photography's repeatability as an automatised mode of image production, Sontag's 'implies' thus points to the fact that individual photographs are themselves repeatable and, often, actually repeated.

SERIES AND SEQUENCES

As photography historians including David Campany and Blake Stimson have recently argued, these technological attributes of photography have, from very early on, determined its development 'as a medium of multiplicity and accumulation'.[67] This development, moreover, makes 'seriality . . . a primary photographic form' – and one which, as Vaccari acutely suggested, may in turn have contributed to new ways of seeing, stimulating 'techniques of comparison' and other strategies for *making* 'sense' in, and of, their abundance.[68] Already introduced at Talbot's presentation of his invention via twenty-four photographs in the publication *The Pencil of Nature* (1844–6), one of photography's most famous points of origin, the series went on to become, as László Moholy-Nagy once put it, 'natural' to photography in the course of the twentieth century.[69] From Alfred Stieglitz's almost abstract articulations of clouds (the photographic series he called *Equivalents*, c. 1923–31), to 'documentary' projects as varied as those by August Sanders in late-1920s Germany, and Walker Evans or Robert Frank in 1930s and 1950s America respectively, to the 'fictional' world of the photonovel, photography largely developed as a medium of series and sequences. If, by the 1960s, seriality and sequentiality had become thoroughly ordinary photographic forms, this was also, to return to this point again, due in great part to their expanding circulation via print media, as the actual multiplication of series themselves across many copies granted them visibility and, with it, 'naturalness' or ordinariness. In slightly different words, this is to say that this 'secondary' mode of photographic reproduction ('secondary', that is, with respect to reproduction from the negative) has often been a 'primary' mode for the diffusion of the photograph – or indeed, precisely, of photograph*s*. The page was certainly conceived as such a primary mode not only in the case of now iconic series such as Evans' *American Photographs* (1938) and Frank's *The Americans* (1958–9), whose original vehicle was the book, but also in the case of the usually more ephemeral and 'consumable' series featured in international or internationally famous magazines such as *Harper's* (a copy of which can be glimpsed in Thomas's studio), *Life* or *Vogue*, whose popularity soared in the 1960s. And, as we have seen, not only is Thomas's activity generally predicated on such serial modes of production and circulation, but, as the film's plot shows, he is specifically engaged in making series for both these kinds of print media – the 'artistic' and 'committed' book, as well as the glossy magazine.

Moreover, around the time of *Blow-Up*'s release, the very ordinariness of series and sequences as photographic forms was being aesthetically and conceptually flaunted by work such as Bernd and Hilla Becher's monumental taxonomy of industrial architecture (started in 1959) and Ruscha's aforementioned prolific series of photographic books, some of which, such as *Crackers* (1969) and *Royal Road Test* (1966), are mocking elaborations of photonovels and other forms of photographic narrative (e.g. step-by-step or 'before' and 'after' demonstrations) common in mass-consumption print-media.[70] For artists such as Ruscha and the Bechers, the photographic series was not only a way of valuing multiplicity over singularity (that is, a means for having the overall effect or meaning of the work reside in a group of pictures rather than in an individual picture, and in reproducible or actually reproduced images rather than in a unique object). It was also a way of engaging formally and theoretically with what was felt to be an open, accretive and expansive medium; a medium, consonant with Sontag's formulation, in which growth and addition are already *implied* in each individual unit.[71] This openness is obvious in the case of the Bechers' extensive, cumulative, inventories – even if their ultimate aim is to individuate a constant 'typology' across many-ness.[72] In Ruscha's books, on the other hand, it is, paradoxically, the relative brevity and the random interruption of each photographic series (ending variously at '*twenty-six* gasoline stations', after '*some* Los Angeles apartments' or, even more oddly, after '*various* small fires *and* milk', and '*nine* swimming pools *and* a broken glass') that suggests the potential expansion and inherent openness of the series themselves. The continuation implied by caesura is not unlike the way in which even the last instalment of a serialised photonovel may exude a certain on-going-ness, the promise of continuation – *mutatis mutandis* – in another story.[73]

Through the series and their potential – if not actual – openness, these works manifest what we have been calling photography's constitutive plurality. Indeed, its plurality is articulated, as it were, 'horizontally', by systematically adding one photo next to or after the other in ways which not only suggest the global, cumulative expansion of the medium but that also replicate, or at least evoke, the mechanical repeatability, the unthinking automation, of photography itself. It is this horizontal axis of photography's plurality – the possibility of following one photograph with another, and the technological and cultural incentive to realise that possibility – that is also called upon in *Blow-Up*. In the

(handwritten marginalia) (not this too how Thomas can't complete photo project)

film, photographs are shown to be taken, made and consumed in – or, even, *as* – series and sequences; accretive, 'open' series and sequences, where one picture leads to and, in fact, almost *produces* another. This is cogently introduced by the rapid camera 'clicks' during the fashion shoot and in the park, suggested by the film's portrayal of Thomas's photobook project (the contact prints, the portfolio he leafs through with Ron) and, finally, most vividly and thoroughly articulated in the sequence dedicated to Thomas's attentive making and studying of his park photographs.

In this central moment in the film, not only does Thomas make (i.e. develop) the series 'naturally' contained in the roll itself (the series *as* shot) but, out of this, he also makes (i.e. generates) a new, further series. The laborious mental and material realisation of this series is dwelled on and explored at length in this remarkable scene. No doubt, we are far from so-called 'real' time: the episode proceeds through temporal ellipses, condensing into minutes a process which, in real life, would have unfolded over a much longer interval. Yet, the film's pace conspicuously slows down, and cinema is as though given over to photography and its stillness as Thomas proceeds to compose this series through a meticulous process of scrutiny, selection, and trips to the dark room. The film shows us the series' gradual emergence as a spatial configuration in Thomas's studio: the physical alignment of photographs along the exposed beams and walls, one next to the other. But, through close-ups, zooms and pans on and between the photographs themselves, the movie camera also directs us to – and itself organises – the series' complementarily emerging configuration in time: for Thomas (and, consequently, plot-wise), this serial arrangement in space also has a temporal, and 'narrative', valence – it is a sequence. Not unlike Ruscha's and the Bechers' deadpan series, but with a narrative momentum perhaps closer to the strips of the *fotoromanzo*, Thomas's sequence presents photography's plurality 'horizontally', as a succession of one photograph after the other. In this sense, the scene's photographic display also, self-reflexively, calls upon that 'horizontal' plurality of photographs which *Blow-Up* itself – and cinema more broadly – is at its literal core. If the physical alignment of the photographs in space and the sense of a forward movement in time that Thomas's reconstruction 'applies' to them represent cinema, then it is also true that cinema is, conversely, as Antonioni had adumbrated at the beginning of *Cronaca di un amore*, presented as a particular intensification of the technological and cultural drive to follow a photograph with another: photography's plurality *is* cinema's very structure.

Thomas's construction of his sequence further plays out this drive to make and engage with a series of photographs rather than one photograph.[74] And, again not unlike the photographic series of photonovels or Ruscha's and the

Bechers', Thomas's series, too, signals openness and accretion, *even as* it may seem to reach a certain 'closure'. The fact that Thomas's series 'ends' twice weakens finality, insinuating a sense that closure may be fundamentally under-scored by openness, the possibility of continuation. For, indeed, Thomas first deems his sequence closed, his (re)construction complete, when, having osten-sibly detected a gunman in the enlarged detail of one of the photographs, he concludes that he has unwittingly averted a murder, as he excitedly tells Ron on the telephone. But, after an 'interlude' (the scene of the sexual frolic with the two aspiring models who turn up at his door to be photographed), Thomas returns to his series and 'opens' it again, adding at least one more pic-ture to it by – as the film now makes a point of showing – re-photographing a detail from a previous enlargement. This second 'end' to his series, a very grainy enlargement (whose resemblance with the semi-abstract paintings by an artist friend of Thomas will later be noted in the film) leads him to think that, rather than having prevented a killing, he has, in fact, witnessed one without quite seeing it – because in this image there seems to be a supine body, half hidden by a bush.[75]

With this addition, the plurality of photography which *Blow-Up* both represents and reflects on becomes apparent under a new light. If Thomas's display – as well as his photographic activity more generally – articulates such plurality by evoking a horizontal vector, a forward movement to the next photograph, then the recursive use of enlargements in his reconstruc-tion also calls into play a vertical vector, a movement *within* individual photographs through which – I believe – the film also proposes a cogent definition of what photography is. For a start, even visually, 'verticality' becomes a marked feature with the introduction of this further enlargement, which Thomas arranges partly 'on top' of the one from which it logically and sequentially derives, and whose logical relation to the previous image is outlined and underlined by the movie camera's descending and ascending panning movement between the two. Quite literally, then, the vertical axis of photography's plurality is configured in superimposition to its horizontal axis. Although enlargements have already featured in Thomas's reconstruc-tion (in fact, all of the prints are, technically, enlargements of the 35 mm negatives), this formal language, coupled with the diegetic role of this image, foregrounds the 'blow up' as the conceptual core of the film – for the blow up crucially performs and epitomises photography's plurality.[76] As the image gives way to the grain, the potential seriality of even a single photograph is brought into relief. In its potential to generate further photographs from 'inside' itself, the individual photograph opens onto plurality by imply-ing another which will be after or next to it, but also, logically, *within* it. Although the real captured by the camera may be lost, what is not only maintained but, in fact, quantitatively and qualitatively (or, numerically and intrinsically) pluralised through the process of enlargement, is the photograph itself. Concomitantly, it is precisely the fact of photography *as* a technology – and, indeed, a process – *of* reproduction which is highlighted, and even proposed as a description or definition of what photography is. Besides, this is a reproduction that – surprisingly, if not paradoxically – begets difference. The very process of reproduction by which *another* photograph is produced is also, at the same time, the generation of *an other* photograph, as the same source data (the same negative) engender a different image. Here, phenomenological abundance is underscored, and motored, by ontological plurality; a plurality which, even as the quintessence of a reproductive technology – a technology, therefore, arguably structured through, and for, repetition – contains difference.

REPETITION AND DIFFERENCE

As I have argued, Antonioni's engagement with the material reality of photography – even the 'technological stuff' which, as Antonioni himself explained, is given particular attention in *Blow-Up* – has tended to be overlooked in favour of a focus on the way in which the film reflects on the medium's ability to represent or 'capture' reality. Two works, however: a film and a photobook produced a few years after its release, stand out not only as particularly cognate with Antonioni's film but, also, as commentaries on what I believe is Antonioni's emphasis on photography's plurality and its status as a process characterised by, as Balsom describes it, both referential and circulatory reproducibility. *Esposizione in tempo reale* (a pun which can translate both as '*Exhibition*' and '*Exposure in Real Time*', 1973), by Vaccari, is a photobook which followed – and completed – the artist's contribution to the 1972 Venice Biennale that I mentioned at the beginning of this chapter, in which viewers were invited to use the photo booth that he had installed in the exhibition space. The book collects and reproduces hundreds of the characteristic four-photograph strips that viewers took of themselves and, originally, affixed onto the walls of the exhibition. *Blow-Up*'s pursuit of photographic plurality resonates with and is, in fact, amplified by Vaccari's intriguing book. For not only has Vaccari reproduced photo-booth polaroids, instantaneous negative-less photos, but the reproduction of the four-unit photo series unfolds – or is complexly 'modulated' – not only horizontally, through telescopic arrangements of as many as sixteen strips per page, but also, indeed, vertically, with enlargements of single images from the strips, recurrently blown-up to fill the approximately A4-size page.[77]

Figure 4.7 From the series *Le montagne incantate*, n.d., courtesy Gallerie d'Arte Moderna e Contemporanea: Fondo Michelangelo Antonioni, Ferrara

A similar dynamic, although pursued by different means, can be detected in *nostalgia* (1971) by Frampton, in which about a dozen of Frampton's own photographs are filmed in close-up as, one after the other, they are burnt on a hotplate. Plurality is, again, played out in various ways: not only, on a first level, in the serialised presentation of the photographic prints but also, secondarily, in the voice-over commentary, whose anecdotes about them make each individual image ripple with plurality (even, indeed, while it is ostensibly being destroyed). The film's commentary produces plurality by linking each individual image to a much larger series (e.g. a photo shoot) to which it belongs, or by presenting each image as one of many copies from the original negative. And, finally – in what seems a direct, tongue-in-cheek homage to Antonioni's film – *nostalgia* calls upon the blow-up as it closes.[78] Here, the narrator recounts having recently taken what will likely be his last photograph (a last photograph, furthermore, which was the only one he managed to take on the particular occasion). Yet, even this mysterious, unique last photograph – which is rhetorically evoked but not shown in the film – is, in fact, plural, as a strange compulsion to unpack it has meant that, as the voice-over tells us, it has been enlarged again and again 'till the grain of the film all but obliterates the features of the image'.

Not unlike Mulas's *Verifiche*, Frampton's and Vaccari's works help to bring into relief how Antonioni's engagement with photography – not only in *Blow-Up* but also, as shown, consistently throughout his cinema – both reflects and reflects *on* the experience of the medium's exponential expansion in the second half of the twentieth century and the conditions through which photographs are made, circulated and consumed in mass-image culture. While generally overlooked, this enables a reflection on the nature of photography as such which is slightly different from – and in excess of – the concern with the real *in* the photograph which most scholarly accounts to date attribute to *Blow-Up* as Antonioni's film *about* photography. Yet, even *Blow-Up* ultimately proposes that plurality structures not only our experience of photography but also the medium itself: it affirms, that is, the plurality intrinsic to photography as such – and constitutive of it as a technology of reproduction. The film's insistence on the figure of the enlargement discloses the 'depth' of such plurality. This pluralisation of photography from 'within' an individual image, through the very processes which should produce a copy, yields difference: reproduction does not suspend or sidestep, but rather generates and sponsors, difference. Antonioni returned to demonstrate this logic with the series *Le montage incantate* [*The Enchanted Mountains*] mentioned in Chapter 1. This pictorial series is also a photographic series, as many of the small abstract watercolour compositions are enlarged photographically, through a procedure which, as Antonioni explains, 'is the same as in *Blow-Up*' and whose aim is to 'produce a photographic enlargement of the image to the point at which this turns into something else'.[79]

Ultimately, *Blow-Up*'s attentive enquiry into photography's 'how' perhaps also turns out to offer an account for 'what' photography is in a way that exceeds the technological specificity of the photochemical era in which it is itself rooted. Clearly, plurality is still – exponentially – the experiential and constitutive condition of 'photography' (or what still largely goes by this name) in our *digital* image culture. Even in the context of the allegedly 'perfect' copy and instant transmission enabled by digital technologies, reproduction, as the low-resolution and heavily compressed images which abound on the Internet prove, still realises photography's plurality not only quantitatively but also qualitatively – as difference.[80]

While noting the pervasiveness of photographic images, not unlike Sontag and Antonioni, Vaccari once suggested that 'as in a homeopathic cure, where, as the etymology suggests, "same" is used to get rid of "same", it is photography itself to provoke a new type of awareness able, after having provoked a congestion of vision, to function as a "decongestant" for it'.[81] Antonioni's reflection on the 'image-world', and the prominent deployment of photographic images in many of his films, has something in common with the 'decongestion' invoked by Vaccari. The director's recurrent and overt inclusion of photography within his cinema is also, in turn, an aesthetic re-articulation of the cinematic image itself: one whose 'uncinematic' qualities and links with boredom I explore in the next and final chapter, by going back to the slightly earlier moment of *L'avventura* (1960) and *L'eclisse* (1962).

Figure 4.8   Franco Vaccari, from photobook *Esposizione in tempo reale 4* (1973)

NOTES

1. Munier, *Contre l'image*, p. 21.
2. Sontag, *On Photography*, p. 178. An earlier version of this last chapter, titled 'The Image-World' in the book, appeared in *The New York Review of Books*, on 23 June 1977, with the title 'Photography Unlimited'.

3. Ibid., p. 179.

4. Flusser, *Into the Universe of Technical Images*; Sorlin, *Les Fils de Nadar*; and Henning, *Photography: The Unfettered Image*, esp. pp. 5–6. As Henning also notes, photography has not tended to be seen as part of mass media, and therefore it has not generally been incorporated within media histories and theories, p. 128.

5. Sontag, *On Photography*, pp, 157, 178.

6. Kracauer, 'Photography', p. 432.

7. Mumford, *Art and Technics*, pp. 96 and 97.

8. Heidegger, 'The Age of the World Picture', pp. 134 and 130.

9. Sontag, *On Photography*, p. 3.

10. Ibid., p. 171.

11. Freund, *Photography and Society*, pp. 207–8.

12. Similarly, in this scene the people seem to be aware of, but relatively indifferent, to Antonioni's movie camera. Only in a striking and uneasy scene in a remote mountain village in the Hanan region, do the people being filmed react with a mixture of curiosity and worry.

13. Sontag, *On Photography*, p. 172.

14. Schaeffer, *L'image précaire*, pp. 9–10.

15. Vaccari citing from Vergine, *Il corpo come linguaggio*, in Vaccari, *Fotografia e inconscio tecnologico*, p. 82.

16. Thorough research on London's artistic and cultural scene was undertaken in preparation for *Blow-Up*, both by Antonioni himself and others. In 1965, a questionnaire was prepared for photographers and artists inquiring about their professional formation, lifestyle and beliefs, Francis Wyndham compiled a report titled 'Fashion Photographers in the East End' (Bailey, Donovan and Duffy), and Anthony Haden-West wrote 'General Notes on the Profession'. Antonioni also attended actual photo shoots. See 8C/48, Michelangelo Antonioni Archive, Ferrara. Much of this material, including the questionnaire, has now been published in Fofi, Franco, Garner and Moser, *Io sono il fotografo. Blow-Up e la fotografia*. For a discussion of *Blow-Up*'s relation to the cultural and artistic milieu of 1960s London, see Garner and Mellor, *Antonioni's Blow-Up*, ch.1; and Lev, 'Blow-Up, Swinging London, and the Film Generation'.

17. For examples of 'existential' readings, see Chatman, *Antonioni*, esp. pp. 138–52 and Grossvogel, '*Blow-Up*: The Forms of an Esthetic Itinerary'. For 'photographic ontology' readings, as well as how this further relates to cinema, see, for example, Jones, 'Seeing Differently: From Antonioni's *Blow-Up* (1966) to Shezad Dawood's *Make It Big* (2005); Lotman, *Semiotics of Cinema*, pp. 97–105; Freccero, '*Blow-Up*: From the Word to the Image'.

18. Talbot, *The Pencil of Nature*.

19. Bazin, 'The Ontology of the Photographic Image'.

20. Peirce, *The Collected Papers*, esp. Chapter 3. Peirce defines 'index' as a type of sign 'we may think of . . . as a fragment torn away from the Object' (p. 137) 'denot[ing] what it does owing to a real connection with its object', thus 'mark[ing] the junction between two portions of experience' (pp.160–1).

Even though an index may *also* be iconic, it doesn't denote by resemblance but by physical connection. This is the case of the photographic image, in which similarity, as Peirce points out, is just a by-product of the photographs 'having been produced under such circumstances that they were physically forced to correspond point by point to nature' (p. 159). For a historical contextualisation of the index in relation to modernity, time and the emergence of cinema, see Doane, *The Emergence of Cinematic Time*, esp. Chapter 3. Peirce's semiotics, and its application to film analysis, was pioneered by Wollen, *Signs and Meaning in the Cinema*, ch. 3. The art historian Rosalind Krauss took up the concept in the 1970s in 'Notes on the Index'. On the basis of Peirce's definition, Krauss concisely summarises 'indexes' as 'the marks or traces of a particular cause, and that cause is the thing to which they refer, the object they signify' (p. 70). The transition to digital technologies and media rekindled thinking on the 'index', and the elimination or transformation of this property in the absence of a photosensitive material support. Among others, the 2007 special issue of *difference*, dedicated *Indexicality*, edited by Doane, which includes Doane's own article, 'The Indexical and the Concept of Medium Specificity'; Rodowick, *The Virtual Life of Film*; Mitchell, 'Image'.

21. Chatman, *Antonioni*, p. 143; Lotman, *Semiotics*, pp. 97–8.
22. Jones, 'Seeing Differently', p. 186.
23. Chatman, *Antonioni*, p. 143.
24. Ibid., p. 149.
25. Lotman, *Semiotics*, p. 98. Lotman is here, selectively if not slightly inaccurately, thinking only of some of the enlargements, such as the one in which Vanessa Redgrave's character is seen raising her hand to hide her face and stop Thomas from taking further pictures. However, some of Thomas's photos actually do show quite a lot of the park and, crucially, it is by enlarging the area of the fenced copse to the right of the couple that Thomas believes he can detect a man holding a gun.
26. Chatman, *Antonioni*, p. 152.
27. Jones, 'Seeing Differently', p. 186 (my emphasis).
28. Ibid., p. 187.
29. Quoted in Huss, *Focus on Blow-Up*, (intro.) p. 5, from the foreword to Antonioni, *Blow-Up*, p. 7. Julio Cortázar's short story 'Las babas del diablo' (literally, 'The Devil's Drool', 1963) was translated as 'Blow-Up' when published in English in the collection *End of the Game and Other Stories*.
30. Freund, *Photography and Society*, p. 217. For discussion of photography as and within mass media, see among others: Beegan, *The Mass Image*; Marien, *Photography: A Cultural History*; Ford, *The Kodak Museum*, esp. David Allison, 'Photography and the Mass Market', pp. 42–59.
31. In addition to Freund, *Photography and Society*, I have relied on, among others, Wade, *A Short History of the Camera*; and Coe, 'The Rollfilm Revolution'.
32. For historical overviews of photojournalism, see Lebeck and Von Dewitz, *Kiosk: A History of Photojournalism*; Lucas and Agliani, *La realtà e lo sguardo*, esp. ch. 4 and 5.

33. Cf. Campany, 'From Ecstasy to Agony'.

34. Parr and Badger, *The Photobook,* vol. 2, p. 6.

35. Bourdieu, *Un Art moyen* (only partially published in English in 1990 as *Photography: A Middle-Brow Art*).

36. Letter from Italo Calvino to Antonioni, 29 September 1965, from Michelangelo Antonioni Archive, published in Païni, *Lo sguardo di Michelangelo*, p. 140.

37. Calvino, 'The Adventure of a Photographer' (first published in *Il contemporaneo*, 1955), p. 52.

38. Calvino, 'The Adventure of a Photographer', p. 43.

39. Ibid., pp. 50, 43.

40. Ibid., p. 52.

41. McCullin, *Unreasonable Behaviour*. For McCullin's contribution to *Blow-Up* see Mellor, 'Fragments of an Unknowable Whole; Garner, 'Gli ingrandimenti di *Blow-Up*'.

42. Szarkowski, *The Photographer's Eye*, p. 8.

43. Ibid., pp. 6–7.

44. For an overview of these developments, see the '1960–1969' section of Foster, Krauss, Bois and Buchloh, *Art Since 1900*. See also Buchloh, 'Conceptual Art 1962–1969'.

45. VanDerBeek's films had been shown at the Festival di Spoleto in 1961.

46. Talbot conjectured on such possibility and adumbrated what came to be developed as the photographic halftone process in the 1880s, see Stulik and Kaplan, *The Atlas of Analytical Signatures of Photographic Processes: Half-Tone*; Twyman, *Printing 1770–1970*, p. 31.

47. Maynard, *The Engine of Visualization*, p. 18. Furthermore, as Maynard notes, processes such as photo and rotogravure were themselves, literally, a kind of photography before the introduction of digital printing. See also Goldberg, *Photography in Print*.

48. For more on the popular press in Italy see Forgacs and Gundle, *Mass Culture and Italian Society from Fascism to the Cold War*, pp. 35–42 and pp. 95–123.

49. See, for example, Brewer, *An Approach to Print*, esp. pp. 33–4; and Hutchings, *A Survey of Printing Processes*.

50. See Lucas and Agliani, *La realtà e lo sguardo*.

51. Precursors of the *fotoromazo*, generally text-based summaries of released films with a number of significant illustrations, had been around since the late 1920s. However, it is from the late 1940s that the photonovel in its photographic comic-strip style emerges and flourishes. See Anelli, Gabbrielli, Morgavi, Piperno, *Fotoromanzo: fascino e pregiudizio* and De Berti, *Dallo Schermo alla carta*.

52. See Nardelli, 'Leafing through Cinema'.

53. See Parr and Badger, *The Photobook*, vol. 1; Drucker, *The Century of Artists' Books*; Thurman-Jaies and Hellmold, *Art Photographica*.

54. McLuhan, *Understanding Media*.

55. Ghirri, *The Complete Essays 1973–1991*; Hollis Frampton's 1970s articles for *Artforum* are now available in his collected writings: Frampton, *The Camera and Consecutive Matters*.

56. Mulas, Solomon and Provinciali, *New York: The New Art Scene*.

57. Mulas, *La fotografia*. The '*Verifiche*' are also available online on Ugo Mulas's website <http://www.ugomulas.org/index.cgi?action=view&idramo=1090232183&lang=engtext> (last accessed 15 November 2019).

58. Siegel, 'Identification of a Medium: *Identificazione di una donna* and the Rise of Commercial Television in Italy', p. 218.

59. For a discussion on the differentiation between 'medium' and 'media', see, for example, Casetti, 'The Relocation of Cinema'.

60. Balsom, *After Uniqueness*, pp. 4–5. See also Batchen, 'Dissemination'.

61. Parigi, 'L'avventura de *I vinti*', esp. pp. 7–8.

62. Flusser, *Towards a Philosophy of Photography*, p. 49.

63. Siegel, 'Identification of a Medium', pp. 218, 226.

64. See Maynard, *The Engine of Visualization*, where he suggests that it may be more useful to think of photography as, broadly, 'a kind of technology' (p. x) rather than as an activity geared to the making of photographs; for indeed, as he argues, from photogravure to microprocessors, 'there is photography that does not consist in making photographs – at least not as we ordinarily understand those terms' (p. 9).

65. Sontag, *On Photography*, p. 166 (my emphasis).

66. Calvino, 'The Adventure of a Photographer', p. 43.

67. Campany, *Photography and Cinema*, p. 60.

68. Stimson, *The Pivot of the World*, p. 30. Vaccari, *Fotografia e inconscio tecnologico*, p. 75.

69. Moholy-Nagy, *Vision in Motion*, p. 208.

70. See Lange, *Bernd and Hilla Becher: Life and Work* (2005); and Marshall, *Ed Ruscha*.

71. Cf. De Salvo, *Open Systems: Rethinking Art c. 1970*.

72. Bernard and Hilla Becher, *Anonyme Skulpturen. Eine Typologie Technischer Bauten* (1970).

73. In addition to the aforementioned books, see also Ruscha's *Various Small Fires* (1964) and *Nine Swimming Pools* (1968), whose series indeed take a 'narrative' twist not introduced in the cover title by ending with these unannounced objects (which are, however, mentioned in the title page inside the cover).

74. Cf. Dubois, *L'Acte photographique et autres essais*, p. 154.

75. Thomas's grainy enlargements, as well as the attempt to find clues to a murder, resonate with the frame enlargements of Abraham Zapruder's 8 mm footage of John F. Kennedy's assassination (in November 1963) published in mass print media.

76. There is a hint of this, for instance, even in *Funny Face*. At a point, ostensibly through progressive enlargement, two glamorous images of Audrey Hepburn's Jo (one of them an extreme close-up) are derived from a shot in whose composition she was only accidentally framed.

77. For a fuller account see Leonardi, *Feedback: Scritti su e di Franco Vaccari*, pp. 29–31.

78. In fact, Frampton himself once denied that his film made direct reference to *Blow-Up*, though he admitted to having been 'entertained' by it: 'An Evening with Hollis Frampton', 8 March 1973. SR, 70.22. The Museum of Modern Art Archives, New York, quoted in Moore, *Hollis Frampton – (nostalgia)*, p. 30.

79. Antonioni, *Antonioni: Le montagne incantate*, p. 17.

80. See Steyerl, 'In Defense of the Poor Image'; Balsom, *After Uniqueness*, pp. 42–7.

81. Vaccari, *Fotografia e inconscio tecnologico*, p. 77.

CHAPTER 5

Uncinematic Provocations and the Pursuit of Boredom

As I mentioned in the Introduction to this book, the invocation of the premiere of *L'avventura* in Cannes in May 1960 as one of the inaugural moments of modern art cinema is well consolidated: Geoffrey Nowell-Smith, as we saw, describes it as a 'watershed separating the world of new cinemas from that of the old'.[1] If there is a resonance with the way in which the famous 1895 screening at the Café Royal in Paris tends to be cited to invoke the very 'birth' of the medium, a crucial difference lies with the type of reaction that these events prompted (and which their respective anecdotal, if not mythological, elaborations have tended to emphasise). While the audience was amazed and excited by the Lumière Brothers' cinematograph films, it was frustrated and bored by *L'avventura*.[2] As is well known, many cried 'cut!' and booed the unnecessary *longueurs* and undramatic 'dead times' of a film which took nearly two and a half hours seemingly *not* to tell a story. In what quickly became an assessment that endures to this day, it was not so much that nothing at all happened, but that narrativity and drama seemed to have broken down or been 'thrown off', as Christian Metz put it a few years later, and cinematic duration was being articulated according to a different rhythm or temporal economy.[3] Drawing specifically on the word 'rhythm', Dudley Andrew, however, characterised it in Antonioni's films, admiringly, as 'a slow and deliberate beat which might be called inexorable', 'load[ed]' with an exorbitant number of lengthy 'stills'.[4] Writing in 1966, in an essay entitled 'Transparencies on Film' in which modern –European, art – cinema is pitted against Hollywood, Theodor Adorno summed up these features as being provocatively 'uncinematic'. Referring in particular to *L'avventura*'s successor, *La notte* (1961), he suggested that these features endowed Antonioni's films with a 'static character' through which the (formal, narrative) motion so distinctive of cinema was paradoxically 'denied and yet preserved, in negative form'.[5]

Besides the initial hostile reaction and critical accolades that soon followed and compensated for it, there is something worth noting in the way in which, not unlike the Lumière's screening, the event of *L'avventura*'s premiere has entered cinema history with the valence of a (new) beginning. What this event contributes to bring into relief is how the initial excitement at moving images which marked the historical birth of cinema is seemingly replaced by the frustration and tedium towards images refusing to move, or to move fast enough, at the birth of *modern* cinema. If movement and speed were the required attributes for being or feeling modern in the first half of the twentieth century, then *L'avventura* crystallises a shift, a moment when cinema sought to renew itself by resisting or restraining such attributes, and embracing seemingly antithetical qualities such as slowness or, even, a stillness that might make *moving* images look somewhat *photographic*.[6]

In his 1961 talk at the Centro Sperimentale di Cinematografia in Rome, Antonioni confessed that what had led him 'along [the] particular road' inaugurated by *L'avventura* had been 'an ever-increasing feeling of boredom with the current standardised methods of filmmaking and the conventional ways of telling a story'.[7] A form of boredom, then, is – not very surprisingly perhaps – offered as a catalyst for what Antonioni self-consciously characterised as 'modern cinema' in his own account of staleness and renewal.[8] Yet, as well as something to escape *from*, boredom at the same time surfaces as something that the new cinema of which Antonioni spoke might run *into*, or even seek to include. Indeed, it may not only be part of its subject matter, as 'La malattia dei sentimenti [The Malady of Feelings]', the title given to the talk on publication a few months later, suggests. It may also somehow incorporate boredom through the very newness of its formal and aesthetic strategies, as Antonioni himself opened the way to by arguing for the cinematic inclusion of the 'pauses' of time – when time itself, as he put it, is 'slow', 'motionless' and even 'appears almost static'.[9] These 'pauses' – the Antonionian *temps morts* referred to by many critics – may include the moments just after the actors have 'completed their performance of the written scene'[10] or, as he further explained in subsequent occasions, those 'moments . . . when, apparently, nothing is happening'.[11] If, then, as Antonioni suggested, the modern cinema (or, at least, *his* modern cinema) emerged as an attempt to find relief from boredom with the old, a layered *production* of boredom (as the Cannes reaction also helps to bring into relief) also seemed to be at stake, not least in the seeming resistance to, or containment of, that which traditionally motored 'the movies'. In 1963, Jean Mitry put his finger on the matter by suggesting that boredom featured as both content and form in that 'modern school of cinema' of which Antonioni is singled out as an exemplar. Not only, he considered, was the audience shown 'people being bored, dragging out an aimless existence' but, through 'the expression of emptiness, the representation of immobility', there was an attempt 'to make us share . . . and experience their boredom'.[12] Hoping to discourage further attempts in this direction, Mitry hastened to suggest that while, to his credit, Antonioni could be 'interesting even when he is being boring', 'he went as far as it is possible to go in this direction'. The attempt to make boredom a matter of both narrative and aesthetics, he warned, was 'bound . . . to end up boring us to death'.[13] Such prospect is effectively what Andrew Sarris complained of by coining the pejorative term 'Antoniennui' in the mid-1960s, to encapsulate not only what he saw as the director's signature style and thematics of alienation and 'malady of feelings', but also, as a spectator, his own sense of fatigue with them, and with their popularity with other filmmakers.[14]

For in many ways, by then, and not only in the movies, there was a lot of boredom, and anxiety about boredom, around. If, with a kind of pendant term to 'Antoniennui', Pauline Kael talked of a 'creeping Marienbadism' (referring to Alain Resnais's 1961 film and listing *La notte* as an example), in some quarters it might even have started to emerge not only as a challenge, but as something to be ostentatiously pursued.[15] Andy Warhol, who, with films such as *Sleep* (1963) and *Empire* (1964), was also during those years contributing to a modern or, as Jonas Mekas called it, a 'new American' cinema, would famously later boast of liking 'boring things', *even as* he was 'bored by them'.[16] John Cage had indirectly praised boredom in his 'Lecture on Indeterminacy' in 1958, when he suggested that 'if something is boring after two minutes', we should keep going and repeat it exponentially.[17]

Yet, though acknowledged or even 'liked' by some, boredom largely remained a problem. When not raised as an outright criticism or fault of a given situation or work, it might most often be invoked only to be negated or disavowed, presented as a reaction arising from a lack of critical discernment or proper engagement. So, for instance, in his famous lecture, Cage suggested that the repetition of the boring is 'not boring at all but very interesting'.[18] And Susan Sontag, citing Antonioni, Samuel Beckett and William Burroughs among others in her 1965 essay outlining the rise of a 'new sensibility', argued that boredom is simply a response to work that challenges 'our sensorium' with new, still unfamiliar, contents and forms.[19]

Although frequently invoked in writings on Antonioni, and in that 'new sensibility' in the arts and culture more broadly for which Sontag used Antonioni's cinema as a key identifier, boredom has nevertheless tended to remain superficially or ambivalently acknowledged. Even though in recent years there has been a flurry of studies offering a general history, philosophy or psychology of boredom as feeling or disposition, the possibility of its presence as something that might inform not only the content or the conception of specific works but, also, their form and their reception – something 'produced' during their consumption, so to speak – continues to be met with some reticence.[20] Aesthetically speaking, boredom is largely seen as an undesirable outcome, and the idea that boredom may itself *have* or *be* an aesthetics does not tend to be considered. While the problematics of boredom have begun to find a sympathetic or fertile ground in emerging debates on 'slowness' in contemporary art and cinema, boredom is still more likely to be met with resistance and criticism than to be seen in itself as a possible form of resistance or critique.[21] So, for instance, in his book *Motion(less) Pictures* (2015), Justin Remes argues that to see 'Warhol's films as explorations of boredom' is reductive, and that '[t]o call . . . *Sleep* and *Empire* boring' is 'to miss the point'; for, as he explains, the films were not meant by Warhol to be watched attentively at all, but distractedly.[22] While for Remes the 'distracted spectatorship' encouraged by Warhol is a defeat of boredom, a less reticent engagement with the phenomenon might help disclose how distraction is not antithetical to boredom but, on the contrary, profoundly entangled with it. Indeed, perhaps the promotion of distraction is precisely a consequence of Warhol's engagement with boredom and the aesthetic articulation of it.

My main aim in this chapter is to explore how Antonioni's cinema might be of particular interest precisely *because of* (rather than despite) boredom in the context of the self-conscious development of a modern art cinema and its provocative pursuit of seemingly uncinematic qualities such as slowness and stillness. It is from this specific perspective that I return to focus on the prominent and recurrent deployment of photographic images addressed in the previous chapter as Antonioni's reflection on the proliferation of the 'image-world' in post-war culture. Here, I explore how such deployment may constitute a way of 'imaging' boredom and articulating it as a question of the 'occupation' of visuality and time in an age of mass production, mass consumption and mass media. If photographic imagery helps to visualise boredom diegetically, as I will show, it is also mobilised in the formal (re)production of the phenomenon. As I want to argue, photography and 'photographic' stillness are implicated in an intermedial re-articulation of the cinematic image through which means – or indeed, media – usually called upon to dispel boredom are harnessed to make it manifest aesthetically, if not even to encourage its emergence in the aesthetic reaction to the work. As another instance of Antonioni's aesthetics of impurity, this uncinematicity manifests both a renewal of cinema through dialogue with, and absorption of, other forms, and a mode of criticality – if not, indeed, of self-critique or reflexivity – of the cinematic image as such, articulated intermedially.

Boredom as Image

If there is a general sense in which Antonioni's 'modern' films such as *L'avventura*, *La notte* and *L'eclisse* (1962) address *ennui*, as Sarris saw it, or boredom (as I will call it for reasons clarified to follow) through narrative themes, there are also moments in which boredom appears to be attentively staged and choreographed within a specific scene. In a sense, Antonioni offers a cinematic vignette or image of boredom, often in turn constructed, as we will see, through a relation of the characters to certain types of image within the *mise en scène*. It is on such instances that I propose to focus, and I shall start by introducing two examples.

The first example occurs just about five minutes before the end of *L'avventura*, and concisely but poignantly begins to draw attention to the question of boredom's key connection with visuality, time and their respective 'occupation' which I propose to explore in the course of this chapter. Claudia (Monica Vitti) has just woken up, alone, in the middle of the night. Her new lover, Sandro, is still presumably at the party she was too tired to join. Waiting for him to return and the night to end, she tries to find ways of occupying herself. At one point, we see her slumped over a pile of newspapers and illustrated magazines. Seemingly, these have failed to divert her (even if only superficially) from her boredom, for Claudia has resorted to counting time – literally. Having failed to occupy herself and time with images, she is, in a way, occupying time with time itself. Watch in hand, she is counting out aloud the passing seconds and writing them down, over a full-bleed image of Jean Seberg on a page.

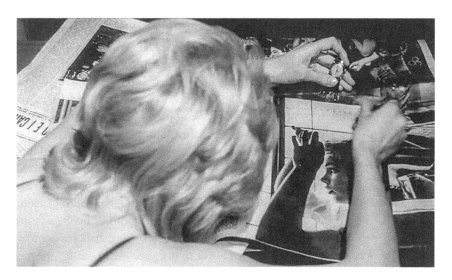

Figure 5.1 *L'avventura* (1960)

Not unlike the flicking through the illustrated pages which, though not shown, is likely to have preceded it, Claudia's counting is an attempt to occupy time with a view to making it pass. Yet, she is doing something that, in addition to making time more strongly felt (she can't become unaware of it, because she is counting it) and, to some extent, visible in the digits she jots down, is in fact also a way of keeping time. As she counts to the rhythm of the clock and 'fixes' seconds on the page, she seems to hold on to time, rather than letting go of it; yet she is also paradoxically distracted from her experience of time's emptiness or painfully slow progress by her very activity of monitoring such experience. There is, then, a strange frisson in this particular scene, which, moreover, despite thematising an unbearable lingering of time, lasts only for about a minute, but comes towards the end of a film in which established economies of cinematic duration and narration seem (or were largely perceived) to have been upset – diluted, elongated or slowed down. Time is slow *and* fast, static and moving, at the same time. 'Nothing' happens, Claudia is in despair at the long, empty stretch of night still ahead, yet the seconds tick away rapidly: time is something that fails to pass soon enough, but whose passing she finds hard to keep up with in her writing and counting, endlessness nested in finitude.

The second example occurs about thirty minutes into *L'eclisse*. The scene or image of boredom that it offers is longer and more complex than my first example, and is in a way complementary to it. For, here, unlike in *L'avventura*, the occupation of the visual field and of time is more successful and, from a diegetic point of view, boredom is seemingly overcome, or made latent, through distraction. The scene starts with a long shot of the façade of a building at night. On the second floor, a light comes on and the camera quickly cuts to a close-up of a poster (for an exhibition of French artists' drawings) on a wall: this is the first of the many photographic images constituting the core visual motif of the scene. Even though it is late at night, Vittoria (Vitti again) is awake and banging a nail into the wall in order to hang a newly bought artefact in her modern apartment. Soon Anita, her neighbour and friend, is at the door. Although complaining about the noise on behalf of her husband, she herself, seemingly also unable to sleep, seems rather relieved to have found an excuse to have a chat and moan about her comfortable yet uneventful life. For her part, Vittoria recounts how she spent the whole of the previous night awake too, breaking up with her long-term fiancé. She is tired, but of a tiredness, she specifies, which is *not* sleepiness: 'There are days', she tries to explain, 'in which to have in your hands a needle, a piece of cloth, a book, a man, is the same thing'. While they are talking, the phone rings. It is yet another neighbour, Marta, a white Kenyan who lives in the opposite building. She too cannot sleep, since a mixture of loneliness and frustrated homesickness keep her awake – her husband is temporarily away, and she will later explain that her life in Italy is empty: she never goes out and has nothing to do all day. Now, having seen the two conversing in Vittoria's illuminated flat through her window, she is calling to invite them over to her place for company.

At this point, the scene cuts again to a wall in a dark interior. On it is tacked a large, unframed photographic image of an African, seemingly Maasai woman in tribal dress. Just like the exhibition poster in Vittoria's flat, it is through this silent and static shot of a still image that Marta's apartment, as yet unidentified, is first introduced on the screen. Marta's flat is a place full to the brim with things to look at: 'a modern space', as Mark Betz has put it, 'festooned with the paraphernalia of colonial kitsch'.[23] Large images of Africa are pinned to the walls, and a multitude of safari-type trophies, spears and artefacts (including an elephant-foot coffee table and zebra skins) is arranged all around the layout. Vittoria browses around the flat, perusing the objects and, above all, the pictures lining the walls; Anita, reclining on the bed, looks unexcitedly at the images of some illustrated books through which Marta leafs as she talks of Kenya.

Whether some of the photographs were taken by Marta herself is not explained: whether on the page or the wall, the images – of sunsets over Lake Naivasha, Mount Kilimanjaro, the savannah with lions, a baobab tree, Maasai men and women in full tribal attire – look spectacular yet anonymous and clichéd, of the kind that might circulate in publications such as *The National Geographic*, tourists brochures or guides (at a time when, in a country that had been a tourist destination since Victorian times, mass air travel and organised holiday tours would begin to make experiences such as the 'leisure safari' more widely accessible).[24] With Marta or her off-screen voice occasionally commenting on the views and locations, in what does indeed sound like travel-agent speak ('Kenya has everything: the jungle, the snow, the savannah . . .'), the camera alternates between the women and the photos. It is on the photos in particular that it emphatically lingers, whether with a static close-up, by gently zooming into a detail, or by unhurriedly panning across their whole surfaces. Moving and zooming protractedly (almost torpidly, it might seem) onto and across these stills, the camera emphasises their nature as photographic objects – flat, static, grainy – almost more than it does their actual images. This is not the end of this scene of boredom, which in fact continues, and concludes, with a shocking turn: Vittoria's black-face dance – to which I will return. But, for the moment, I want to pause on this image of women awake at night, passing the time by looking at photographic images (several of which, such as the book illustrations if not the prints on the walls, are in fact photomechanical, mass-circulation reproductions). In a nutshell, both here and in *L'avventura*, this is how boredom is itself 'put into image' in these scenes.

Figure 5.2a   *L'eclisse* (1962)

Figure 5.2b   *L'eclisse* (1962)

Figure 5.2c   *L'eclisse* (1962)

The co-presence of the boredom of these women and the photographic imagery is not incidental. On the contrary, it is precisely through the women's relation to the photographs that their boredom is articulated. Via the photographs, boredom is presented not only, as I have already highlighted, in its crucial relation to visuality and time but also, more specifically, as a problem with these categories at a specific moment in the twentieth century. This is a moment which, in this scene, *L'eclisse* in fact also visibly conjugates in terms of colonialism – at the very point of its demise. Furthermore, it is again through the women's engagement with images (with seemingly at least partial success in one case, less so in the other) that boredom's relation to 'distraction' – a term with which the critical history of boredom is closely linked – is crystallised. As boredom is articulated through distraction and other states, such as restlessness, wakefulness and insomnia, that might appear antithetical to it, these scenes encapsulate the contradiction inherent in the condition and the increased temporal awareness that characterises it. In boredom, time itself comes to be felt as heterogeneous or 'contradictory', an uncomfortable exposure to both stasis and movement, slowness and speed, endlessness and finitude: an excess, something that falters, yet is nevertheless spent.

Boredom is featured in these scenes not only at the level of the diegetics of the image, but also of its aesthetics – perhaps as an instance of what Adorno (not referring to Antonioni's cinema specifically) once described as the 'sedimented content' of form.[25] These scenes point to a symmetry between form and content, diegetics and aesthetics, so that, through the kind of strategy that Mitry perceptively adumbrated but dismissed, in the viewing experience boredom may be both reproduced *and* produced. If the photographic images are a hinge for the women's state represented in the film's story, they also have a key role in its 'formal' rendering. Through them is engendered an oscillation, a tension between stasis and motion, speed and slowness, that resonates with boredom's oxymoronic temporality. In this respect, the prominence of these still images also functions more emblematically as a 'disclosure' of the seemingly cinematically impure – if not *un*cinematic – intermedial strategies through which Antonioni self-consciously articulates a modern cinema. Not unlike in the famous central sequence of *Blow-Up* (1966) considered in Chapter 4 in which the photographer studies at length the stills pinned all around his studio, in *L'eclisse*'s longer scene in particular the cinematic tempo slows down with the introduction of the photographs. (This is so notwithstanding the presence of cuts and temporal ellipses, as we shall see.) Adorno's provocative 'static quality', then, is provocatively on display. For what Adorno characterised as the paradox of cinematic movement being 'denied and yet preserved' in seemingly 'static' films like *La notte*, whose 'uncinematic' quality gives them 'the power to express, as if with hollow eyes, the emptiness of time', holds here too. Even more strongly perhaps, this paradox is played out, revealed in its mechanism, and played with.[26] But before we consider this in further detail, some remarks on boredom are in order.

Bored and Distracted: the Occupation of Time and Visuality

Often described in terms of lack, negation and absence (as in psychoanalyst Adam Phillips's epigrammatic definition of it as 'the wish for a desire'), boredom belies a fullness, and is in fact the consequence of historically and geo-politically specific conditions of abundance – if not excess.[27]

These conditions are subtly evoked in Alberto Moravia's novel *La noia* [*Boredom*], published in 1960. Through its first-person narrator, the prologue draws the outlines of a meta-reflection on boredom and adumbrates a sense of its historical evolution and specificity. Despite the use of a word – *noia* – which, like the French *ennui*, is of medieval origin, a difference is drawn between the form that had affected the narrator's father, and the one afflicting the narrator himself. Whereas the former was an ordinary, passing disposition which could be alleviated by 'new and rare sensations', the latter is presented as an ambiguous and slippery, yet profound and ultimately insurmountable, state of mind. Already as a child, when the movies were suggested to the narrator by his mother as a diversion – a distraction – from his boredom, he knew all too well that they were not a solution.[28] Even though it is, typically, described in negative terms – as an 'insufficiency' or 'scarcity' of reality, or a 'withering away' of objects, among other things – this newer form of boredom by which the narrator is affected seems to be crucially underscored not by a want of objects, diversions and time, but by an abundance of them. Beyond an intense affliction during boyhood (in the 1920s and 1930s – which in Italy, of course, also meant fascism and its visual spectacles), the point at which the narrator's boredom reaches its most violent, profound and, henceforth, permanent manifestation is given, fairly precisely, as 'around 1957'.[29]

Italy was in the midst of its 'economic miracle' then, transformed at an unprecedented rate by processes of technological and social modernisation, urban and infrastructure construction, industrialisation, and a new affluence and availability of consumer products. 'Headlong, dramatic and breathless' is how, in her influential study *Fast Cars, Clean Bodies*, Kristin Ross, writing about the comparable situation in France (which moreover, like Italy, had been a beneficiary of the European Recovery Programme, or Marshall Plan, from 1948 to 1952) has described the intensity and speed of these processes; such, indeed, that they may even qualify as '*events*' – more sudden and unexpected than a *process*.[30] But, like in *L'avventura* and, especially, *L'eclisse*, where this reality provides (more overtly than in Moravia's novel) the setting for the films' stories, boredom does not seem to be incompatible with the intensity and speed of these radical transformations.

In this respect, even as it presents the condition as a withdrawal from the world and an indifference to reality, Moravia's *story* about boredom is indeed also, similarly to Antonioni's films, an account that frames it *historically*, as a problem of modernisation and, even, 'modernity' broadly intended. The very naming of boredom points to this, as the English word started to appear around the middle of the nineteenth century.[31] While recognising its connection with other, historically anterior, moods and dispositions (such as *ennui*, acedia and melancholia), most recent studies of boredom have concurred in seeing it inextricably linked to the socio-economic developments of the past two centuries. Boredom may perhaps even be one of the epiphenomena through which 'modernity' and 'modernisation' themselves come to be known and recognised as viable descriptors for experiences which, though changing throughout this period, may still hold key common traits.[32] From this perspective, the differentiation between forms of boredom made by Moravia's narrator both locates the mood in history and outlines a sense of the mood's own history.

Even though the perception of boredom in terms of lack, negation or emptiness may tend to 'efface its historicity',[33] boredom '*has* a history', as several recent studies have sought to emphasise.[34] Such history points not only to its growth in intensity and yield as modernity unfolds and changes, but also to the transformation of the condition itself. If the outlines of this 'new way of feeling' emerged during the Enlightenment, boredom came to be 'democratised' with the industrial and consumer revolutions.[35] In his unfinished *The Arcades Project*, writing about boredom in the 1930s (if most often through the lens of nineteenth-century Paris), Walter Benjamin commented on its 'epidemic proportions' and described it as an 'index to participation to the sleep of the collective'.[36] By the late 1950s, when Maurice Blanchot compared the spread of the condition to that of the accumulation of carbon dioxide 'in a closed space when too many people find themselves together there', boredom is perceived to be such a 'mass' phenomenon that even the possibility of contagion seems to have become a thoroughly banal and unavoidable fact, like breathing.[37]

The epidemic, democratic and 'levelling' aspect of boredom is important in Antonioni's recurrent thematisation of the phenomenon. In a slightly earlier film such as *Le amiche* (1955), boredom seems only to affect the upper-middle classes; well-off, non-working women especially. Clelia, the working woman protagonist busy setting up a fashion salon in Turin, has no time for it, as she herself explains. Yet, by *L'eclisse* or, later, *Blow-Up*, no such differences seem to be in place. Boredom affects equally affluent housewives, working 'new' women (Vittoria is a translator who, as shown through the character of her mother, has climbed the social ladder from a more modest background) and celebrity professionals (while not even having the time to 'have his appendix out', as he puts it, the super-busy fashion photographer of

Antonioni's London film is nevertheless bored by the city or, as he puts it, he has gone 'off' the city, among other things). Indeed, in this respect, the very situation of night wakefulness of the women in *L'avventura* and *L'eclisse*, even while conveying the oppressiveness of being awake at the 'wrong' time, in the enclosed space of Marta's crowded apartment, points to how boredom might, paradoxically, also be the index of a new social mobility, of gender as well as class (and in Italy, women only obtained full voting rights from 1946).[38]

It is partly as a consequence of a perceived epidemic that boredom began to acquire not only representational exposure (as in Antonioni's films) but also critical attention. This started in the late 1920s and early 1930s, with Benjamin, Siegfried Kracauer and, if from a different perspective, Martin Heidegger, and continued up to Adorno, with and without Max Horkheimer, Henri Lefebvre and Blanchot into the 1960s. Where Heidegger dwelled at length on boredom as a 'fundamental mood' in his lecture course *The Fundamental Concepts of Metaphysics* (delivered in 1929–30 but first published nearly ten years later), Lefebvre repeatedly announced the need for a systematic 'sociology of boredom' in his three volumes of *Critique of Everyday Life* (1947, 1961 and 1981).[39] Even though Lefebvre did not himself deliver such systematic analysis, calls such as this suggest, as critical-studies scholar Jonathan Flatley has argued, that, along with boredom itself, *anxiety* about it peaked towards mid-century.[40] Arguably, its spectre loomed in a range of publications addressing, from different perspectives, both the routinisation and the spectacularisation of life in advanced capitalism, from studies of work (e.g. Charles White Mills's *White Collar: The American Middle Class*, 1951) and organisational management (e.g. William Whyte's *The Organization of Man*, 1956) to studies of mass culture including Edgar Morin's *L'Esprit du temps* (1962), philosophical treaties on time such as Emil Cioran's *The Fall into Time* (1964) and indictments of consumer capitalism from Herbert Marcuse's *One Dimensional Man* (1964) to Guy Debord's *The Society of the Spectacle* (1967).

Across the mid-decades of the twentieth century, in the wake of the boom of mass production, mass consumption and of what Adorno and Horkheimer described as the industrialisation of culture and leisure in their famous essay of the mid-1940s, boredom came not only to be seen to be spreading like wildfire, but also to have found modulation as something inextricable from the provision of *distractions*, in the sense of commercial forms of (mass) entertainment, as well as from *distraction* as a mode of perceptual and cognitive engagement developed in response to a world of abundance and sensorial (over)stimulation.[41] As is well known, according to Benjamin, distraction in this latter sense, as a form of disengaged or half-engaged 'reception' which doubles as a form of protection from and training for over-stimulation, had found 'its true means of exercise' in the distraction, in the former sense of entertainment, of the cinema, where '[t]he film with its shock effect' is met by a public which is 'an examiner, but an absent-minded one'.[42] Boredom's intertwinement with distractions (as entertainment) and distraction (as a mode of reception), as we will see further, is indeed a recurrent – inescapable, almost – feature of representations and reflections on the phenomenon.

In a country such as Italy that had somewhat lagged behind other Western countries in the first half of the twentieth century, the transformations to landscape, society, culture and the economy underway during the 1950s and 1960s were, as I began to note earlier, certainly experienced as dramatic, fast and radical. The invocation of the supernatural – the 'miracle' – in the expression used to sum up these changes certainly contributes to suggest as much. From the early 1950s, modernising projects included infrastructure development, such as the state-owned petrol-processing plants (e.g. SAROM, ANIC) built around the port of Ravenna which Antonioni captured in *Il deserto rosso/ Red Desert* (1964) and Europe's then longest motorway, the *Autostrada del Sole* connecting Milan and Rome from the late 1950s and extending to Naples by 1964. It additionally entailed intense building programmes, whose often shady legality, speed and greediness is piercingly captured in Italo Calvino's 1957 novella *La speculazione edilizia* [*Building Speculation*] and Vittorio De Sica's 1963 film *Il boom/The Boom*. Yet if, similarly to Calvino's and De Sica's representations of the Ligurian Riviera and Rome respectively, Ormanno Olmi's *Il posto* (1961), for instance, focuses on Milan as a city of building sites to capture some of the magnitude and impact of the transformations underway, Antonioni's *La notte*, although starting with the famous tracking shot descending along the side of the *just* completed Pirelli tower there (the highest building in Italy at the time besides the pinnacled Mole Antonelliana), presents us with a newness which, at least apparently, is already firmly in place. This is not so much a modernisation that is happening, but one that has *already*, even if only just, happened. Like in Moravia's story, the situations presented in Antonioni's films show (as even Benjamin, despite his focus on notions of 'shock', knew) that dramatic, sudden and perceptually rich or overwhelming experiences do not exclude the possibility of feelings of routine, stagnation and boredom. On the contrary, they may in fact co-exist with them or even possibly at some level be involved in their very generation. After all, '[m]onotony', as Benjamin wrote in the 'Boredom, Eternal Return' *convolute* of *The Arcades Project*, 'feeds on the new'.[43]

In 1903, in his famous essay 'The Metropolis and Mental Life', Georg Simmel had outlined how the external stimulation of the new might lead quickly not to a reaction of surprise, amazement or confusion, but of apathy and distraction: a 'blasé attitude' characterised by a 'blunting of discrimination' and sense of indifference.[44] As Simmel observed, it is the 'money economy' itself that, 'express[ing] all qualitative distinctions between [things] in the distinction of how much', and thus promoting a sense of their *inter*-changeability as well as of their *ex*changeability, generates such sense of indifference.[45] This is so even as, paradoxically, it stimulates the constant production and reproduction of the new. If Simmel's sense of indifference to, and between, objects chimes with that of Moravia's narrator in *La noia* and Vittoria's description of her apathy in the night scene of *L'eclisse* – when, as she puts it, 'to have in your hands a needle, a piece of cloth, a book, a man is the same thing' – it is overtly evoked in the definition of boredom that Adorno gave in the 1960s. 'Boredom', he wrote then, is 'the reflection of objective dullness' – a mental dullness in the human subject that responds to, indeed *mimics*, the dullness of objects in a world where capital stimulates their proliferation and circulation while also reducing their unique qualities to exchangeable qualities, and both labour and leisure are factories of the 'eversame'.[46]

The co-existence of seemingly incompatible experiences such as newness and monotony, sensorial stimulation and distraction, shock and indifference invoked by the reflections above is perhaps best encapsulated in what the film scholar Patrice Petro has termed 'after shock'. '*After shock*', she explains, designates an intermediary zone *after* the initial impact of the new: it 'retains an element of shock, but nonetheless signals the fading of its initial intensity'. 'Not unlike the term *afterimage*', Petro continues, 'after shock invokes an impression, or experience, or affect that persists long after an image or stimulus has passed from view'.[47] As well as calling into play a visual field, after shock points to:

> a moment when the new ceases to be shocking, when leisure as well as labour time becomes routinized, fetishized, commodified, and when the extraordinary, the unusual, and the unfamiliar are inextricably linked to the boring, the prosaic, the everyday.[48]

As Petro considers, Weimar Germany constitutes an important manifestation of 'after shock' in which a 'culture of boredom' spread, with Kracauer's impressions of city life in particular offering compelling textual snapshots of this. In his Berlin essays, the enjoyment of forms of mass culture (such as the 'optical fairylands' of grand movie houses and the 'blizzard of photographs' of illustrated magazines) and organised leisure is inseparable from waiting, habituation, repetitiousness – also since, ultimately, as Kracauer puts it, 'the form of free time busy-ness corresponds to the form of business'.[49]

But 'after shock' also fits well the slightly later moment at issue in my discussion. Both the temporality and the sense of visual stimulation suggested by 'after shock', precisely because, as Petro suggests, the notion still retains an element of bewilderment and surprise, seem especially evocative of the particular reality of the modernising and booming Italy of the 1950s and 1960s. Furthermore, the routinisation of work and leisure, and the conditions of affluence and abundance of consumer products, services and 'spare' time which describe Petro's 'after shock' obviously become all the more intense in the decades after the war in advanced capitalist economies more generally.

If automation contributed at this point to making the time *of* work increasingly standardised, routinised and monotonous (as, among others, Hannah Arendt's *The Human Condition* begun to denounce in the late 1950s, and Harry Braverman's study of the 'degradation of work' in the twentieth century analysed in concrete detail in the 1970s), it also freed up much more time *from* work, renewing the question of time's occupancy.[50] Writing an entry for the term 'automation' in a 'dictionary' of current themes published in the 1959 *Almanacco letterario Bompiani*, the sociologist Ottiero Ottieri (who was soon to collaborate on the script for *L'eclisse*) considered not only how automation may make work repetitious and boring, but how it may reduce and eventually eliminate the need for work as such. Yet, the possibility of being paid *not* to work – of 'paid *otium*' (or what may today be called 'universal basic income') – is raised as a prospect as grave as, or graver than, unemployment: 'a new alienation'.[51] While Ottieri's consideration of work's total elimination is relatively unusual, the significant shortening of the work day and expansion of time off work – 'spare', 'leisure' or, as Adorno addressed it in his famous essay of 1969, 'free' time – is a crucial preoccupation in the course of the 1950s and 1960s, as the attention given to its growth in critical discourse shows. For instance, in *L'Esprit du temps* Morin commented, not unlike Adorno in 'Free Time', on the dramatic and progressive reduction of the working week (literally halved, as he points out, between the 1860s and the 1960s). He then argued, not unlike Lefebvre, that free or leisure time itself – once a rarer and more special occurrence in a life dominated by work and other necessary chores – had undergone a process of 'quotidianization' and come to crucially inform the time of *every* day.[52]

Yet, rather than an affirmative presence, this quotidian free time may often seem to be more of a gaping hole, a void to be filled, an oxymoronically *empty excess*. In the 1930s, the psychoanalyst Otto Fenichel had begun to outline the problem of boredom's relation to free time through the case of 'Sunday neurotics', 'whose symptom is merely that on Sundays, or during vacations, they *are* bored'.[53] When the day is not regimented by work, boredom creeps in as an experience where time is excessively felt, or felt to be in excess. As Fenichel pointed out by drawing (not unlike others, such as Heidegger) on the German word for boredom – *Langeweile*, literally 'long while' – in boredom 'the "while" is long'.[54] In a slightly later context when free time, and its abundance or excess, have become not only a matter of Sundays, but, as Morin noted, of everydayness, the obsessive 'hobby' photographer of Calvino's short story 'The Adventure of a Photographer' (1955) mentioned in Chapter 4, or Warhol's intensive film and video making from the mid-1960s onwards, which he described as 'just a way of taking up time', and Bruce Nauman's filming of banal, iterative activities in his studio, such as *Walking in an Exaggerated Manner Around the Perimeter of a Square* (1968), come to mind.[55] Unsurprisingly perhaps, it is at this occupational void that forms of leisure, as more or less organised and commodified entertainment, entered the scene with increased impetus. These spanned from the hands-on engagement with media technologies themselves, increasingly available as consumer products to foster the filling of time and the 'hobbies' that Adorno disparagingly considered in 'Free Time', to what may be described as the 'off the shelf' products, from movies to packaged holidays, of the culture or tourist industries. Indeed, according to Morin, these industries mirrored each other, for tourism is nothing but a 'great travel-spectacle' whose 'precipitous succession of images' and 'uninterrupted voyeurism' bear 'striking affinities' with mass media such as cinema.[56] For Adorno, not unlike for Kracauer, such forms of leisure have brought 'free time' towards 'its own opposite': they are, effectively, 'compulsory' forms of 'organised freedom'.[57] In 'late capitalism', as Adorno put it with Horkheimer in 'The Culture Industry' essay, where it is 'the rhythm of mechanical production and reproduction' that sets the pace and 'everything has to run incessantly, to keep moving', 'amusement' is in fact an 'exertion' for the resting worker and (as he further argued in 'Free Time') it is but 'afterimages of the work process itself'.[58]

The complexity of boredom's relation to distraction should have started to come into sharper focus by now. The replication of the structures, patterns and rhythms of labour in organised leisure and amusement also contributes, as Kracauer, Horkheimer and Adorno suggested, to make these alleged forms of distraction *from* work not only as tiring as work itself but also as intimately associated *with* the boredom of work's monotony and routine. Moving 'rigorously in the worn grooves of association', the distraction of entertainment is bound to quickly become boring itself – if it does not perhaps already, more radically, constitute a manifestation of boredom *as such*. For, as Moravia surmised in *La noia*, 'boredom is not the opposite of amusement' but actually 'resembles' it – as the narrator discovered as a child on being taken 'to the cinema', a distraction which was 'neither the opposite of boredom nor its remedy'.[59] In many ways, this is a position with which even more sympathetic commentators, such as Morin, more or less overtly concur across the mid-decades of the twentieth century: though the offerings of the 'culture industry', organised leisure and mass media may superficially seem to relieve boredom, they in fact keep boredom going. They *are* boredom, since they arise from the same socio-economic context, life conditions, and modalities of production and consumption as everything else, even though they mask themselves as 'distractions'. In fact, while boredom is profoundly entangled with the 'distractions' of entertainment in this sense, there is also the possibility, as we shall see, that this inextricable pairing may foster a different intertwinement of boredom and distraction: one where a state of perceptual distraction (à la Benjamin) towards the boredom at once masked and incarnated by (mass) entertainment may lead, as we will see, to *another* form of boredom.

As well as pointing to a replication of work in leisure (so that leisure emerges as a shadow or spectre of work in consumer capitalism), by invoking the idea of 'afterimage' Adorno also brings into relief the visual propensities of the leisure offerings that may help to fill 'free time' – propensities that had also already been in evidence to Kracauer and Benjamin in the 1930s, and Adorno himself or Lefebvre in the 1940s. Although 'The Culture Industry' addresses radio, it mostly dwells on the movies. And, in 1947, Lefebvre, even while considering reading (and listing readers' digests, picture and travel books, and strip cartoons among the items of choice), concluded that 'the constitutive elements of leisure are more likely to be images and films'.[60] According to Morin, the kind of 'industrialization' of 'images and dreams' that started with nickelodeons amounts, by the 1960s, to a 'nervous system' whose leisure offerings have a capillary reach and, from the images available through 'the screens of cinema' and 'the monitors of television', to those experienced through the 'bay windows of modern apartments, the Plexiglas of Pullman cars and the portholes of aeroplanes', a strongly visual bent.[61] Developments such as the diffusion of television, cheap colour-printing methods for wide-circulation publications, affordable 'point-and-shoot' still, film and (from the mid-1960s) video cameras (which Kodak adverts often presented as so easy to use that *even* women could do so), mass air travel and tourism concurred to seal, if not the sense of a dominance of visuality, then of a dramatically increased occupation – a saturation – of the visual field, as such. Television is particularly important here, of course, because of its domestic presence and its perceived valence as a 'new hearth'. This particular view was argued, among other places, in a special issue of the technology and culture-oriented *Pirelli* magazine on the success of the relatively new mass medium published in 1961.[62] In an article on the diffusion of the TV set, a series of photographs of families across Italy, in various domestic settings, but all generally 'glued' to the luminous screen, contributes to generate a sense that the storytelling and conversations promoted by the traditional hearth were being replaced by the absorbed consumption of a flow of images (and words).

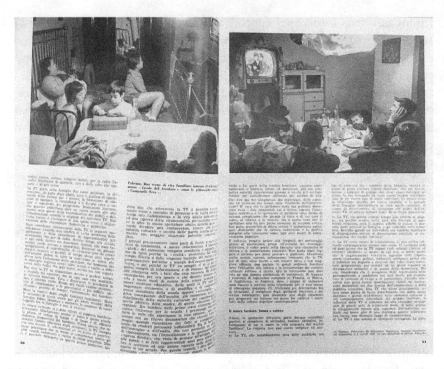

Figure 5.3   Double-page spread from article 'Il teleschermo nuovo focolare [The TV monitor as new hearth]', in *Pirelli* magazine (January–February 1961)

As noted at other points in this book, some, such as Umberto Eco in the very same issue, or the editor of the 1963 *Almanacco letterario Bompiani*, talked with relative enthusiasm of a definitive turn towards a 'civilization of vision' or 'of the image'; others, more alarmed, hoped to rally support 'against the image'.[63]

This increased 'occupation' of visuality bears on boredom not only because it is absorbed into everydayness, but also because visuality's occupation as such generates everydayness. While, from photography onwards, visual media technologies have been seen to expand the field of the visible by prosthetically helping to preserve or reveal what might otherwise be forgotten or remain invisible, they have also, for these same reasons, been implicated in the growth – if not, as some have argued, even in the very 'construction' – of the categories of the clichéd, the banal, the everyday.[64] Blanchot dwelled on this connection in 'Everyday Speech' (1959), aligning visual mass media, the everyday and boredom: '[B]oredom', he argued, is nothing other than 'the everyday become manifest: as a consequence of having lost its essential – constitutive – trait of being *unperceived*.'[65] For indeed, while, as Blanchot considered, the everyday tended to 'escape', visual media (photography – in its diffusion via print media – film and television are mentioned in particular) have from very early on contributed not simply to its capture but to its 'exposition': 'everything is to be put into the limelight'.[66] For sceptical, if not critical, observers such as Blanchot, this capture and exposure of the everyday – its visualisation – are, together with the growth and quotidianisation of free time, leisure and mass media, symptoms of the increasingly commodified and spectacularised conditions of life. This was a situation that Debord, Lefebvre and Morin started at around this time to describe, in what have become well-known refrains, as a 'colonization' of the 'everyday' and 'of the human soul'. As Debord requested in his short film *On the Passage of a Few People Through a Rather Brief Moment in Time* (1959), this was a colonisation from which it was imperative to seek 'liberation', by 'destroy[ing]', among other things, cinema, or a certain cinema.[67]

The term 'colonisation' was, for these critics, meant to invoke the idea of the 'Americanisation' of life – acutely felt not only financially but also culturally, as a promotion of American values and ways of life, in post-war European countries that were beneficiaries of the Marshall Plan – and, with it, of a total subjugation to consumer capitalism. Yet, as Ross has pointed out, such catchphrases were not coined casually or accidentally, and their invocation of processes of 'colonisation' of the everyday and the soul crucially stems from their historical coincidence with the peak of anti-colonial struggles against European imperialism in Africa and Asia.[68] Ross pursued precisely this coincidence in her landmark study of post-war France, considering consumerist modernisation – 'a growth without precedent of capitalism' throughout the 1950s and 1960s – as a form of 'interior colonialism', where 'rational administrative techniques developed in the colonies were brought home and put to use side by side with new technological innovations such as advertising in reordering metropolitan, domestic society, the "everyday life" of its citizens'.[69]

And so, having considered the historical specificity of boredom in its entanglement with distraction and the occupation of time and visuality, we are brought back to the images of boredom offered by the scenes from *L'avventura* and *L'eclisse* that I introduced earlier. In addition to being articulated in its relation to temporality and visuality, boredom in Antonioni's staging seems to relate to the double-edgeness of the term 'colonisation' invoked by the French critics. On the one hand, the women's engagement with (mass) photographic imagery – the illustrated magazine in *L'avventura*, the photobooks, posters and prints in *L'eclisse* – contributes to present the women as subjects of consumption and as representatives of the gender most often interpellated, and responsible, for it.[70] (The photos might be of 'home' for Marta, but for Vittoria and Anita they represent a place of escape to which tourism might grant them access by turning it into a 'product' buyable as a holiday.) If a sense of consumerism's 'colonisation' of life is called into play here – and, perhaps, in

L'avventura, even challenged in its efficacy by Claudia's seeming disinterest in, and boredom with, the magazine – *L'eclisse* seems to make overt reference to the conditions of imperial colonialism that arguably inflect the French critics' condemnation of the 'colonisation' of the everyday and the soul.

BECOMING LIKE

As mentioned, *L'eclisse*'s scene of boredom that I have considered does not end with the women looking at the photographs. If they at first kill time by doing so, there comes a point where a different way of filling it is devised, and a different dynamic of boredom in relation to the photographs emerges. An abrupt cut interrupts the protracted pan across the photos of Maasai people being contemplated by Vittoria. Even in a scene which, as Karen Pinkus has noted, is structured through a 'kind of edit that calls attention to itself' – a 'series of [radical] cuts' whose 'effect is disorienting, but deliberately so' – this cut is 'of such radicalness and momentary disorientation in time and space that the first-time viewer might even imagine that the film's print itself has been damaged'.[71] For indeed, the shot after this cut, announced by a more high-pitched and sustained percussion rhythm (diegetically coming from records of 'African' music on a turntable) reveals an almost unrecognisable Vittoria, whose lengthy process of 'transformation' is omitted in the film. In 'black face', minstrel-like, with pendant earrings and a thick choker around her neck, Vittoria stands next to a photograph of a Maasai woman that has served as a 'model'. Wrapped in a white sheet and spear in hand, she is now a tribeswoman herself or, at least, so thinks Anita who (also partially dressed up), pointing at the photo, exclaims: 'Doesn't she look like her?' 'Identical!', replies Vittoria, before setting off dancing and chanting around the flat, and on the bed, until Marta takes the needle off the record and stops her: 'Enough of playing negroes, please [Adesso basta fare i negri, per favore]'. After another cut, the women are seen lying on the bed (Vittoria is now wrapped in a towel, and still has a flannel in her hand, presumably used to wipe away the make-up). Sipping drinks, they discuss the anticolonial struggle in Kenya (the country gained independence from Britain in 1963, in the wake of the Mau-Mau uprisings of the mid-1950s), which Marta describes as 'six million monkeys' wanting 'to throw out the 60,000 whites'.

Betz has described this moment in the scene as 'one of the most shocking examples of colonial/racist representation combined with modern femininity in all of European art cinema'.[72] Through his discussion of *L'eclisse*, as well as other contemporaneous examples of modern European cinema, Betz seeks to demonstrate how, while generally seen 'as an alternative or resistant mode of film practice to that of Hollywood', these films cannot be merely understood as 'national responses to US cultural imperialism in Europe', since they are, in fact, themselves entangled in national narratives of, and debates on, colonialism, decolonisation and recolonisation.[73] From this perspective, both Betz and Pinkus have offered compelling analyses of *L'eclisse*'s scene in particular. Pinkus concentrates on how the scene gestures towards the problematic questions of colonialism and decolonisation in the post-war decades. While affecting Italy directly too as a colonial power (both before and during fascism), these questions, Pinkus shows, are raised by the scene yet also disavowed and displaced, both narratively and formally. Content-wise, colonialism and its aftermaths are alluded to but, at the same time, tied to the foreign character of Marta (she speaks Italian with an accent, interspersing it with English words) and the then still British colony of Kenya. Not unlike in RAI's newly launched second-channel programme *Anni d'Europa*, which, from February 1962, while *L'eclisse* was in production, dedicated five episodes to 'The Apogee and Decline of Colonialism' and contributed to bringing debate about such questions into the public sphere, the issue of *Italian* colonialism and decolonisation more specifically remains eclipsed in the film.[74] At the formal level, what Pinkus describes as the attention-seeking editing strategy of the scene, distances Vittoria's minstrel dance from the main story of the film, almost like a 'foreign' moment in the film. Through a different focus, Betz has considered how Vittoria's masqueraded dance, as it has her enact (if not, indeed, temporarily become) a colonial, racialised 'other', also functions as a kind of allegory for the nexus between modernisation, geopolitical decolonisation and the 'interior colonialism' – or colonisation *at* and *of* the home – of which Ross writes in *Fast Cars, Clean Bodies* in relation to French national culture in the post-war decades.[75]

Neither photography nor boredom is particularly at issue in Betz's and Pinkus's discussions. However, their important observations on how questions of race and colonialism inform this scene diegetically and aesthetically can be brought to bear on the problematics of temporal and visual occupation at issue in this chapter. I think that an awareness of the interrelation of photography, coloniality and boredom is insinuated in this scene.

Considering the photographs' 'bridging' function between the first and second moment of this scene's diegesis brings into view both boredom's connection to the occupation of time and visuality in consumer capitalism and its intertwinement with distraction. In this sense, the radical cut that delivers the viewer to Vittoria in black face functions as a marker of another sort of spatial and temporal dislocation: that of Vittoria's imaginary escape *into* the space and time of the photographic images and their mediated, if not mediatised, spectacle. While for Marta the photographs may well have significance as 'props' for remembering, tools for managing her personal memories, for the other two women, on the contrary, they belong to an impersonal dimension and function as objects of entertainment and distraction: aids, we could say, for forgetting oneself and one's boredom. As Morin considered in *L'Esprit du temps*, the ever-increasing access to mass media means that when engaging with them – even indeed, at home, flicking through an illustrated publication or watching television – their consumers or public are, like never before, transported 'elsewhere'.[76] What, in their white, Eurocentric positioning, Vittoria and Anita seem to value in Marta's clichéd, holiday-brochure kind of imagery is precisely the kind of spatial and temporal ambiguities that allow them to receive and construe these images as elsewheres and outsides of (Western) modernity. Yet of course, as Morin among others also notes, the very abundance of such imagery is inevitably leading to the elimination of the category of the 'elsewhere', fast subsuming it under that of the 'familiar' instead, in what might in fact be a form of visual and aesthetic 'colonisation' which, while implicating capitalism and consumer culture, is not wholly reducible to or exhausted by a charge of American cultural imperialism.[77] According to Adorno in 'Free Time', this familiarisation or domestication of the elsewhere is what distinguishes Baudelerian *ennui* from twentieth-century boredom: in *ennui* 'distant places' (from a Western or Eurocentric viewpoint) were still 'different places', but in boredom they are part of 'the eversame' – a condition certainly summoned by the abundance and visual redundancy of Marta's images, many of which look, as one might put it, 'the same'.[78]

With this in mind, I want to focus in particular on how, while the scene stages a *becoming other* of Vittoria in the racialised terms considered by Betz, such endeavour is also at the same time an attempt to *become like* on Vittoria's part.

Figure 5.4 Vittoria 'like' the photograph in *L'eclisse* (1962)

Vittoria's masqueraded spectacle is an act of mimicry, crucially pegged to an interaction with the many photographs in Marta's apartment. It not only recalls the subjective, mental 'reflection of objective dullness' that defines boredom in Adorno's terms, but it offers an embodied instantiation, a literal acting out, of the mimicry crucial to Adorno's definition. In fact, Vittoria's transformation and dance are an attempt to become like *the images* of the photographs from which she takes inspiration.[79] What she imitates is an image, a representation. If we wanted to describe accurately what happens in this scene, we would have to say that the object of her mimicry is not the referent existing 'beyond' the images, but the way in which that referent is imaged – that is, the kind and mode of representation (in a formal as well as a technological sense) provided by photographs and these photographs in particular. Rather than temporarily becoming a Maasai woman, Vittoria enacts the colonialist, ethno-touristic mode of representation through which Maasai women have been made 'available' to a Western audience – an often de-historicised 'other' whose difference is at the same time constructed, displayed and erased, through the very anonymity, frontality and repetitiousness of the images, and whose 'elsewhere' has nevertheless been brought 'here'.[80] Tellingly, the primitivising images on Marta's walls are at odds with her own account of Kenya, where, as she tells her friends, she opted to return to give birth because of very 'modern' hospitals. Vittoria's shocking performance to an extent *activates* this representational mode, in the sense of beginning to make the mode itself visible by playing it out, not unlike the ways in which the photographic portraits of August Sander's *People of the Twentieth Century* (1920s–1940s) or Jean Rouch's documentary *Les Maîtres Fous* (1955) had started to challenge and make visible the very modalities of Eurocentric ethnographic representation by turning it on itself. (Some of what I think this scene gestures towards is more overtly addressed in the moment in *The Passenger*, 1975, in which the West African 'tribe witch doctor' being interviewed by David Locke says: 'Mister Locke, your questions are much more revealing about yourself than my answers would be of us', before turning the camera onto the journalist and concluding: 'now we can have an interview, you can ask me the same questions as before'.)[81]

The entanglement with (inter)national narratives of colonialism, decolonisation and recolonisation at work in the scene also bears on its articulation of boredom. Boredom itself comes into image at – or as – the intersection of these phenomena. Vittoria's imitation of photographic images mimes a mass medium and form of entertainment through which, though ostensibly evaded, boredom is in fact, at the same time, made manifest. As she literally makes herself spectacle, her boredom does not simply become like, but is actually embodied *as* distraction. Through this act of mimicry of photographic images, the women's boredom is geared to the economy of mass (re)production and consumption, and the technologies and aesthetics of repetitions, in which it is historically rooted. Vittoria's reproduction of the photographs invokes both the reproducibility of this mass medium and the tendency towards repetitiousness and visual redundancy of many of its applications. The women's unfolding engagement with photographs links boredom to the problematics of temporal and visual occupation of which boredom itself is a manifestation. Boredom emerges as a symptom or consequence of capitalism's colonising drive. And in fact, at a specific level, the photographs' subject matter, what I have called their ethno-touristic representational mode, and the way in which this in turn inspires Vittoria's dance, contribute to bring into view the intimate link between capitalism and colonialism: how capitalism's occupational drive requires colonisation geo-politically, socio-economically and culturally, and is, indeed, colonially inflected. In particular, in addition to a colonisation *by* images, as Morin, Debord and Lefebvre lamented, capitalism's occupation of visuality is a colonisation *of* images: the imposition and diffusion of regimes and modalities of representations which, as this scene in part suggests, are also the product of Western imperialism and white colonial and racial discourse.

TIME DILATED: FORMS OF BOREDOM

Most considerations of boredom, as we have seen, emphasise its intimate link with temporality. Boredom is understood as a condition that affects the experience of time or is itself, more strongly, an intensified temporal awareness – a state whose crucial unease is due not so much to the fact that there is too much time but that time itself is felt too much, as it were. Yet, the temporality affected or made manifest by boredom is not homogenous and uniform. Most accounts present it as a polarity of action and inaction, restlessness and apathy, motion and stasis.[82] For instance for Warhol, who, as we have seen, confessed to enjoying 'being bored', boredom – and its temporality – consists of a hovering between action and inaction.[83] 'Everyone knows how it is', he explained, 'some days one can sit and look out of the windows for hours and hours and some days one can't sit still for a single second'.[84] As well as outlining a co-existence of apparent opposites within boredom – such as social mobility and stagnation, psychic aboulia and restlessness, physical motion and stasis – Moravia laid emphasis on the recursive structure of its temporality. In *La noia*, Dino compares the condition to the 'repeated and mysterious interruption of the electric current inside a house', whereby one moment there is light and the next 'darkness and an empty void'.[85] Through these metaphors of intermittence, boredom's temporality is presented not only as repetitive but also as heterogeneous, a flow that includes – or, in fact, *contains*, in both the sense of comprising *and* of limiting – its own interruptions or negations.

Dino's metaphor of a recurrent black-out, not unlike Warhol's descriptions of an alternation of repose and action, draws attention to the *how*, to the dynamics by which, as Benjamin put it in relation to the similar yet antecedent condition of 'spleen', time becomes 'palpable'. [86] In many ways, as the scenes from *L'avventura* and *L'eclisse* on which I have focused contribute to show, what materialises time in boredom, renders it evident and felt, is precisely an unresolved tension between stillness and movement. For, in boredom, as Claudia's killing *and* feeling time by counting time itself encapsulate perhaps most compellingly, time is experienced as just this painful inextricability: something that fails to pass *while* passing, nevertheless. This same tension – or suspension? – is at play, more overtly, in *L'eclisse*.

As in *L'avventura*, photographs are not only a key diegetic element through which the women's boredom is put into image, they also contribute to making boredom's temporal problematics – the palpability, heterogeneity and tensions of and within time that characterise it – a *matter* of aesthetics. In this sense, boredom is addressed both representationally and formally. It is figured as image – an image that, as we have seen, in turn implicates boredom within a regime of representation and mode of image production whose colonialist and racialised connotations are also symptomatically made visible. Yet, the content of that image also informs the scene's aesthetics. That is, the emphatic focus on the stills in this scene – a remarkable aesthetic motif that, with greater or lesser degrees of intensity, recurs in Antonioni's films, and is reprised, most famously, in *Blow-Up* – functions formally, to paraphrase Adorno, as a precipitate or sediment of content.[87] Even more broadly, the formal incorporation and display of still images works as a reflexive commentary on the aesthetics of the film as a whole and, in so doing, as a reflexive commentary on the aesthetic strategies felt to be necessary to the development of a 'modern' cinema to which Antonioni, as we have seen, was at the time overtly committing himself. In this sense, then, this scene of boredom with the stills is not only a narrative, visual and formal exploration of the phenomenon of boredom, it is also a scene that crystallises and discloses the way in which Antonioni's self-consciously modern cinema might have adopted boredom *as* an aesthetics. If the photographs have a part in the representation or imaging of boredom, they also, I want to suggest, are a crucial tool in its aesthetic articulation, if not, indeed, in the pursuit of boredom as a modern cinematic aesthetic – one which, as we have seen Antonioni put it, should include the 'pauses' of time. In other words, what, following Jay David Bolter and Richard Grusin's well-known McLuhanesque concept, we could describe as 're-mediations' of photography in cinema, introduce a provocatively 'uncinematic' *frisson* within the cinematic that helps to configure boredom in the form of film itself.[88] Not unlike the *frisson* of still images within moving images, boredom is itself, as we have seen, a condition of temporal *frisson* between stillness and movement, as in the oscillation between apathy and restlessness, or the contradictory experience of time standing still yet passing nevertheless.

To think about this, we need to look briefly at the use of photography in *L'eclisse*'s scene through a different lens. With its emphasis on photographic imagery, the scene in Marta's apartment stages an 'encounter' between photography and cinema. Although deeply imbricated with time since their very emergence, from its capture and representation, to its reconceptualisation and management, these media have usually been related to two different aspects of it. While digital developments – and, especially, the convergence of previously relatively separate functions for the realisation of still and moving images onto singular devices – have contributed to a blurring and interchangeability of these different aspects, historically they have been attributed to photography and cinema separately.[89] On the one hand, as in André Bazin's or Roland Barthes's famous accounts in 'The Ontology of the Photographic Image' (1945) and *Camera Lucida* (1980) respectively, photography (or, more precisely, photography after the technological developments of the 1880s which enabled drastically reduced exposure times) has been linked to the instant and stillness: a moment seized, as if frozen, out of the durational flow of life. If, according to Bazin, photography could only give us the object 'enshrouded . . . in an instant, as the bodies of insects are preserved . . . in amber', cinema had enabled the overcoming of the frozen and disconnected instants of photography in a representation of events in their unfolding – an 'image of things' *and* 'of their duration', or 'change mummified', as he called it.[90] In their respective differences, these media technologies have not simply 'made manifest' these seemingly incompatible attributes of time but, in fact, actively contributed to *configure* them as such. If photography seizes the instant, the very notion of the instant is, in turn, dependent on the photographic: our sense of it might be different without Eadweard Muybridge's image of the galloping horse with all four hooves off the ground, or Henri Cartier Bresson's man leaping over a very large puddle in *Behind the Gare Saint-Lazare* (1932).

In a 1990 essay titled 'The Film Stilled', Raymond Bellour analysed the scenario in which, within the terrain of the moving image, cinema and photography meet, as it were.[91] For Bellour, the focus on, or imitation of, a photographic image within cinema, as in the filming of a photograph or the recourse to the freeze-frame effect, leads not only to moments of aesthetic stillness in which, not unlike Adorno had argued in 'Transparencies on Film', the mobility of the cinematic seems to be negated, but also to the possibility of experiencing the time of the photographic within cinematic time. 'These instants that suspend the time of movement', as Bellour puts it, reveal and 'open up, inside of time, another time'.[92] Where Bazin admired cinema for the possibility it offered to supersede the instant, Bellour seemed to admire instead cinema's contrary capacity to return the frozen instant to full presence through strategies of inclusion of photography and its stillness. For Bellour, these strategies that 'open up' the time of the photograph within cinema become 'both the pose and the pause of the film':[93] they are important because, as the title of the essay intimates, the film is 'stilled', giving viewers time to reflect (on cinema and its photographic historical origin and material basis perhaps above all, in Bellour's account).

But this inclusion or 'remediation' of one medium within another changes both media. While the moving image may seemingly be taken against its own grain by such incorporation, a filmed photograph (like a freeze frame) may *seem* still yet is, of course, still *moving* – it is a stillness *in* movement. As Stanley Cavell remarked in *The World Viewed* (1971), '[t]he current of frames through the projector cannot be stilled (unless for analysis), so that the liveness of a motionless camera on a motionless subject remains altogether different in its significance from the stillness of a still depiction'.[94] According to Gilles Deleuze, there is a fundamental difference 'at the point where the cinematographic image most directly confronts the photo', as he observed in *Cinema II*, 'it also becomes most radically distinct from it'. For, in cinema, the still image '*endure[s]*, has a duration' that it lacks as a paper print or photomechanical reproduction in a magazine, the most common formats through which photographic imagery would be encountered before its migration to screens that got underway with the 'digital revolution' of the mid-1990s (when, arguably, the more durational mode of experience of still images now dominant also started to take hold).[95] The remediation – the mimicry, perhaps – of photography or its stillness in cinema endows such imagery with a *set* duration, a precise *screen time* ('over ten seconds of the vase', as Deleuze comments, evoking a fixed shot, or 'still life', by Japanese director [Yasujiro] Ozu).[96] This is the case even with montages of still images in rapid succession, as in Antonioni's own *I vinti/The Vanquished* (1953), mentioned in Chapter 4, or Alan Pakula's *The Parallax View* (1974). But, most often, the movie camera 'holds' a still image for a length of time outlasting the 'instant' traditionally embodied by the photographic or necessary for the impression on the negative of the specific image on view. In other words, the 'instant' of the photographic is dragged out in an aesthetic strategy that seems to implicate, as art historian George Baker has suggested, the other meaning of the word still – 'continuation' – and to invoke the sense of prolongation and repetition of the French '*encore*'.[97]

The sense of duration outlined by Deleuze, as well as the prolongation and repetition described by Baker, are at work in *L'eclisse*. As in *Blow-Up*, in whose famous central sequence the quick fire photographs taken by Thomas in the park with his Nikon F camera are held in view for a time long in excess of the fractions of seconds of which they are both indices and representations, the photographic instant is, here too, '*encored*'. It is not only elongated and prolonged, but repeated, as it is not one still photograph, but many, that are filmed. Indeed, while there is a surfacing of the still time of the photographic in *L'eclisse*, the film is not so much *stilled* by this emergence as, rather, I would argue, *slowed down*, over a period of a few minutes during which the camera continues to alternate between the African images and the women. Moreover, the camera does not fix upon the photographs statically. Rather, it zooms leisurely in on them and then lingers, perhaps focusing on a detail, or it gradually reveals their surface by unhurriedly scanning across one or a series of photos pinned next to each other on the wall, as in the shot preceding Vittoria's dressing up. The cumulative effect of the recurrence of the photographs lingered over, zoomed in, panned across, is a still*ing* that does not quite stop the film; it is the production, indeed, of a certain cinematic slowness.

As David Campany has noted, the correct tempo for being or feeling 'modern' underwent a shift roughly mid-way through the last century. Whereas in the first half of the twentieth century to be modern, 'contemporary and progressive' was 'to be reactive, instantaneous, *fast*', in the second half, when the industrial rhythms of mechanical production and reproduction seemed to become dominant and entrenched in all aspects of life, including, as Adorno and Horkheimer considered, the arts and culture, to be modern, as Campany explains, meant 'to be *slow*'.[98] To demonstrate this point, Campany sketches a synoptic genealogy of cinematic 'resistance to speed' that starts with representatives of Italian neorealism, and goes on to include Antonioni, alongside directors such as Ingmar Bergman, Pier Paolo Pasolini, Andrei Tarkovsky and Bela Tarr, as well as experimental filmmakers such as Hollis Frampton and Warhol.[99]

It is worth expanding on Campany's claim for slowness as a marker for being 'modern', and the alignment of intent he suggests across a range of practitioners, by considering briefly the case of Warhol. As the British experimental filmmaker Malcolm Le Grice saw it in the late 1970s, Warhol's filmmaking endeavours from the early 1960s contributed to define a moment when boredom became a 'cinematic principle'.[100] The paradox is evident, for Warhol's cinema, and the early films to which Le Grice is alluding in particular, are in many respects not very cinematic, if not, indeed, provocatively *un*cinematic, and share – and can be seen to take to further extremes – some of the features that prompted Adorno to characterise Antonioni's and other feature cinemas in these terms in the mid-1960s. *Empire* and *Sleep*, the best known among the dozens of films that Warhol made in the early 1960s, may be seen to deliver exactly – and perhaps, on some accounts, no more than – what they promise in their titles, but with unexpected temporal abundance: fixed-camera shots of the Empire State Building in one and of the poet John Giorno sleeping in the other (where in fact we have a montage of shots from different angles, some of them repeated), that continue for several hours. Referring to these early films in a late interview, Warhol said that his 'old stuff is better to talk about than to see. It always sounds better than it really is'.[101] If their withdrawal from circulation in the late 1960s meant that these films could literally not be seen for a couple of decades, even now – when they are widely available as digital files on the Internet – they are probably still more talked about than watched in their entirety. For, if they fulfil the expectation raised by their titles, they also exceed it, presenting us with their subjects for over eight and five hours in a gentle slow-motion effect engendered by the prescribed speed of projection of sixteen frames per second, rather than the standard twenty-four at which they were shot. Outraged when seeing *Sleep* at standard speed, Stan Brakhage was apparently won over when Jonas Mekas convinced him to sit down again and watch it at the required lower rate.[102] What may this slowing down reveal?

While not literally, as in *L'eclisse*, *Blow-Up* and *L'avventura*, Warhol's films too can be seen to stage an encounter between photography and cinema. The overt if not, for 'a movie', seemingly excessive static qualities of films such as *Empire* and *Sleep* in a sense remediates one medium within the other, the photographic within the cinematic. Remediation here may even seem to call into play the idea of a 'reversion' of the moving to the still image. Yet, this convergence, this assimilation between the two media is at once evoked and negated: it is, in a way, permanently 'in process', and suspended, within the films themselves (in whose static shots on seemingly static subject matter, as Cavell might put it, there is always nevertheless a liveness, from the changing appearance of film grain to micro movements or events themselves, such as, in *Empire*, atmospheric changes and city lights going on and off). This is perhaps even better encapsulated by the more than 500 *Screen Tests* that Warhol produced between 1964 and 1966. Length-wise at the opposite end of the spectrum from *Empire* and *Sleep*, these short films are portraits of visitors to the Factory whom Warhol deemed to have a 'star' quality, who would be seated in front of a 16 mm movie camera, fixed on a tripod, and asked to keep as still as possible for the time – approximately three minutes – taken by a 100-foot reel of film to run through the camera at standard sound speed.[103] Among the first to note the 'primitive' qualities of these and other Warhol's films, Mekas argued that Warhol was 'taking cinema back to its origins, to the days of Lumière, for a rejuvenation and a cleansing'.[104] Yet, as the film historian Paul Arthur subsequently retorted, 'the remark does not go far enough. In truth Warhol took cinema back to the dawn of still photography', to the formal stillness required by the long-exposure times of early photographic portraiture and the social function of *cartes-de-visite* as 'passports' to desired milieux.[105] However still the sitters might have tried to be, these prolonged static portraits are riddled with movements, even if only those of breathing, blinking, small twitches, a sniffle or a parting of the lips.

This may be cinema that mimics or approximates photography, yet, precisely at this point, it becomes 'radically distinct' from it, as Deleuze might put it. For, beyond a superficial static quality, Warhol's films move, unfold – and *endure*. While durations such as those of *Empire* and *Sleep* which may be described as monumental in comparison with the average length of feature films in commercial cinema may suggest an inevitable link with the 'long while' of boredom, the crux of the matter, as the relative brevity of the *Screen Tests* helps to bring into relief, is how such duration is structured. This duration is structured not via a substitution of movement with stillness, but through an ongoing tension between the two (as in the attempt to reduce or eliminate 'pro-filmic' and camera movements, or in the reduction of projection speed). It is not incidental, in this respect, that Warhol's cinema is seen as a crucial forerunner of that new tendency in experimental cinema that P. Adams Sitney in his famous essay of 1969 defines as 'structural', and whose 'aesthetic crux', as he writes, is 'the principle of elongation rather than condensation'.[106] With respect to boredom, the consideration of Warhol's aesthetic strategies contributes to draw attention to how the phenomenon might be constituted into a 'cinematic principle', as Le Grice suggests, when cinema becomes, in a way, less like itself, and more, but *not quite*, like the photograph.

While Campany is thinking mainly about cinema – and, indeed, about cinema that may seem to be contaminated by, or in pursuit of, photographic qualities – slowness as a modern gesture comes to be found, at this juncture, even in ostensibly unlikely categories or types of work: such as 'sculpture', for example.

Antonioni almost certainly saw the show of 'programmed' and kinetic art that Bruno Munari curated for Olivetti in 1962, and which was first shown in the company's shop in Milan in May before travelling to Venice, Rome and other venues in Europe and the United States in the mid-1960s. Although famous for its typewriters, the firm, as we saw in Chapter 2, was actively involved in the development of computers during the decade of Italy's economic miracle, when it also started a cultural and art programme of which Munari's show was a part.[107] Not only was Antonioni interested in everything industrial, automated and cybernetic, as I discuss specifically in Chapters 1 and 2, but he also admired Munari's work (he had planned a documentary on the artist's mobile sculptures, the *Macchine inutili* [*Useless Machines*], in the 1940s)[108] and had by the early 1960s become friends with Eco, whose essay in the catalogue for the Olivetti exhibition contains one of the first outlines of the scholar's concept of 'open work'.[109] What interests me here is how the work of Munari and other kinetic artists constituted one of the most innovative, if not daring, developments in art at the time, especially, as in the Olivetti's touring show, with the adoption of electromechanical motors and other devices to introduce movement into 'sculptural' or, as with some of Gianni Colombo's 'moving' surfaces, such as *Superficie pulsante* [*Pulsating Surface*] (1959), 'pictorial' objects. Yet, for all the insistence on kinetics and dynamism, the pace of these works was fairly slow. The hanging *Macchine inutili* are not motored at all: they simply move, lightly and slowly, in response to changes in the air currents in their surrounding environment – if people enter the room, for instance. *Nove sfere in colonna* [*Nine Spheres in a Column*] (1962), the piece which Munari exhibited at the *Arte programmata/Arte cinetica* [*Programmed Art/Kinetic Art*] show in Milan, consists of nine Plexiglass spheres one on top of the other, encased within a see-through cylindrical structure in whose base is hidden a motor. Activation of the motor causes the first sphere to rotate on itself and, through the friction progressively transmitted from one sphere to the one above, the rotation of all the spheres. A short documentary of the show in the Olivetti archive shows a young girl seated and looking up at the piece: the movement is torpid, slow, and the girl looks lulled rather than thrilled.

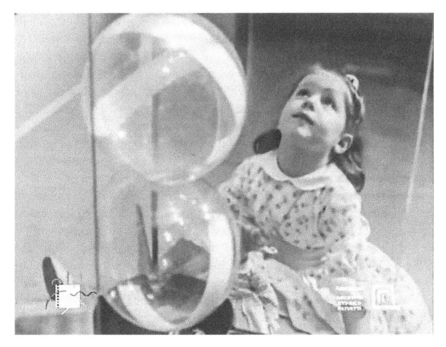

Figure 5.5   Little girl looking at Bruno Munari's *Nove sfere in Colonna* [*Nine Spheres in a Column*] (1962), in Olivetti documentary film of the show (1962)

This is one of the most self-consciously modern and up-to-date forms of art around in the early 1960s, inspired by the cybernetic and technological euphoria of the period; yet, while movement is key, the tempo and dynamics at play are very different from the ones eulogised by the Futurists a couple of generations earlier. This is a trait shared by many of the kinetic artists, of different inspirations, at the time. The Swiss Jean Tinguely, who had set off his kinetic, self-destroying sculpture *Homage to New York* (1960) in the grounds of the Museum of Modern Art at the beginning of the decade, and was to close it with *La vittoria* [*Victory*] (1969), a more monumental self-destructing construction set off in Milan's Cathedral Square, delivered a lecture at the Institute of Contemporary Arts in London in which, though celebrating 'movement', asserted that this was 'static'. 'Be static!', it exhorted, 'Believe in movement's static quality'.[110] The Belgian kinetic artist Pol Bury was somewhat less provocatively paradoxical. In a short manifesto of 1964 entitled 'Time Dilated', he praised that which lay 'between the immobile and mobility': 'slowness'. Revealed as a paradoxical suspension between these antithetical poles, slowness is, for Bury, a *positive* 'quality' that 'dilates' time.[111]

These examples from kinetic art bring into relief a convergence towards the different tempo for being 'modern' of which Campany speaks, even in fields other than cinema. Or, perhaps, they point to intermedial dialogues through which, in the second half of the twentieth century, the medium of movement *par excellence* is rethought by a conspicuous number of filmmakers in terms of a new dynamics and a new pace that seemingly – if not ostentatiously – takes it against its own grain. In many ways, what characterises instances of incorporation of photographic stillness within the moving image, such as the scene in *L'eclisse* or the *Screen Tests*, is precisely a formal tension 'between mobility and immobility' by which time is 'dilated' – made to 'endure' or 'continue' as Deleuze or Baker put it. What is produced is slowness as a paradoxical dynamic of stillness. Additionally, the slowness of *L'eclisse*'s scene can also be seen as a concentrated demonstration of the overall slowness of the film, and of Antonioni's 'new' aesthetic strategies more generally. So, for example, not only, as we have seen, is Vittoria's apartment, like the cut to the photograph re-locating to Marta's, introduced by a protracted shot of a poster on one of its walls, but Vittoria herself is often framed standing still within the frame of a window. And, narratively too, *L'eclisse* is threaded through with the 'pauses' of time, when time itself, as Antonioni put it, is 'slow', 'motionless' or 'appears almost static', and 'apparently, nothing is happening' – from the dialogue-less opening sequence chronicling not 'the end' of a love affair, but the moments just afterwards, to the long concluding one from which the protagonists have vanished – that Antonioni asserted that he 'liked' in films and wanted to include in his own.[112] Where the reaction of Cannes's audience may have been the result of experiencing such tension in *L'avventura*, Adorno noted it in *La notte*, in whose pursuit of the 'uncinematic' within the cinematic, movement was both 'denied and . . . preserved', a paradox through which, as we have seen, the film was, as Adorno put it, empowered to express 'the emptiness of time'.[113] As boredom is a problem of time's abundance and how to fill it, it is precisely *L'eclisse*'s literal remediation of the photographic that encapsulates and discloses the dynamics by which Antonioni's cinema adopts boredom and its heterogeneous, unresolved temporal structure as an aesthetics. Or, as Le Grice suggests in relation to Warhol, boredom is elevated to 'cinematic principle': a slowing down, elongation and dilution of narrative and cinematic time that might also invite boredom, encourage its production in the very act of cinematic consumption.

But a contradiction emerges here. On the one hand, as I have argued, Antonioni's 'modern' films often thematise boredom and even, indeed, seek to visualise it or put it into image in certain scenes as a problem of the occupation of time and visuality in an age of mass consumerism and mass media. Yet, on the other, these very same films court an aesthetic (re)production of boredom. As I have suggested, the same photographic imagery that helps to represent or visualise boredom diegetically is also mobilised to articulate it formally in the aesthetics of the film and perhaps promote it in the viewer. But if boredom is made manifest within, and as a reaction to, the distractions of mass culture and the culture industry, why would a cinema that poses itself as different in some way – as an instantiation of the medium at the 'high-quality' or 'art' end of its spectrum – court boredom in its turn? The way in which Antonioni's films, through a paradoxical dynamic of stillness, may seek to weave boredom in cinematic form and elicit it as an experiential response to cinema points to a valorisation of boredom as a possible form of resistance and critique, rather than as something to be resisted and critiqued.

In most reflections, boredom itself is not one and 'static' but, rather, is understood as itself a temporal condition that may develop into different moments or levels of intensity. Within its recursive yet heterogeneous manifestation there is, in other words, a 'narrative' of boredom, wherein the condition may tip from negative to positive connotations. Not unlike Heidegger, who subdivided boredom into three different levels, from a more superficial to a 'profound' form, Kracauer distinguished between 'the vulgar boredom of daily drudgery' and 'real boredom': where the former pushes people 'deeper and deeper into the hustle and bustle until eventually they no longer know where their head is', the latter is 'the extraordinary, radical boredom that might be able to reunite them with their head'.[114] While the lower form of boredom is coupled with distractions (such as, in Kracauer's account, advertisement, movies, radio, or, in Heidegger, waiting for a train or spending the evening at a party) which both seemingly alleviate it and produce it, the more radical from of boredom, for which, as Kracauer points out, one needs 'patience', entails distraction in another way: one becomes profoundly absorbed in one's own boredom. Boredom itself, that is, becomes *the* distraction and 'occupation'.[115] If the lower – or 'bad' – forms of boredom imply a loss in the objective world, in the external world of objects, this radical – and 'good' – form of boredom is a loss into oneself. Here is how Benjamin describes it:

> Boredom is a warm grey fabric lined on the inside with the most lustrous and colourful of silks. In this fabric we wrap ourselves when we dream. We are at home in the arabesque of its lining. But the sleeper looks bored and grey within his sheath. And when he later wakes and wants to tell of what he dreamed, he communicates by and large only this boredom. For who would be able at one stroke to turn the lining of time to the outside?[116]

The non-pejorative, almost desirable terms in which Benjamin describes boredom in the convoluted description above as a luxuriously textured fabric is in many ways echoed by Bazin, who, addressing boredom specifically as a spectatorial response to cinema, talks of it as 'a time that can be embroidered'.[117] Bazin makes these reflections on boredom and its time writing about Charlie Chaplin's *Limelight* (1952), by which he confesses to having been 'bored' at points, during each of the three times he saw it. Yet, as he adds, he 'never wished for any shortening of these periods of boredom. It was rather a relaxing of attention'.[118] As Karl Schoonover and Rosalind Galt, who discuss Bazin's text at length, suggest, the critic's reflections on his reaction to Chaplin's film posit 'the political productivity of boredom as a mode of spectatorial practice' that 'opens up time'.[119] In other words, boredom emerges, as Schoonover has put it elsewhere, as a 'special kind of work', an activity where consumption may turn into production, while resisting traditional understandings of both (and veering perhaps towards the state that Jacques Rancière described as 'free play').[120] Intriguingly, Antonioni's 'modern' cinema may succeed in stimulating the 'good' viewer's boredom that 'opens up time' and engenders a 'relaxing of attention' precisely through a representation of the 'bad' boredom of consumer capitalism, and with the very mass media often called upon to alleviate it. A cinematic critique of boredom that itself produces boredom as a form of critique.

This uncinematic provocation, then, emerges as another manifestation of what this book has called the aesthetics of impurity of Antonioni's cinema. At a first level, this aesthetics simply demonstrates that 'constant interplay' with an *other* from which *any* medium, as McLuhan put it, gains 'meaning or existence'.[121] But as complex engagements of those (mass) media and art forms in which, as Bazin suggested, cinema must 'irrigate its banks' in order not to dry up, this aesthetics is also a strategy of renewal – and, indeed, a strategy of renewal through intermedial dialogue in a cinema that is so often upheld as exemplary of a purification of the medium.[122] And most captivatingly and significantly perhaps, as this impure aesthetics deploys a tension between resistance and absorption, it affords both a critical exploration of the forms other than cinema it engages with and a self-critique of cinema itself: an intermediality at once critical and reflexive.

NOTES

1. Nowell-Smith, *Making Waves*, p.159. See also, for example, Nowell-Smith, *L'avventura*; Rascaroli and Rhodes, 'Interstitial, Pretentious, Alienated, Dead', esp. pp. 3–4; and Betz, *Beyond the Subtitle*, esp. pp. 5–6.
2. See, for example, Nowell-Smith, *Making Waves*, p. 159.
3. Metz, *Film Language*, p.185.
4. Andrew, 'The Stature of Objects in Antonioni's Films', p. 40.
5. Adorno, 'Transparencies on Film' (first published in *Die Zeit*, 18 November 1966), p. 201.
6. This is in part the argument that Deleuze makes in his *Cinema* books, and *Cinema II* in particular, as will be discussed further in what follows.
7. Antonioni, 'A Talk with Michelangelo Antonioni on His Work', p. 23.
8. Antonioni, 'A Talk', p. 26. Antonioni's project is of course related to neorealism's pursuit of the ordinary and the everyday. His early documentaries *Gente del Po* (*People of the Po*, shot 1942–3; edited and released 1947) and *Nettezza Urbana* (*N. U.*,1948) informed, and were informed by, the neorealist programme and aesthetics. However, Antonioni's focus in the later films is significantly different from neorealism. Where the latter aimed to highlight the tragedies to be found *within* the lives of ordinary people (as Zavattini once put it, 'I'm interested in the dramas of things we happen to encounter, not those we plan') Antonioni sought to show that the real problem was, in a way, the very absence of drama. See Zavattini, 'Some Ideas on the Cinema', p. 69. For a discussion of the ways in which neorealism's emphasis on the ordinary may be seen to inform the aesthetics of boredom of 1960s and 1970s filmmaking, see Margulies, *Nothing Happens*, esp. ch.1.
9. Antonioni, 'A Talk', p. 26.
10. Ibid., p. 25.
11. Tassone, 'Conversation', p. 237.
12. Mitry, *The Aesthetics and Psychology of the Cinema*, p. 362.
13. Ibid.
14. Sarris, 'No Antoniennui', where in fact he wrote enthusiastically about *Blow-Up* and its avoidance of what he saw as the filmmaker's characteristic form of *ennui*.
15. Kael, 'Are Movies Going to Pieces? (originally in *The Atlantic Monthly*, December 1964), p. 351.
16. Warhol and Hackett, *Popism*, p. 50.

17. 'If something is boring after two minutes', Cage suggested, 'try it for four. If still boring, try it for eight, sixteen, thirty-two and so on.' In Cage, *Silence*, p. 93. The quote appears as a filler in the book, but is part of the one-minute stories constitutive of Cage's 'Lecture on Indeterminacy', first performed in Brussels in 1958. Consisting of thirty such stories initially, the performative lecture had tripled to ninety by the following year, when performed in the United States.

18. Ibid.: 'Eventually one discovers that it's not boring at all but very interesting.'

19. Sontag, 'One Culture and the New Sensibility' (first published in abridged form in *Mademoiselle*, 1965), p. 303.

20. See Dalle Pezze and Salzani, *Essays on Boredom and Modernity*; Goodstein. *Experience without Qualities*; Svendsen *A Philosophy of Boredom*; Toohey, *Boredom: A Lively History*; Meyer Spacks, *Boredom: The Literary History of a State of Mind*; Martin, Sadlo and Stew, 'The Phenomenon of Boredom'.

21. See, for example, Koepnick, *On Slowness* and de Luca and Barradas Jorge, *Slow Cinema*. Within this broader area of inquiry, for positions more sympathetic towards boredom, and which suggest its potential as critique or form of resistance, see Schoonover, 'Wastrels of Time'; and Fujiwara 'Boredom, *Spasmo*, and the Italian System'.

22. Remes, *Motion(less) Pictures*, pp. 53 and 40.

23. Betz, *Beyond the Subtitle*, p. 174.

24. See Mónica Cejas, 'Tourism "Back in Time"', pp. 121–34.

25. Adorno, *Aesthetic Theory*, p. 5.

26. Adorno, 'Transparencies on Film', pp. 200–1.

27. Phillips, *On Kissing, Tickling, and Being Bored*, p. 68.

28. Moravia, *La noia*, pp. 14–16. Initially published in English under the title *The Empty Canvas* (1961), the novel has more recently been republished under the title *Boredom* (1999).

29. Ibid., p. 19.

30. Ross, *Fast Cars, Clean Bodies*, p. 7 (my emphasis).

31. Dickens might have coined the term in *Bleak House* (1852) (e.g. pp. 324 and 128). In French, Flaubert modified the older '*ennui*' with the adjective '*moderne*', and Baudelaire opted for the English 'spleen'. See, for example, Healy, *Boredom: Self and Culture*, p. 28ff.

32. Goodstein describes it as 'less a new feeling than a new way of feeling', *Experience Without Qualities*, p. 3.

33. Ibid., p. 7.

34. Dalle Pezze and Salzani, *Essays on Boredom and Modernity*, p. 12. Toohey, *Boredom*, provides an exception to the historicist view.

35. Goodstein, *Experience without Qualities*, p. 18.

36. Benjamin, *The Arcades Project*, p. 108.

37. Blanchot, 'Everyday Speech', p. 16.

38. For a discussion of boredom in terms of gender, and as a feminist question, see Petro, 'Historical *Ennui*, Feminist Boredom'; Pease, *Modernism, Feminism and the Culture of Boredom*, esp. ch. 1.

39. See, for example, Lefebvre, *The Critique of Everyday Life*, vol. 2, p. 75. A fully-fledged sociology or analysis of the condition is not carried out in the volumes, but Gardiner, in 'Henri Lefebvre and the 'Sociology of Boredom', has argued that this can be pieced together looking across his oeuvre.

40. Flatley, 'Allegories of Boredom', p. 53.

41. Adorno and Horkheimer, 'The Culture Industry: Enlightenment as Mass Deception'.

42. See Benjamin's famous essay 'The Work of Art in the Age of Mechanical Reproduction', esp. pp. 233–4.

43. Benjamin, *The Arcades Project*, p. 111.

44. Simmel, 'The Metropolis and Mental Life', p. 413.

45. Ibid., p. 414.

46. Adorno, 'Free Time', p. 166.

47. Petro 'After Shock/Between Boredom and History,' p. 265.

48. Ibid. See also Hansen, 'America, Paris, the Alps'.

49. Kracauer, 'The Cult of Distraction', pp. 323, 325.

50. Arendt, *The Human Condition*, p. 131, pp. 149–53; Braverman, *Labour and Monopoly* Capital.

51. Ottiero Ottieri, 'Automazione', p. 149. Ottieri's autobiographical novel Donnarumma all'assalto, on his experience and observation of mechanised labour at Pozzuoli's Olivetti's plant in the late-1950s as a 'human-resources' consultant, was also published in 1959 and inspired Red Desert. The novel appeared in English as *At the Gate*.

52. Morin, *L'Esprit du temps*, pp. 85–6. At around the same time, Roberto Rossellini's expressed a more utopian view of the expansion of free time and the concomitant diffusion of television as a tool of knowledge and discovery. See Rossellini, 'Cinema: Nuove prospettive di conoscenza'. Cramer, *Utopian Television*, explores Rossellini's hopes for the medium.

53. Fenichel, 'On the Psychology of Boredom', pp. 300–1. Fenichel is also in fact drawing on an earlier paper by Ferenczi, 'Sunday Neurosis', who had first drawn attention to the phenomenon.

54. Fenichel, 'On the Psychology of Boredom', p. 301.

55. Quoted in Gidal, *Andy Warhol: Films and Paintings*, p. 84.

56. Morin, *L'Esprit du temps*, p. 93.

57. Adorno, 'Free Time', pp. 163, 165.

58. Adorno, 'The Culture Industry', p. 137; 'Free Time', p. 163, 165.

59. Moravia, *La noia*, p. 7.

60. Lefebvre, *Critique of Everyday Life*, vol. 1, pp. 32–3.

61. Morin, *L'Esprit du temps*, pp. 9 and 90.

62. Bellotto, 'Il teleschermo nuovo focolare'. For a study of television and domesticity, see Spigel, 'Media Home: Then and Now', as well as her book *Make Room for TV*.

63. Eco, 'Verso una civiltà della visione'. See also *Almanacco letterario Bompiani* 1963, dedicated to the 'civilisation of the image'. It is, however, in these same years that McLuhan, in *The Gutenberg Galaxy*, begins to think of the emergence

of television as a steering away from the predominance of visuality in culture, and a move towards aurality.

64. Roberts, *The Art of Interruption*, p. 14. A more recent correlation is discussed by Shinkle, 'Boredom, Repetition, Inertia'.

65. Blanchot, 'Everyday Speech', p. 16.

66. Ibid., p. 18.

67. Lefebvre refers to Debord in *Critique of Everyday Life*, vol. 2, p. 11. See also, for example, Debord, 'Perspectives de modifications coscientes dans la vie quotidienne', where 'everyday life' is termed 'a colonised sector' (p. 22), and Morin, *L' Esprit du temps* on 'the second colonization . . . [which] enters that grand reserve which is the human soul' (p. 9).

68. Ross, *Fast Cars, Clean Bodies*, p. 7. For broader discussions, see, among others, Scrivano, 'Signs of Americanization in Italian Domestic Life'; McKenzie, *Remaking France*; Fritsche, *American Marshall Plan Film Campaigns and the Europeans*; Mansoor, *Marshall Plan Modernism*.

69. Ross, *Fast Cars, Clean Bodies*, p. 7.

70. Ibid., p.77. See also Huyssen's now classic essay 'Mass Culture as Woman'.

71. Pinkus, 'Empty Spaces', pp. 308 and 309 cited.

72. Betz, *Beyond the Subtitle*, p. 170.

73. Ibid., p. 96.

74. Italy's post-war trusteeship over its former colony in Somalia came to an end in 1960 with the declaration of the country's independence. In the aforementioned episodes of *Anni d'Europa*, Italy was presented as 'a fair coloniser' and decolonisation as a conflict-free, diplomatic and relatively unproblematic process. See Deplano, 'Decolonisation Will Be Televised'.

75. Betz, *Beyond the Subtitle*, p. 175.

76. Morin, *L'Esprit du temps*, p. 89.

77. Ibid., p. 247.

78. Adorno, 'Free Time', p. 166.

79. In a well-known essay of 1935, 'Mimicry and Legendary Psychastenia', Roger Caillois described acts of mimicry as a kind of photography.

80. Henning, *Photography*, pp. 111–15. For a broader discussion, see Maxwell, *Colonial Photography*; Behdad and Gartlan, *Photography's Orientalism*. In relation to Italy specifically, see Farnetti and Novelli, *Images of colonialism and decolonisation in the Italian Media*; Giuliani, *Race, Nation and Gender in Modern Italy*.

81. In the film, this moment is presented as part of the footage that Locke's wife is being shown, having been informed of her husband's alleged death (which he has in fact faked to embrace the opportunity of a new identity).

82. See, for example, Kracauer, 'Boredom'; Benjamin, *The Arcades Project* (esp. pp. 107ff.); Fenichel, 'On the Psychology of Boredom'; Heidegger, *The Fundamental Concepts of Metaphysics* (ch. 2).

83. For a discussion of Warhol and boredom alternative to the one I pursue here, see Svendsen, *A Philosophy of Boredom*, pp. 100–6.

84. Warhol and Hackett, *POPism*, p. 50.

85. Moravia, *La noia*, p. 7.
86. Benjamin, 'Some Motifs in Baudelaire', p. 180.
87. Adorno, *Aesthetic Theory*, p. 5.
88. Bolter and Grusin, *Remediation*.
89. See Doane, *The Emergence of Cinematic Time*; Sutton, *Photography, Cinema, Memory*; Green and Lowry, *Stillness and Time*; Beckman and Ma, *StillMoving*.
90. Bazin, 'The Ontology of the Photographic Image', pp. 14–15.
91. Bellour, 'The Film Stilled', p. 105 cited. Mulvey's *Death 24 x Second* responds to and develops Bellour's reflection.
92. Bellour, 'The Film Stilled', p. 108.
93. Ibid.
94. Cavell, *The World Viewed*, p. 202.
95. Deleuze, *Cinema II*, p. 17 (my emphasis); Nardelli 'End(ur)ing Photography'.
96. Deleuze, *Cinema II*, p. 17.
97. Baker, 'Re-Animations (I)', p. 34. Baker's article is on the films and slide-projections of James Coleman. He draws on Silverman's essay 'Growing Still', which reflects on the double use of the word 'still' in one of Coleman's works.
98. Campany, 'Introduction', p.10. See also Koepnick, *On Slowness*.
99. Campany, *The Cinematic*, p. 11.
100. Le Grice, *Abstract Film and Beyond*, p. 121.
101. O'Brian, 'Interview: Andy Warhol' (first in *High Times*, August 1977), p. 247. On Warhol's dissatisfaction with his films, see also Koestenbaum, *Andy Warhol*, p. 56.
102. Jonas Mekas, 'Notes After Re-seeing the Films of Andy Warhol', in John Coplans (ed.), *Andy Warhol* (New York: New York Graphic Society, 1970), pp. 28–30.
103. See Angel, *Andy Warhol's Screen Test* and Arthur, 'No Longer Absolute', which discusses them within the genre of the 'portrait film' (esp. pp. 106–9). See also Smith, *Andy Warhol's Art and Films*, pp. 154–6.
104. Mekas, 'The Independent Film Award' (originally a speech for the Sixth Award, 1964), p. 427.
105. Arthur, 'No Longer Absolute', p. 107. Benjamin, in a 'A Small History of Photography' suggests that, because of the long exposure time, 'the subject as it were grew into the picture', pp. 245 and 247.
106. Sitney 'Structural Film', p. 335.
107. Rubino, 'Bruno Munari Versus Programmed Art'; Caplan, 'From Collective Creation to Creating Collectives'.
108. Quaresima, 'Making Love on the Shores of the Rivero Po', p. 119. The reference to this unrealised film also appears in Di Carlo, *Il primo Antonioni*, pp. 15–16 and in Di Carlo, *Il mio Antonioni*, p. 350.
109. Antonioni was a friend of both Eco and Munari, and Eco wrote the essay for the Olivetti show, one of the places in which he first outlined his notion of 'open work' ['*opera aperta*']. The *Almanacco Letterario Bompiani* for 1962, for which Munari provided the graphics and curated a 'paper' exhibition in the central section, had been dedicated to cybernetics.

110. Hultén, *Jean Tinguely – Méta*, p. 107. During a 'cyclo-matic' evening at the Institute of Contemporary Arts in London on 16 November 1959, on the occasion of his solo exhibition at the Kaplan Gallery, Tinguely was invited to give a lecture, billed as 'Art, Machines, and Motion: a Lecture by Tinguely'.
111. Bury, 'Time Dilated', p. 107.
112. Tassone, 'Conversation', p. 237.
113. Adorno, 'Transparencies on Film', p. 156.
114. Kracauer, 'Boredom', p. 331; Heidegger, *The Fundamental Concepts of Metaphysics*, pp. 97, 160. See also Misek, 'Dead Time: Cinema, Heidegger and Boredom'.
115. Kracauer, 'Boredom', p. 332.
116. Benjamin, *The Arcades Project*, pp. 105–6.
117. Bazin, 'The Grandeur of *Limelight*', quoted by Schoonover and Galt in *Queer Cinema in the World*, p. 284.
118. Ibid.
119. Ibid., p. 284.
120. Schoonover, 'Wastrels of Time', pp. 70–3; Rancière, *Aesthetics and Its Discontents*, p. 27.
121. McLuhan, *Understanding Media*, p. 35.
122. Bazin, 'In Defense of Mixed Cinema', p. 74.

Bibliography

Adorno, Theodor W., *Aesthetic Theory* [1970], trans. Robert Hollot-Kentor (Minneapolis: University of Minnesota Press, 1997).

Adorno, Theodor W. and Max Horkheimer, 'The Culture Industry: Enlightenment as Mass Deception', in *Dialectic of Enlightenment* [1944], trans. John Cumming (London: Verso, 1997), pp. 120–67.

Adorno, Theodor W., 'Free Time' [1969], trans. Thomas Y. Levin, in *The Culture Industry: Selected Essays on Mass Culture*, ed. J. M. Bernstein (London: Routledge, 1993), pp. 162–70.

Adorno, Theodor W., 'How to Look at Television', *The Quarterly of Film Radio and Television*, 8/3 (Spring 1954), pp. 213–35.

Adorno, Theodor W., 'Transparencies on Film' [1966], trans. Thomas Y. Levin, *New German Critique*, 24/25, Special Double Issue on New German Cinema (Autumn–Winter 1981–2), pp. 199–205.

Agamben, Giorgio, 'What Is the Contemporary?', in *'What is an apparatus?' and Other Essays*, trans. David Kishik and Stefan Pedatella (Stanford: Stanford University Press, 2009), pp. 40–54.

Allison, David, 'Photography and the Mass Market', in Colin Ford (ed.), *The Kodak Museum: The Story of Popular Photography* (London: Century Hutchinson, 1989) pp. 42–59.

Alloway, Lawrence, *The Venice Biennale 1895–1968: From Salon to Goldfish Bowl* (London: Faber and Faber, 1969).

Ameline, Jean-Paul, *Lex Nouveaux Réalistes* (Paris: Centre Georges Pompidou, 1992).

Andrew, J. Dudley, 'The Stature of Objects in Antonioni's Films', *TriQuarterly* 11 (Winter 1968), pp. 40–61.

Anelli, Maria Teresa, Paola Gabbrielli, Marta Morgavi and Roberto Piperno, *Fotoromanzo: fascino e pregiudizio. Storia, documenti e immagini di un grande fenomeno popolare (1948–1979)* (Milan: Savelli, 1979).

Anfam, David, *Mark Rothko: The Work on Canvas Catalogue Raisonnée* (New Haven: Yale, 1998).

Angel, Callie, *Andy Warhol's Screen Tests: Catalogue Raisonné* (New York: Harry Abrams, 2006).

Anon., 'Questions à Antonioni', *Positif: Revue de Cinéma* 30 (July 1959), pp. 7–10.

Antonello, Pierpaolo, *Il menage a quattro* (Florence: Le monnier, 2005).

Antonioni, Michelangelo, Bernardo Bertolucci, Pier Paolo Pasolini, Gillo Pontecorovo et al., 'Amalfi Manifesto' [1967], in Scott McKenzie (ed.), *Film Manifestos and Global*

Cinema Cultures: A Critical Anthology (Berkeley: University of California Press, 2014), p. 572.

Antonioni, Michelangelo, 'Apropos of Eroticism' [1967], in Michelangelo Antonioni, *The Architecture of Vision: Writings and Interviews on Cinema*, ed. Carlo Di Carlo, Giorgio Tinazzi and Marga Cottino-Jones (Chicago: University of Chicago Press, 2007), pp. 148–67.

Antonioni, Michelangelo, *The Architecture of Vision: Writings and Interviews on Cinema*, ed. Carlo Di Carlo, Giorgio Tinazzi and Marga Cottino-Jones (Chicago: University of Chicago Press, 2007).

Antonioni, Michelangelo, *Blow-Up* (Turin: Einaudi, 1968).

Antonioni, Michelangelo, 'Conclusioni sul doppiato' [1941], in Michelangelo Antonioni, *Sul cinema*, ed. Carlo Di Carlo (Venice: Marsilio, 2004), pp. 162–4.

Antonioni, Michelangelo, 'Del colore' [1942], in Michelangelo Antonioni, *Sul cinema*, ed. Carlo Di Carlo (Venice: Marsilio, 2004), pp. 185–7.

Antonioni, Michelangelo, 'Dichiarazioni di Michelangelo Antonioni', *Cinema* 60 (October 1964), pp. 63–4.

Antonioni, Michelangelo, *Fare un film è per me vivere. Scritti sul cinema*, ed. Carlo Di Carlo and Giorgio Tinazzi (Venice: Marsilio, 2009).

Antonioni, Michelangelo, 'From a Thirty-Seventh Floor Over Central Park: Soundtrack for a Film in New York' [1961], in Michelangelo Antonioni, *That Bowling Alley on the Tiber*, trans. William Arrowsmith (New York and Oxford: Oxford University Press, 1986), pp. 189–94.

Antonioni, Michelangelo, *Il deserto rosso* (Bologna: Cappelli 1964).

Antonioni, Michelangelo, 'Il mondo è fuori dalla finestra' [1975], in Michelangelo Antonioni, *Fare un film è per me vivere. Scritti sul cinema*, ed. Carlo Di Carlo and Giorgio Tinazzi (Venice: Marsilio, 2009), pp. 156–65.

Antonioni, Michelangelo, 'La malattia dei sentimenti' [1961], in Michelangelo Antonioni, *Fare un film è per me vivere. Scritti sul cinema*, ed. Carlo Di Carlo and Giorgio Tinazzi (Venice: Marsilio, 2009), pp. 20–46.

Antonioni, Michelangelo, *Le Montagne incantate* (Venice: Electa/Edizioni Biennale di Venezia, 1983).

Antonioni, Michelangelo, 'Let's Talk about *Zabriskie Point*' [1970], in Michelangelo Antonioni, *The Architecture of Vision: Writings and Interviews on Cinema*, ed. Carlo Di Carlo, Giorgio Tinazzi and Marga Cottino-Jones (Chicago: University of Chicago Press, 2007), pp. 94–106.

Antonioni, Michelangelo, 'Letter to Rothko' (27 May 1962), in Oliver Wick (ed.), *Mark Rothko* (Milan and London: Skira and Thames & Hudson, 2007), p. 55.

Antonioni, Michelangelo, 'On Color' [1942], trans. Marguerite Shore, *October* 128 (Spring 2009), pp. 111–20.

Antonioni, Michelangelo, 'Pazienza del cinema' [1949], in Michelangelo Antonioni, *Sul cinema*, ed. Carlo Di Carlo and Giorgio Tinazzi (Venice: Marsilio, 2004), pp. 148–53.

Antonioni, Michelangelo, 'Per un film sul fiume Po', *Cinema* (25 April 1939), pp. 254–7.

Antonioni, Michelangelo, 'Preface to Six Films' [1964], in Michelangelo Antonioni, *The Architecture of Vision: Writings and Interviews on Cinema*, ed. Carlo Di Carlo, Giorgio Tinazzi and Marga Cottino-Jones (Chicago: University of Chicago Press, 2007), pp. 57–68.

Antonioni, Michelangelo, *Quel bowling sul Tevere* (Turin: Einaudi, 1983).

Antonioni, Michelangelo, *Sei film* (Turin: Einaudi, 1964).

Antonioni, Michelangelo, 'The Silence' [c. 1950?], in Michelangelo Antonioni, *That Bowling Alley on the Tiber: Tales of a Director*, trans. William Arrowsmith (New York and Oxford: Oxford University Press, 1986), pp. 23–6.

Antonioni, Michelangelo, *Sul cinema*, ed. Carlo Di Carlo (Venice: Marsilio, 2004).

Antonioni, Michelangelo, 'A Talk with Antonioni on His Work' in Michelangelo Antonioni' [1961], *The Architecture of Vision: Writings and Interviews on Cinema*, ed. Marga Cottino Jones (Chicago: University of Chicago Press, 2007), pp. 21–47.

Antonioni, Michelangelo, *Tecnicamente dolce*, ed. Aldo Tassone (Turin: Einaudi, 1976).

Antonioni, Michelangelo, *That Bowling Alley on the Tiber: Tales of a Director*, trans. William Arrowsmith (New York and Oxford: Oxford University Press, 1986).

Antonioni, Michelangelo, *Unfinished business: Screenplays, Scenerios, and Ideas*, ed. Carlo Di Carlo and Giorgio Tinazzi, trans. Andrew Taylor (New York: Marsilio, 1998).

Antonioni, Michelangelo, 'Vita impossibile del signore Clark Costa' [1940], in Michelangelo Antonioni, *Sul cinema* (Venice: Marsilio, 2004), pp. 155–60.

Arendt, Hannah, *The Human Condition* [1958], (Chicago: University of Chicago Press, 1970).

Aristarco, Guido, 'Literary Cinema' [1961], in Pierre Leprohon (ed.), *Michelangelo Antonioni: An Introduction* [1961] trans. Scott Sullivan (New York: Simon and Schuster, 1963), pp. 160–2.

Arnheim, Rudolf, 'Film and Reality' [1933], in *Film as Art* (Berkeley: University of California Press, 1957), pp. 8–33.

Arnheim, Rudolf, 'The New Laocoön', Artistic Composites and the Talking Film' [1938], in *Film as Art* (Berkeley: University of California Press, 1957), pp. 199–230.

Arnheim, Rudolf, *Film as Art* (Berkeley: University of California Press, 1957).

Arrowsmith, William, *Antonioni: The Poet of Images* (Oxford: Oxford University Press, 1995).

Arrowsmith, William, 'Translator's Preface', in Michelangelo Antonioni, *That Bowling Alley on the Tiber: Tales of a Director* (New York and Oxford: Oxford University Press, 1986).

Arthur, Paul, *A Line of Sight: American Avant-Garde Film Since 1965* (Minneapolis: University of Minnesota Press, 2005).

Arthur, Paul, 'No Longer Absolute: Portraiture in American Avant-Garde Documentary Films of the Sixties', in Ivone Margulies (ed.), *Rites of Realism: Essays on Corporeal Cinema* (Durham NC: Duke University Press, 2003), pp. 93–118.

Asaro, Peter M., 'From Mechanisms of Adaptation to Intelligence Amplifiers: The Philosophy of W. Ross Ashby', in Philip Husbands, Owen Holland and Michael Wheeler (eds.), *The Mechanical Mind in History* (Cambridge MA: MIT, 2008), pp. 149–84.

Ashby, William Ross, *Design for a Brain* (London: Chapman and Hall, 1952).

Ashby, William Ross, 'Design for a Brain', *Electronic Engineering* 20 (December 1948), pp. 379–83.

Ashby, William Ross, 'Homeostasis' [1952], in Claus Pias (ed.), *Cybernetics. The Macy Conferences 1946–1953: Complete Transactions* (Zurich: Diaphanes, 2003), pp. 593–619.

Ashby, William Ross, 'Simulation of a Brain' [1962], in Harold Borko (ed.), *Computer Applications in the Behavioural Sciences* (London: Prentice Hall, 1962), pp. 452–66.

Ashton, Dore, *About Rothko* (Oxford: Oxford University Press, 1983).

Associazione Archivio Storico Olivetti, 'Alle origini del personal computer: l'Olivetti Programma 101', <https://www.storiaolivetti.it/articolo/39-elettronica-della-olivetti-p101-e-dei-piccoli-s/> (last accessed January 2020).

Badiou, Alain, 'The False Movement of Cinema' [1994], in *Handbook of Inaesthetics*, trans. Alberto Toscano (Stanford: Stanford University Press, 2005), pp. 78–88.

Baker, George, 'Re-Animations (I)', *October* (Spring 2003), pp. 28–70.

Balázs, Bela, *Theory of the film: Character and Growth of a New Art)* [1930], trans. Edith Bone (London: Dobson, 1952).

Ballard, J. G., 'The Sound-Sweep' [1960], in *The Voices of Time* [1961] (London: Phoenix, 1992), pp. 41–79.

Balsom, Erika, *After Uniqueness: A History of Film and Video Art in Circulation* (New York: Columbia University Press, 2017).

Barad, Karen, *Meeting the Universe Half-Way: Quantum Physics and the Entanglement of Matter and Meaning* (Durham NC: Duke University Press, 2007).

Barbaro, Umberto, *Poesia del film* [1955] (Rome: Bulzoni, 1999).

Barker, Rachel and Browny Ormsby, 'Conserving Rothko's *Black on Maroon* 1958: The Construction of a "Representative Sample" and the Removal of Graffiti Ink', *Tate Papers* 23 (Spring 2015), <https://www.tate.org.uk/research/publications/tate-papers/23/conserving-mark-rothkos-black-on-maroon-1958-the-construction-of-a-representative-sample-and-the-removal-of-graffiti-ink> (last accessed 19 March 2019).

Barker, Timothy, *Against Transmission: Media Philosophy and the Engineering of Time* (London: Bloomsbury, 2018).

Barthes, Roland (with Roland Havas), 'Listening' [1976], in *The Responsibility of Form*, trans. Richard Howard (Berkeley: University of California Press, 1991), pp. 245–60.

Batchen, Geoffrey, 'Dissemination' (2012) <https://www.fotomuseum.ch/en/explore/still-searching/articles/26929_dissemination> (last accessed 15 April 2019).

Baudry, Jean-Louis, 'Ideological Effects of the Basic Cinematographic Apparatus' [1970], trans. Alan Williams, *Film Quarterly*, vol. 28, 2 (Winter 1974–5), pp. 39–47.

Bazin, André, 'In Defense of Mixed Cinema' [1951], in André Bazin, *What Is Cinema?*, trans. Hugh Gray, vol. 1 (Berkeley: University of California Press, 1967), pp. 53–75.

Bazin, André, 'The Grandeur of *Limelight*' [1953], in André Bazin, *What Is Cinema?*, trans. Hugh Gray, vol. 2 (Berkeley: University of California Press, 1967), pp. 128–39.

Bazin, André, 'The Ontology of the Photographic Image' [1945], in André Bazin, *What Is Cinema?* trans. Hugh Gray, vol. 1 (Berkeley: University of California Press, 1967), pp. 9–16.

Bazin, André, 'Painting and Cinema' [1943–51], in André Bazin, *What Is Cinema?*, trans. Hugh Gray, vol. 1 (Berkeley: University of California Press, 1967), pp. 164–9.

Beckman, Karen and Jean Ma (eds), *StillMoving: Between Cinema and Photography* (Durham NC: Duke University Press, 2008).

Beegan, Gerry, *The Mass Image: A Social History of Photomechanical Reproduction in Victorian London* (Basingstoke: Palgrave Macmillan, 2008).

Bellotto, Adriano, 'Il teleschermo nuovo focolare', *Pirelli. Rivista d'informazione e di tecnica* (January–February 1961), pp. 48–53.

Bellotto, Adriano, *La television inutile* (Milan: Comunità, 1962).

Bellour, Raymond, 'The Film Stilled', trans. Alison Rowe and Elisabeth Lyon, *Camera Obscura* 24 (1990), pp. 99–123.

Benci, Jacopo, '"All that is Behind Colour": Antonioni and Painting (three case studies)', *Journal of Contemporary Painting* 1/1 (2015), pp. 65–89.

Benjamin, Walter, *The Arcades Project* [1927–40], trans. Howard Eiland and Kevin McLaughlin (Cambridge MA: The Belknap Press, 1999).

Benjamin, Walter, 'A Small History of Photography' [1931], in *One-Way Street and Other Writings*, trans. Edmund Jephcott (London: Verso, 2000), pp. 240–57.

Benjamin, Walter, 'Some Motifs in Baudelaire' [1939], in *Illuminations*, trans. Harry Zorn (London: Pimlico, 1999), pp. 152–96.

Benjamin, Walter, 'The Work of Art in the Age of Mechanical Reproduction' [1936], in Walter Benjamin, *Illuminations*, trans. Harry Zorn (London: Pimlico, 1999), pp. 211–44.

Bergson, Henri, *Time and Free Will: An Essay on the Immediate Data of Consciousness* [1889] (London: Routledge, 2014).

Berio, Luciano, 'Agli amici degli "Incontri musicali"' [1958], in Luciano Berio, *Scritti sulla musica*, ed. Angela Ida de Benedictis (Turin: Einaudi, 2013), pp. 14–17.

Berio, Luciano, 'Commenti al rock' [1967], in Luciano Berio, *Scritti sulla musica*, ed. Angela Ida de Benedictis (Turin: Einaudi, 2013), pp. 108–20.

Berio, Luciano, 'La nuova musicalità' [c. 1956, previously unpublished], in Luciano Berio, *Scritti sulla musica*, ed. Angela Ida de Benedictis (Turin: Einaudi, 2013), pp. 7–13.

Berio, Luciano, 'Musica per *Tape Recorder*' [1953], in Luciano Berio, *Scritti sulla musica*, ed. Angela Ida de Benedictis (Turin: Einaudi, 2013), pp. 173–9.

Berio, Luciano, 'Note sulla musica elettronica' [1957], in Luciano Berio, *Scritti sulla musica*, ed. Angela Ida de Benedictis (Turin: Einaudi, 2013), pp. 196–209.

Berio, Luciano, 'Prospettive nella muisca. Richerche e attività dello Studio di Fonologia Musicale di Radio Milano' [1956], in Luciano Berio, *Scritti sulla musica*, ed. Angela Ida de Benedictis (Turin: Einaudi, 2013), pp. 180–95.

Berio, Luciano, *Scritti sulla musica*, ed. Angela Ida de Benedictis (Turin: Einaudi, 2013).

Bernardini, Aldo, *Michelangelo Antonioni da Gente del Po a Blow-Up* (Milan: Edizioni i 7, 1967).

Bertocci, Carlo, 'Il profeta e il burattino' [transcription of exchange between John Cage and Mike Bongiorno, *Lascia o Raddoppia*, 26 February 1959), *Gong* (October 1975).

Betz, Mark, *Beyond the Subtitle: Remapping European Art Cinema* (Minneapolis: University of Minnesota Press, 2009).

Beugnet, Martine, *L'attrait du flou* (Crisneé: Yellow Now, 2017).

Billard, Pierre, 'An interview with Michelangelo Antonioni' [1965], in Michelangelo Antonioni, *The Architecture of Vision: Writings and Interviews on Cinema*, ed. Carlo Di Carlo and Marga Cottino-Jones (Chicago: University of Chicago Press, 2007), pp. 141–7.

Bíro, Yvette, *Turbulence and Flow in Film: The Rhythmic Design*, trans. Paul Salamon (Bloomington: Indiana Unversity Press, 2008).

Blanchot, Maurice, 'Everyday Speech' [1959], trans. Susan Hanson, *Yale French Studies* 73, *Everyday Life* (1987), pp. 12–20.

Bolter, Jay David and Richard Grusin, *Remediation: Understanding New Media* (Cambridge MA: MIT, 1999).

Bonitzer, Pascal, *Décadrages: Peinture et* Cinéma (Paris: Éditions de l'Étoile, 1985).

Bonitzer, Pascal, *Le Champ aveugle: Essais sur le cinema* (Paris: Gallimard, 1982).

Boschi, Alberto, '"La musica che meglio si adatta alle immagini": suoni e rumori nel cinema di Antonioni', in Alberto Achilli, Alberto Boschi and Gianfranco Casadio (eds), *Le sonorità del visibile: immagini, suoni e musica nel cinema di Michelangelo Antonioni* (Regione Emilia Romagna, Ravenna: Assessorato alla cultura, 1999), pp. 83–92.

Bourdieu, Pierre, *Photography: A Middle-Brow Art*, trans. Shaun Whiteside (London: Polity, 1990).

Bourdieu, Pierre, *Un Art moyen: essai sur les usages sociaux de la photographie* (Paris: Editions de minuit, 1965).

Braun, Emily, 'Aftermath', in *Alberto Burri: The Trauma of Painting* (New York: Guggenheim, 2015), pp. 24–37.

Braun, Emily (ed.), *Alberto Burri: The Trauma of Painting* (New York: Guggenheim, 2015).

Braverman, Harry, *Labour and Monopoly Capital: The Degradation of Work in the Twentieth Century* [1974] (New York: Monthly Review Press, 1988).

Breslin, James E., *Mark Rothko: A Biography* (Chicago: University of Chicago Press, 1993).

Brewer, Roy, *An Approach to Print: A Basic Guide to the Printing Processes* (London: Blandford Press, 1971).

Bruno, Edoardo, 'Le responsabilità della Biennale', *Filmcritica* 113 (August–September 1961), pp. 455–6.

Bucarelli, Palma, 'Mark Rothko', in Palma Bucarelli (ed.), *Mark Rothko* (Rome: De Luca, 1962), pp. 7–12.

Buchloh, Benjamin H. D., 'Conceptual Art 1962–1969: From the Aesthetic of Administration to the Critique of Institutions', *October* 55 (Winter 1990), pp. 105–43.

Bury, Pol, 'Time Dilated' [1964], in Dore Ashton, *Pol Bury* (Paris: Maeght Editeur, 1970), p. 107.

Butor, Michel, *Inventory* (New York: Simon and Schuster, 1968).

Butor, Michel, 'Le moschee di New York. O l'arte di Mark Rothko' [1961], in Michel Butor, *Saggi sulla pittura*, trans. Massimo Porfido (Milan: Abscondita, 2001), pp. 129–54.

Buzzati, Dino, *Il grande ritratto* [1960] (Milan: Mondadori, 2018).

Cage, John, 'Erik Satie' [1958], in John Cage, *Silence: Lectures and Writings* (Middletown: Wesleyan University Press, 1961), pp. 76–82.

Cage, John, 'Experimental Music' [1958], in John Cage, *Silence: Lectures and Writings* (Middletown: Wesleyan University Press, 1961), pp. 7–13.

Cage, John, *Fontana Mix* (New York: Henmar Press, 1960).

Cage, John, *For the Birds: In Conversation with Daniel Charles* [1976] (Boston: Maryon Boyars, 1981).

Cage, John, 'The Future of Music: Credo' [1958], *Silence: Lectures and Writings* (Middletown: Wesleyan University Press, 1961), pp. 3–7.

Cage, John, 'Lecture on Nothing', *Incontri musicali* (*Quaderni Internazionali di musica contemporanea diretti da Luciano Berio*) 3 (August 1959), pp. 128–49.

Cage, John, 'Letter to Peter Yates – 28 December 1959', in John Cage, *The Selected Letters of John Cage*, ed. Laura Kuhn (Middletown: Wesleyan University Press, 2016), pp. 210–13.

Cage, John, 'On Film' [1956, previously unpublished], in Richard Kostelanetz (ed.), *John Cage* (London: Allen Lane, 1971), pp. 115–16.

Cage, John, *The Selected Letters of John Cage*, ed. Laura Kuhn (Middletown: Wesleyan University Press, 2016).

Cage, John, *Silence: Lectures and Writings* (Middletown: Wesleyan University Press, 1961).

Cage, John, 'Williams Mix' [1952], in Richard Kostelanetz (ed.), *John Cage* (London: Allen Lane, 1971), pp. 109–11.

Caillois, Roger, 'Mimicry and Legandary Psychastenia' [1935], trans. John Shepley, *October* 31 (Winter 1984), pp. 17–32.

Calabretto, Roberto, 'Giovanni Fusco musicista per il cinema di Antonioni', in Alberto Achilli, Alberto Boschi and Gianfranco Casadio (eds), *Le sonorità del visibile: immagini, suoni e musica nel cinema di Michelangelo Antonioni* (Regione Emilia Romagna: Assessorato alla Cultura, 1999), pp. 45–75.

Calvino, Italo, 'The Adventure of a Photographer' [1955], in *Difficult Loves* [1957], trans. William Weaver (London: Vintage Books, 1999), pp. 40–52.

Calvino, Italo, 'Cybernetics and Ghosts' [1967], in *The Uses of Literature*, trans. Patrick Creagh (San Diego: Harcourt Brace and Co, 1986), pp. 3–27.

Campany, David, 'From Ecstasy to Agony: The Fashion Shoot in Cinema', *Aperture* 190 (Spring 2008), pp. 40–7.

Campany, David, 'Introduction: When to be Fast? When to be Slow?', in David Campany (ed.), *The Cinematic* (London: Whitechapel Gallery, 2007), pp. 10–17.

Campany, David, *Photography and Cinema* (London: Reaktion, 2008).

Canudo, Ricciotto, 'The Birth of the Sixth Art' [1911], trans. Ben Gibson and others, in *Framework: The Journal of Cinema and Media* 13 (Autumn 1980), pp. 3–7.

Caplan, Lindsay, 'From Collective Creation to Creating Collectives: Arte Programmata and the Open Work', in *Grey Room* 73 (Autumn 2018), pp. 54–81.

Caramel, Luciano, *M. A. C.: Movimento Arte Concreta 1948–1952* (Milan: Electa, 1984).

Carpi, Fabio, 'Il Film Letterario', *Pirelli. Rivista d'informazione e di tecnica*, vol. 14/2 (March–April), pp. 45–9, p.112.

Casadei, Delia, 'Milan's Studio di Fonologia: Voice Politics in the City, 1955–8', *Journal of the Royal Musical Association* 141:2 (2016), pp. 403–43.

Casetti, Francesco, 'Back to the Motherland: The Film in the Theatre Postmedia Age', in *Screen* 52:1 (Spring 2011), pp. 1–12.

Casetti, Francesco, 'The Relocation of Cinema', in *NECSUS: European Journal of Media Studies*, special issue on 'Tangibility' (Autumn 2012), <https://necsus-ejms. org/the-relocation-of-cinema/#_edn4> (last aaccessed 15 April 2019).

Cavell, Stanley, 'The Fact of Television' in *Daedalus* 111/4 (Autumn 1982), pp. 75–96.

Cavell, Stanley, *The World Viewed: Reflections on the Ontology of Film* [1971] (Cambridge MA: Harvard University Press, enlarged edition 1979).

Ceccato, Silvio, 'Adamo II', *Congresso Internazionale dell'automatismo* (Milan, 8–13 April 1956), pp. 1–8.

Ceccato, Silvio, *Cibernetica per tutti* (Milan: Feltrinelli, 1968).

Ceccato, Silvio, 'Da cibernetica a filosofia', *Pirelli. Rivista d'informazione e di tecnica* 3 (May–June 1962), pp. 82–4.

Ceccato, Silvio, *Il perfetto filosofo* (Bari: Laterza, 1988).

Ceccato, Silvio, *La mente vista da un cibernetico* (Turin: Nuovi Quaderni ERI/ Edizioni RAI, 1972).

Ceccato, Silvio, 'La storia di un modello meccanico dell'uomo che traduce', *Almanacco Letterario Bompiani* 1962 (Milan: Bompiani, 1961), pp. 122–34.

Ceccato, Silvio, *Linguistic Analysis and Programming for Mechanical Translation* (Milan and New York: Feltrinelli/Gordon And Reach Science Publishers, 1960).

Ceccato, Silvio, 'A Model of the Mind', in Eduardo Renato Caianiello (ed.), *Cybernetics of Neural Processes* (Course Held at the International School of Physics, sponsored by NATO, at the Istituto di fisica teorica, Università di Napoli, 26 April to 13 May 1962) (Rome: CNR, 1965), pp. 21–79.

Ceccato, Silvio, *Un tecnico fra i filosofi* vol.1 (Padua: Marsilio, 1964).

Cejas, Mónica, 'Tourism "Back in Time": Performing "the Essence of Safari" in Africa', *Intercultural Communication Studies* 16/3 (2007), pp. 121–34.

Celant, Germano, 'Alberto Burri and Material', in Germano Celant (ed.), *Alberto Burri* (New York: Mitchell-Innes and Nash, 2007), pp. 7–16.

Ceruzzi, Paul E., *Computing: A Concise History* (Cambridge MA: MIT, 2012).

Chanan, Michael, *Repeated Takes: a Short History of Recording and Its Effects on Music* (London: Verso, 1995).

Chatman, Seymour, *Antonioni: Or the Surface of the World* (Berkeley: University of California Press, 1985).

Chiaretti, Tommaso (ed.), *L'avventura* (Bologna: Cappelli, 1960).

Chiarini, Luigi, *Arte e tecnica del film* (Bari: Laterza, 1962).

Chion, Michel, *The Voice in the Cinema* [1982], trans. Claudia Gorbman (New York: Columbia University Press, 1999).

Christov-Bakargiev, Carolyn and Marcella Cossu (eds), *Fabio Mauri. Opere e azioni, 1954–1994* (Rome: Galleria Nazionale d'Arte Moderna e Contemporanea, 1994).

Christov-Bakargiev, Carolyn and Marco Scotini (eds), *Gianni Colombo* (Milan: Skira, 2010).

Christov-Bakargiev, Carolyn, 'Thrust into the Whirlwind: Italian Art Before Arte Povera', in Richard Flood and Frances Morris (eds), *Zero to Infinity: Arte Povera 1962–1972* (London and Minneapolis: Tate Publishing/Walker Art Center, 2001), pp. 21–40.

Coe, Brian, 'The Rollfilm Revolution', in Colin Ford (ed.), *The Kodak Museum: The Story of Popular Photography* (London: Century Hutchinson, 1989) pp. 61–89.

Cohen-Séat, Gilbert, 'Civiltà dell'immagine', in Sergio Morando (ed.), *Almanacco Letterario Bompiani 1963. Civiltà dell' imagine* (Milan: Bompiani, 1962), pp. 137–43.

Comolli, Jean-Louis, 'Machines of the Visible', in Teresa de Lauretis and Stephen Heath (eds), *The Cinematic Apparatus* (London: Macmillan, 1980), pp. 121–42.

Cortázar, Julio, 'Blow-Up' [1963], in Julio Cortázar, *End of the Game and Other Stories*, trans. Paul Blackburn (London: Collins and Harvill Press, 1968).

Cortázar, Julio, *End of the Game and Other Stories*, trans. Paul Blackburn (London: Collins and Harvill Press, 1968).

Cox, Christoph and Daniel Warner (eds), *Audio Culture: Readings in Modern Music* (New York: Continuum, 2004).

Cramer, Michael, *Utopian Television: Rossellini, Watkins, and Godard beyond Cinema* (Minneapolis: University of Minnesota Press, 2017).

Cuccu, Lorenzo, *La visione come problema: Forme e svolgimento del cinema di Antonioni* (Rome: Bulzoni, 1973).

Dalle Pezze, Barbara and Carlo Salzani (eds), *Essays on Boredom and Modernity* (Amsterdam: Rodopi, 2009*)*.

Dalle Vacche, Angela, *Cinema and Painting: How Art Is Used in Film* (Austin: University of Texas, 1996).

D'Amato, Giuseppe, 'Antonioni: la poetica dei materiali', *Bianco e Nero* 62 (January–April 2001), pp. 154–81.

David, Michel, *La psicoanalisi nella cultura italiana* (Turin: Boringhieri, 1974).

D'Ayala Valva, Giuseppe, 'Funzione del colore', *Civiltà delle macchine* 6/2 (March–April 1958), pp. 26–32.

De Benedictis, Angela Ida, 'Opera prima: Ritratto di città e gli esordi della musica elettroacustica in Italia', in Veniero Rizzardi and Angela Ida De Benedictis (eds), *Nuova musica alla radio: Esperienze allo Studio di Fonologia della RAI di Milano, 1954–1959* (Rome: RAI-Eri, 2000), pp. 27–56.

De Benedictis, Angela Ida, *Radiodramma e arte radiofonica: storia e funzioni della musica per radio in Italia* (Turin: EDT, 2004).

De Berti, Raffaele, *Dallo Schermo alla carta: Romanzi, fotoromanzi, rotocalchi cinematografici* (Milan: Vita e pensiero, 2000).

De Latil, Pierre, *Thinking by Machine: A Study of Cybernetics* [1953], trans. Y. M. Golla (London: Sidgwick and Jackson, 1956).

De Luca, Tiago and Nuno Barradas Jorge (eds), *Slow Cinema* (Edinburgh: Edinburgh University Press, 2016).

De Salvo, Donna, *Open Systems: Rethinking Art c. 1970* (London: Tate, 2005).

Debord, Guy, 'Perspectives de modifications coscientes dans la vie quotidienne', *Internationale Situationiste* 6 (August 1961), pp. 20–7.

Deleuze, Gilles, *Cinema I: The Movement Image* [1983], trans. Hugh Tomlinson and Barbara Habberjam (London: Athlone Press, 1992).

Deleuze, Gilles, *Cinema II: The Time Image* [1985], trans. Hugh Tomlinson and Robert Galeta (London: Athlone Press, 1989).

Deplano, Valeria, 'Decolonisation Will Be Televised: *Anni d'Europa* and the Fall of European Colonialism', in Paolo Bertella Farnetti and Cecilia Dau Novelli (eds), *Images of Colonialism and Decolonisation in The Italian Media* (Newcastle: Cambridge Scholars Press, 2017), pp. 81–94.

Deren, Maya, 'Cinematography: The Creative Use of Reality' [1960], in P. Adams Sitney (ed.), *The Avant-Garde Film: A Reader of Theory and Criticism* (New York: Anthology Film Archives, 1978), pp. 60–73.

Dewey, John, *Art as Experience* [1934] (London: Penguin, 2005).

Di Carlo, Carlo, 'Antonioni', in Carlo Di Carlo (ed.), *Michelangelo Antonioni* (Rome: Edizioni Bianco e Nero, 1964), pp. 8–41.

Di Carlo, Carlo (ed.), *Il mio Antonioni* (Rome: Istituto Luce/Cinecittà, 2018).

Di Carlo, Carlo, *Il primo Antonioni* (Bologna: Cappelli, 1973).

Di Carlo, Carlo (ed.), *Michelangelo Antonioni* (Rome: Bianco e Nero, 1964).

Di Pietrantonio, Giacinto, 'Non ero nuovo', in Fabio Mauri, *Arte per legittima difesa* (Bergamo: Gamec Books, 2016).

Dickens, Charles, *Bleak House* [1852] (Ware: Wordsworth Editions, 1993).

Doane, Mary Ann (ed.), *differences* 18/1, special issue: *Indexicality: Trace and Sign* (Summer, 2007).

Doane, Mary Ann, *The Emergence of Cinematic: Modernity, Contingency, the Archive* (Cambridge MA: Harvard University Press, 2002).

Doane, Mary Ann, 'The Indexical and the Concept of Medium Specificity', *differences* 18/1, special issue: *Indexicality: Trace and Sign* (Summer, 2007), pp. 128–52.

Doane, Mary Ann, 'Information, Crisis, Catastrophe', in P. Mellencamp (ed.), *Logics of Television: Essays in Cultural Criticism* (London: BFI, 1990), pp. 222–39.

Dorfles, Gillo, 'Biennale' [1958], Oliver Wick (ed.), *Mark Rothko* (Milan and London: Skira and Thames & Hudson, 2007), p. 3.

Dorfles, Gillo, 'Civiltà (e inciviltà) dell'immagine', in *Almanacco Letterario Bompiani 1963: La Civiltà dell'immagine* (Milan: Bompiani, 1962), pp. 67–74.

Dorfles, Gillo, 'A Song without Words . . . an Encounter with Mark Rothko', in Oliver Wick (ed.), *Mark Rothko* (Milan and London: Skira and Thames & Hudson, 2007), pp. 40–3.

Drucker, Joanna, *The Century of Artists' Books* [1994] (New York: Granary Books, 2004).

Dubois, Philippe, *L'Acte photographique et autres essais* [1983] (Bruxelles: Labor, 1990).

Eco, Umberto, *Apocalittici e integrati* [1964] (Milan: Bompiani, 2017).

Eco, Umberto, *Apocalypse Postponed* [1964], ed. Robert Lumley (London: Flamingo, 1995).

Eco, Umberto, 'Del modo di formare come impegno sulla realtà', *Menabò* 5 (1962), pp. 198–237.

Eco, Umberto, 'L'opera in movimento e la coscienza dell'epoca', *Incontri musicali* 3 (Agosto 1959), pp. 32–54.

Eco, Umberto, *The Open Work* [1962], trans. Anna Cancogni (Cambridge MA: Harvard University Press, 1989).

Eco, Umberto, *Opera aperta: forme indeterminate nelle poetiche contemporanee* [1962] (Milan: Bompiani, 2013).

Eco, Umberto, 'The Phenomenology of Mike Bongiorno' [1961], in *Misreadings*, trans. William Weaver (London: Picador, 1994), pp. 156–64.

Eco, Umberto, 'Verso una civiltà della visione', in *Pirelli. Rivista d'informazione e di tecnica* 14/1 (January–February 1961), pp. 32–41.

Eisenstein, Sergei, Vsevolod Pudovkin and Grigori Alexandrov, 'A Statement' [1928], trans. Jay Leida, in Elisabeth Weis and John Belton (eds), *Film Sound: Theory and Practice* (New York: Columbia University Press, 1985), pp. 83–5.

Eisenstein, Sergei, 'Synchronization of the Senses', in *The Film Sense* [1942], trans. Jay Leida (London: Faber and Faber, 1986), pp. 60–91.

Ellis, John, *Visible Fictions: Cinema, Television, Video* (London: Routledge and Kegan Paul, 1982).

Eno, Brian, 'The Recording Studio as Compositional Tool' [1979], in Christoph Cox and Daniel Warner (eds), *Audio Culture: Readings in Modern Music* (New York: Continuum, 2004), pp. 127–30.

Epstein, Jean, 'The Counterpoint of Sound' [1955], trans. Franck Le Gac, in Sarah Keller and Jason N. Paul (eds), *Jean Epstein: Critical Essays and New Translations* (Amsterdam: Amsterdam University Press, 2014), pp. 362–4.

Espinosa, Julio García, 'For an Imperfect Cinema' [1969], trans. Julianne Burton, *Jump Cut: A Review of Contemporary Media* 20 (1979), pp. 24–6.

Eugeni, Ruggero, 'La modernità a disagio. Michelangelo Antonioni e la cultura psichiatrica italiana tra gli anni Cinquanta e gli anni Sessanta del Novecento', in Alberto Boschi e Francesco Di Chiara (eds), *Michelangelo Antonioni: Prospettive, culture, politiche, spazi* (Milan: Il Castoro, 2015), pp. 49–68.

Everett, Wendy, 'Mapping Colour: An Introduction to the Theories and Practices of Colour', in Wendy Everett (ed.), *Questions of Colour in Cinema: From Paintbrush to Pixel* (Oxford: Peter Lang, 2007), pp. 7–38.

Fagiolo dell'Arco, Maurizio, *Rapporto 1960* (Rome: Bulzoni, 1966).

Farina, Franco (ed.), *Michelangelo Antonioni. Le montagne incantate ed altre opera* (Ferrara: Comune di Ferrara, 1993).

Farnetti, Paolo Bertella and Cecilia Dau Novelli (eds), *Images of Colonialism and Decolonisation in The Italian Media* (Newcastle: Cambridge Scholars Press, 2017).

Fenichel, Otto, 'On the Psychology of Boredom' [1934], *The Collected Papers of Otto Fenichel*, ed. Hanna Fenichel and David Rapaport (London: Routledge, 1954).

Fer, Briony, *The Infinite Line: Remaking Art After Modernism* (New Haven: Yale University Press, 2004).

Ferenczi, Sándor, 'Sunday Neurosis' [1919], in John Rickman (ed.), *Further Contributions to the Theory and Technique of Psychoanalysis* (London: Hogarth Press, 1926), pp. 174–7.

Feuer, Jane, 'The Concept of Live Television: Ontology as Ideology', in E. A. Kaplan (ed.), *Regarding Television: Critical Approaches – An Anthology* (Los Angeles: American Film Institute, 1983), pp. 12–22.

Field, Simon, 'Interview with Hollis Frampton', *Afterimage* 4 (Autumn 1972), pp. 44–77.

Flatley, Jonathan, 'Allegories of Boredom', in Ann Goldstein (ed.), *A Minimal Future?: Art as Object 1958–1968* (Cambridge MA: MIT, 2004), pp. 50–75.

Flusser, Vilém, *Into the Universe of Technical Images* [1985], trans. Nancy Ann Roth (Minneapolis: University of Minnesota Press, 2011).

Flusser, Vilém, *Towards a Philosophy of Photography* [1983], trans. Anthony Mathews (London: Reaktion, 2000).

Fofi, Goffredo, Ernesto Franco, Philippe Garner and Walter Moser, *Io sono il fotografo. Blow-Up e la fotografia fotografia* (Rome: Contrasto, 2018).

Foot, John, *The Man Who Closed the Asylums: Franco Basaglia and the Revolution in Mental Health Care* (London: Verso, 2015).

Ford, Colin (ed.), *The Kodak Museum: The Story of Popular Photography* (London: Century Hutchinson, 1989).

Forgacs, David, 'Cultural Consumption, 1940s to 1990s', in David Forgacs and Robert Lumley (eds), *Italian Cultural Studies: An Introduction* (Oxford: Oxford University Press, 1996), pp. 273–90.

Forgacs, David, *Italian Culture in the Industrial Era 1880–1980: Cultural Industries, Politics and the Public* (Manchester: Manchester University Press, 1990).

Forgacs, David and Stephen Gundle, *Mass Culture and Italian Society from Fascism to the Cold War* (Bloomington: Indiana University Press, 2007).

Forgacs, David, commentary, *Red Desert* (DVD) (London: BFI Video, 2011).

Forleo, Francesco, *La cibernetica italiana della mente nella civiltà delle macchine* (Mantova: Universitas Studiorum, 2017).

Foster, Hal, Rosalind Krauss, Yve-Alain Bois and Benjamin H. D. Buchloh, *Art Since 1900: Modernism, Antimodernism, Postmodernism* (London: Thames and Hudson, 2004).

Fox Talbot, William Henry, *The Pencil of Nature* (London: Longman and Co., 1844).

Frampton, Hollis, 'Incisions in History/Segments of Eternity', *Artforum* 13 (October 1974), pp. 39–50.

Frampton, Hollis, *On the Camera and Consecutive Matters: The Writings of Hollis Frampton*, ed. Bruce Jenkins (Cambridge MA: MIT, 2009).

Frampton, Hollis, 'The Withering Away of the State of the Art' [1974], in *On the Camera and Consecutive Matters: The Writings of Hollis Frampton*, ed. Bruce Jenkins (Cambridge MA: MIT, 2009), pp. 261–8.

Freccero, John, '*Blow-Up*: From the Word to the Image' [1970], in Roy Huss (ed.), *Focus on Blow-Up* (Englewood Cliffs: Prentice Hall, 1971), pp. 116–28.

Freud, Sigmund, 'Beyond the Pleasure Principle' [1920], *The Freud Penguin Library*, vol. 11 (London: Penguin Books, 1991), pp. 269–338.

Freud, Sigmund, 'Letter to Abraham, 9th June 1925', in *A Psychoanalytic Dialogue: The Letters of Sigmund Freud and Karl Abraham 1907–1926*, ed. Hilda C. Abraham and Ernst L. Freud (New York: Basic Books, 1964), pp. 546–7.

Freud, Sigmund, 'A Note Upon the "Mystic Writing-Pad"' [1925], *The Penguin Freud Library*, trans. James Strachey, vol. 11 (London: Penguin Books, 1991), pp. 427–34.

Freud, Sigmund, 'Remembering, Repeating and Working-Through' [1914], *Standard Edition of the Complete Psychological Works of Sigmund Freud*, trans. and ed. James Strachey, vol. 12 (London: The Hogarth Press, 1953–74), pp. 147–56.

Freud, Sigmund, 'Screen Memories' [1899], *Standard Edition of the Complete Psychological Works of Sigmund Freud*, trans. and ed. James Strachey, vol. 3 (London: The Hogarth Press, 1953–74), pp. 301–22.

Freund, Gisèle, *Photography and Society* [1974] (London: Gordon Fraser, 1980).

Fried, Michael, 'Art and Objecthood' [1967], in *Art and Objecthood: Essays and Reviews* (Chicago: University of Chicago Press, 1988), pp. 148–72.

Fritsche, Maria, *American Marshall Plan Film Campaigns and the Europeans: A Captivated Audience* (London: Bloomsbury, 2017).

Fujiwara, Chris, 'Boredom, *Spasmo*, and the Italian System', in Jeffrey Sconce (ed.), *Sleaze Artists: Cinemas at the Margin of Taste, Style and Politics* (Durham NC: Duke University Press, 2007).

Galt, Rosalind and Karl Schoonover (eds), *Global Art Cinema* (New York: Oxford University Press, 2010).

Galt, Rosalind and Karl Schoonover, 'Introduction: The Impurity of Art Cinema', in Rosalind Galt and Karl Schoonover (eds), *Global Art Cinema* (New York: Oxford University Press, 2010), pp. 3–28.

Galt, Rosalind, 'On *L'avventura* and the Picturesque', in Laura Rascaroli and John David Rhodes (eds), *Antonioni: Centinary Essays* (London: Palgrave/BFI, 2011), pp. 134–53.

Gandy, Matthew, 'The Cinematic Void: Desert Iconographies in Michelangelo Antonioni's *Zabriskie Point*', in *Landscape and Film*, ed. Martin Lefebvre (London: Routledge, 2006), pp. 315–32.

Gardiner, Michael E., 'Henri Lefebvre and the 'Sociology of Boredom', in *Theory, Culture and Society* 29/2 (2012), pp. 37–62.

Garner, Philippe, 'Gli ingrandimenti di *Blow-Up*', in Ernesto Franco Fofi, Philippe Garner and Walter Moser, *Io sono il fotografo. Blow-Up e la fotografia fotografia* (Rome: Contrasto, 2018), pp. 54–69.

Gelatt, Roland, *The Fabulous Phonograph 1877–1977* (London: Cassell, 1977).

Gelmetti, Vittorio, 'Musica-Verità?', *Filmcritica* 1985 (January 1968), pp. 21–8.

Ghirri, Luigi, *The Complete Essays 1973–1991* (London: Mack Books, 2012).

Gianclaudio Lopez (ed.), *Il sogno delle tre faraone: Silvio Ceccato da filosofo a tecnico della mente* (Viterbo: Stampa alternativa, 2015).

Gidal, Peter, *Andy Warhol: Films and Paintings* [1971] (New York: Da Capo, 1991).

Gidal, Peter, 'Interview with Hollis Frampton', *October* 32 (Spring 1985), pp. 93–117.

Gilman, Richard, 'About Nothing – with Precision', *Theater Arts* 46:7 (July 1962), pp. 10–12.

Giuliani, Gaia, *Race, Nation and Gender in Modern Italy: Intersectional Representations in Visual Culture* (London: Palgrave/Macmillan, 2018).

Godard, Jean-Luc, 'The Night, the Eclipse, the Dawn' [1964], in Michelangelo Antonioni, *The Architecture of Vision: Writings and Interviews on Cinema*, ed. Carlo Di Carlo and Marga Cottino-Jones (Chicago: University of Chicago Press, 2007), pp. 287–97. In Italian as 'La notte, l'eclisse, l'aurora' in Michelangelo Antonioni, *Fare un film è per me vivere. Scritti sul cinema*, ed. Carlo Di Carlo and Giorgio Tinazzi (Venice: Marsilio, 1994), pp. 255–63.

Goldberg, Vicki (ed.), *Photography in Print: Writings from 1816 to the Present* (Albuquerque: University of New Mexico Press, 1988).

Goodstein, Elizabeth S., *Experience without Qualities: Boredom and Modernity* (Stanford: Stanford University Press, 2005).

Gould, Glenn, 'The Prospects of Recording' [1966], in Tim Page (ed.), *The Glenn Gould Reader* (New York: Knopf, 1984), pp. 331–53.

Green, David and Joanna Lowry (eds), *Stillness and Time: Photography and the Moving Image* (Brighton: Photoworks/Photoforum, 2006).

Greenberg, Clement, 'After Abstract Expressionism' [1962], in Clement Greenberg, *The Collected Essays and Criticism, Vol. 4: Modernism with a Vengeance 1957–1969*, ed. John O'Brien (Chicago: University of Chicago Press, 1993), pp. 121–34.

Greenberg, Clement, '"American-Type" Painting' [1955], in Clement Greenberg, *Art and Culture: Critical Essays* [1961] (Boston: Beacon Press, 1989), pp. 208–29.

Greenberg, Clement, 'Avant-Garde and Kitsch' [1939], in Clement Greenberg, *The Collected Essays and Criticism: Vol. 1: Perceptions and Judgments, 1939–1944*, ed. John O'Brian (Chicago: University of Chicago Press, 1986), pp. 5–22.

Greenberg, Clement, 'The Case for Abstract Art' [1959], in Clement Greenberg, *The Collected Essays and Criticism, Vol. 4: Modernism with a Vengeance 1957–1969*, ed. John O'Brian (Chicago: University of Chicago Press, 1993), pp. 75–84.

Greenberg, Clement, 'Modernist Painting' [1961], in Clement Greenberg, *The Collected Essays and Criticism Vol. 4*, ed. John O'Brian (Chicago: University of Chicago Press, 1993), pp. 85–93.

Greenberg, Clement, 'Post-Painterly Abstraction' [1964], in Clement Greenberg, *The Collected Essays and Criticism, Vol. 4: Modernism with a Vengeance 1957–1969*, ed. John O'Brien (Chicago: University of Chicago Press, 1993), pp. 192–7.

Greenberg, Clement, 'Towards a Newer Laocoon' [1940], Clement Greenberg, *The Collected Essays and Criticism: Vol. 1: Perceptions and Judgments, 1939–1944*, ed. John O'Brian (Chicago: University of Chicago Press, 1986), pp. 23–38.

Griffiths, Paul, *Modern Music: The Avant-Garde since 1945* (London: J. M. Dent and Sons, 1981).

Grossvogel, Ian, 'Blow-Up: The Forms of an Esthetic Itinerary', *Diacritics* 2/3 (Autumn 1972), pp. 49–54.

Hansen, Miriam, 'America, Paris, the Alps: Kracauer (and Benjamin) on Cinema and Modernity', in Leo Charney and Vanessa Schwartz (eds), *Cinema and the Invention of Modern Life* (Berkeley: University of California Press, 1995), pp. 362–402.

Healy, Seán Desmond, *Boredom: Self and Culture* (London: Associated University Presses, 1984).

Heidegger, Martin, 'The Age of the World Picture' [1938], in Martin Heidegger, *The Question Concerning Technology and Other Essays*, trans. William Lovitt (New York: Harper, 1977), pp. 3–35.

Heidegger, Martin, *The Fundamental Concepts of Metaphysics: World, Finitude, Solitude* [1983], trans. William McNeill and Nicholas Walker (Bloomington: Indiana University Press, 1995).

Henning, Michelle, 'Image Flow: Photography on Tap', *photographies* 11/2–3 (Summer 2018), pp. 133–48.

Henning, Michelle, *Photography: The Unfettered Image* (London: Routledge, 2018).

Higgins, Dick, 'Intermedia' (1966), in *Leonardo* 34/1 (2001), pp. 49–54.

Holland, Owen and Phil Husbands, 'Pioneers of Cybernetics: Grey Walter's robot tortoises and the Ratio Club', in Ben Russell (ed.), *Robots: The 500-year Quest to Make Machines Human* (London: Science Museum/Scala Arts and Heritage, 2017), pp. 86–99.

Hultén, K. G. Pontus, *Jean Tinguely – Méta* [1972], trans. Mary Whittall (London: Thames and Hudson, 1975).

Hultén, Pontus and Frank Königsberg (eds), *9 Evenings: Theater and Engineering* (New York: Experiments in Art and Technology: The Foundation for Contemporary Performance Arts, 1966).

Huss, Roy (ed.), *Focus on Blow-Up* (Englewood Cliffs: Prentice Hall, 1971).

Hutchings, Ernest A. D., *A Survey of Printing Processes* (London: Heinemann, 1970).

Huxley, Aldous, *The Perennial Philosophy* [1944] (London: Flamingo, 1994).

Huyssen, Andreas, 'Mass Culture as Woman: Modernism's Other', in Andreas Huyssen, *After the Great Divide: Modernism, Mass Culture, Postmodernism* (Bloomington: Indiana University Press, 1986), pp. 44–62.

International Society of Cybernetic Medicine, *Proceedings of the International Congress on Cybernetic Medicine* (Naples: Società internazionale di medicina cibernetica, 1960).

Jacobs, Steven, 'Between EUR and LA: Townscapes in the Work of Michelangelo Antonioni', in Ghent Urban Studies Team, *The Urban Condition: Space, Community, and Self in the Contemporary Metropolis* (Rotterdam: 010 Publishers, 1999), pp. 324–42.

James, David E., *Allegories of Cinema: American Film of the Sixties* (Princeton: Princeton University Press, 1989).

James, William, *The Principles of Psychology* vol. 1 [1890] (New York: Henry Holt and Co., 1918).

Jones, Amelia, 'Seeing Differently: From Antonioni's *Blow-Up* (1966) to Shezad Dawood's *Make It Big* (2005)', *Journal of Visual Culture* 7/2 (August 2008), pp. 181–203.

Jones, Caroline A., *Eyesight Alone: Clement Greenberg's Modernism and the Bureaucratization of the Senses* (Chicago: University of Chicago Press, 2005).

Judd, Donald, 'Specific Objects' [1965], in *Complete Writings 1959–1975* (Halifax and New York: The Press of the Nova Scotia College of Art and Design and New York University Press, 2005).

Kael, Pauline, 'Are Movies Going to Pieces?' [1964], in Richard Dyer MacCann (ed.), *Film: a Montage of Theories* (New York: E. P. Dutton, 1966), pp. 341–54.

Kahn, Douglas, *Noise, Water, Meat: A History of Sound in the Arts* (Cambridge MA: MIT, 1999).

Kaizen, William, 'Live on Tape: Video, Liveness and the Immediate', in Tanya Leighton (ed.), *Art and the Moving Image: A Critical Reader* (London: Afterall/Tate Publishing, 2008), pp. 258–72.

Kandinsky, Wassily and Franz Marc (eds), *Der Blaue Reiter* (Munich: R. Piper and Co. Verlag, 1914).

King, Geoff, *Positioning Art Cinema: Film and Cultural Value* (London: IB Tauris, 2019).

Kittler, Friedrich, *Gramophone, Film, Typewriter* [1986], trans. Geoffrey Winthrop-Young and Michael Wutz (Stanford: Stanford University Press, 1999).

Klüver, Billy, Julie Martin and Barbara Rose (eds), *Pavilion: Experiments in Art and Technology* (New York: E. P. Dutton, 1972).

Koepnick, Lutz Peter, *On Slowness: Toward an Aesthetic of the Contemporary* (New York: University of Columbia Press, 2014).

Koestenbaum, Wayne, *Andy Warhol* (London: Weidenfeld and Nicolson, 2001).

Kostelanetz, Richard, *Conversing with Cage*, 2nd ed. (New York: Routledge, 2002).

Kostelanetz, Richard (ed.), *John Cage* (New York: Praeger, 1970).

Kracauer, Siegfried, 'Boredom' [1924], in *The Mass Ornament: Weimar Essays*, ed. and trans. Thomas Y. Levin (Cambridge MA: Harvard University Press, 1995), pp. 331–6.

Kracauer, Siegfried, 'The Cult of Distraction' [1926], *The Mass Ornament: Weimar Essays*, ed. and trans. Thomas Y. Levin (Cambridge MA: Harvard University Press, 1995), pp. 323–8.

Kracauer, Siegfried, *The Mass Ornament: Weimar Essays*, ed. and trans. Thomas Y. Levin (Cambridge MA: Harvard University Press, 1995).

Kracauer, Siegfried, 'Photography' [1927], trans. Thomas Y. Levin, *Critical Inquiry* 19/3 (Spring 1993), pp. 421–36.

Kracauer, Siegfried, *Theory of Film* (New York: Oxford University Press, 1960).

Krauss, Rosalind, 'Notes on the Index: Seventies Art in America', *October* 3 (Spring 1977), pp. 68–81.

Kuntzel, Thierry, 'A Note Upon the Filmic Apparatus', *Quarterly Review of Film Studies* 1 (August 1976), pp. 266–71.

Labarthe, André, 'All'origine del cinema c'è una scelta' [1960], in Michelangelo Antonioni, *Fare un film è per me vivere. Scritti sul cinema*, ed. Carlo Di Carlo and Giorgio Tinazzi (Venice: Marsilio, 1994), pp. 121–8.

Labarthe, André, 'A Conversation with Michelangelo Antonioni' [1960], in Michelangelo Antonioni, *The Architecture of Vision: Writings and Interviews on Cinema*, ed. Carlo Di Carlo and Marga Cottino-Jones (Chicago: University of Chicago Press, 2007), pp. 133–40.

Labarthe, André and Jacques Rivette, 'Entretien avec Alain Resnais et Alain Robbe-Grillet', *Cahiers du Cinéma* 21 (September 1961), pp. 1–22.

Lange, Susanne, *Bernd and Hilla Becher: Life and Work* [2005], trans. Jeremy Gaines (Cambridge MA: MIT Press, 2007).

Lannes, Sophie and Philippe Meyer, 'Identification of a Filmmaker' [1985], in Michelangelo Antonioni, *The Architecture of Vision: Writings and Interviews on Cinema*, ed. Carlo Di Carlo, Giorgio Tinazzi and Marga Cottino-Jones (Chicago: University of Chicago Press, 2007), pp. 245–56.

Laplanche, Jean, *Essays on Otherness*, ed. John Fletcher (London: Routledge, 1999).

Laplanche, Jean, 'Note on Afterwardsness', in Jean Laplanche, *Essays on Otherness*, ed. and trans. John Fletcher (London: Routledge, 1999), pp. 260–5.

Laplanche, Jean, 'Psychoanalysis, Time and Translation' [1990], in *Seduction, Translation and the Drives*, ed. John Fletcher (London: ICA, 1992), pp. 161–77.

Lebeck, Robert and Bodo Von Dewitz (eds), *Kiosk: A History of Photojournalism* (Göttingen: Steidl, 2001).

Lefebvre, Henri, *The Critique of Everyday Life*, vol. 1: *Introduction* [1947], trans. John Moore (London: Verso, 1991).

Lefebvre, Henri, *The Critique of Everyday Life*, vol. 2: *Foundations for a Sociology of the Everyday* [1961], trans. John Moore (London: Verso, 2004).

Lefebvre, Henri, *The Critique of Everyday Life*, vol. 3: *From Modernity to Modernism* [1981], trans. Gregory Elliott (London: Verso, 2006).

Le Grice, Malcolm, *Abstract Film and Beyond* (London: Studio Vista, 1977).

Leonardi, Nicoletta (ed.), *Feedback: Scritti su e di Franco Vaccari* (Milan: Postmedia Books, 2007).

Leprohon, Pierre, *Michelangelo Antonioni: An Introduction* [1961], trans. Scott Sullivan (New York: Simon and Schuster, 1963).

Lessing, Gotthold Ephraim, *Laocoön: a Essay on the Limits of Painting and Poetry* [1766], trans. Edward McCormick (Baltimore: Johns Hopkins, 1982).

Leutrat, Jean-Louis, *L'année dernière à Marienbad*, trans. Paul Hammond (London: BFI, 2000).

Lev, Peter, 'Blow-Up, Swinging London, and the Film Generation', *Literature/Film Quarterly* 17/2 (1989), pp. 134–7.

Lonzi, Carla, *Autoritratto* [1969] (Milan: Abscondita, 2017).

Lotman, Jurij, *Semiotics of Cinema* [1973], trans. Mark E. Suino (Ann Arbor: University of Michigan, 1981).

Lucas, Uliano and Tatiana Agliani, *La realtà e lo sguardo. Storia del fotogiornalismo in Italia* (Turin: Einaudi, 2015).

McCullin, Don, *Unreasonable Behaviour: An Autobiography* (London: Jonathan Cape, 1990).

McDonald, Dwight, 'A Theory of Mass Culture', in *Diogenes* 1/3 (1953), pp. 1–17.

McKenzie, Brian Angus, *Remaking France: Americanization, Public Diplomacy, and the Marshall Plan* (New York, NY: Berghahn Books, 2005).

McLuhan, Marshall and Bruce R. Powers, *The Global Village: Transformations in World Life and Media in the 21st Century* (New York: Oxford University Press, 1989).

McLuhan, Marshall, *The Gutenberg Galaxy: The Making of Typographic Man* (Toronto: University of Toronto Press, 1962).

McLuhan, Marshall, *Understanding Media: The Extensions of Man* [1964] (London: Sphere Book Editions, 1967).MacDonald, Kevin and Mark Cousin, *Imagining Reality* (London: Faber, 1996).

Malraux, André, *La Corde et les souris* (Paris: Gallimard, 1976).

Malraux, André, *Les Voix du silence* (Paris: La Galerie de la Pleiade, 1951).

Mannucci, Cesare, *Lo spettatore senza libertà. Radiotelevisione e comunicazione di massa* (Bari: Laterza, 1962).

Mansoor, Jaleh, *Marshall Plan Modernism: Italian Postwar Abstraction and the Beginning of Autonomia* (Durham NC: Duke University Press, 2016).

Marien, Warner Mary, *Photography: A Cultural History* (London: Laurence King, 2002).

Marcus, Laura, 'Introduction: Histories, Representations, Autobiographics in *The Interpretation of Dreams*', in Laura Marcus (ed.), *Sigmund Freud's The Interpretation of Dreams: New Interdisciplinary Essays* (Manchester: Manchester University Press, 1999), pp. 1–65.

Marcus, Millicent, *Italian Film in the Light of Neorealism* (Princeton: Princeton University Press, 1986).

Maretti, Enrico, 'Adamo II', *Atti della VI sessione delle giornate di scienza: convegno sui problemi dell'automatismo* (Milan, 8–13 April 1956), supplement to *La ricerca scientifica* 26 (Rome: Consiglio Nazionale delle Ricerche, 1956).

Maretti, Enrico, 'Adamo II', in *Civiltà delle macchine* 3 (1956), pp. 25–32.

Margulies, Ivone, *Nothing Happens: Chantal Akerman's Hyperrealist Everyday* (Durham NC: Duke University Press, 1996).

Marotti, Ferruccio, 'La Televisione come fenomeno sociale', *Civiltà delle macchine* (January –February 1962), pp. 29–34.

Marotti, Ferruccio, 'Tecnica ed estetica dell'espressione televisiva', *Civiltà delle macchine* (September–October 1961), pp. 19–24.

Marshall, Richard D., *Ed Ruscha* (London: Phaidon, 2003).

Martin, Marion, Gaynor Sadlo and Graham Stew, 'The Phenomenon of Boredom' in *Qualitative Research in Psychology* 3/3 (2006), pp. 193–211.

Massironi, Gianni, *Dear Antonioni. Arena*, BBC, episode 33, 18 January 1997.

Maurin, Francois, '*Il deserto rosso*' [1964], in Michelangelo Antonioni, *Fare un film è per me vivere. Scritti sul cinema*, ed. Carlo Di Carlo and Giorgio Tinazzi (Venice: Marsilio, 1994), pp. 251–4.

Maurin, François, '*L'avventura*' [1960], in Michelangelo Antonioni, *The Architecture of Vision: Writings and Interviews on Cinema*, ed. Carlo Di Carlo and Marga Cottino-Jones (Chicago: University of Chicago Press, 2007), pp. 269–73.

Maurin, Francois, '*Red Desert*' [1964], in Michelangelo Antonioni, *The Architecture of Vision: Writings and Interviews on Cinema*, ed. Carlo Di Carlo and Marga Cottino-Jones (Chicago: University of Chicago Press, 2007), pp. 283–6.

Maxwell, Anne, *Colonial Photography and Exhibitions: Representations of the 'Native' and the Making of European Identities* (London: Leicester, 1999).

Maynard, Patrick, *The Engine of Visualization: Thinking Through Photography* (Ithaca: Cornell University Press, 1997).

Mekas, Jonas, 'The Independent Film Award' [1964], in P. Adams Sitney, *Film Culture Reader* [1970] (New York: Cooper Square Press, 2000), pp. 423–9.

Mekas, Jonas, 'Notes After Re-seeing the Films of Andy Warhol', in John Coplans (ed.), *Andy Warhol* (New York: New York Graphic Society, 1970), pp. 139–57.

Mellor, David Alan, '"Fragments of an Unknowable Whole": Antonioni's Incorporation of Contemporary Visualities – London, 1966', in *Visual Culture in Britain* 8/2 (2007), pp. 45–61.

Metz, Christian, *Film Language: A Semiotics of Cinema* [1968], trans. Michael Taylor (Chicago: University of Chicago Press, 1991).

Metz, Christian, 'The Imaginary Signifier', *Screen* 16 (Summer 1975), pp. 14–76.

Michelson, Annette, 'Toward Snow', *Artforum* 9 (June 1971), pp. 29–34.

Millard, Andre, *America on Record: a History of Recorded Sound* (Cambridge: Cambridge University Press, 1995).

Mirzoeff, Nicholas, *How to See the World* (London: Pelican, 2015).

Misek, Richard, 'Dead Time: Cinema, Heidegger and Boredom', in Julia Vassilieva and Constantine Verevis (eds), *After Taste: Cultural Value and the Moving Image* (London: Routledge, 2012), pp. 133–41.

Mitchell, W. J. T., 'Image', in W. J. T. Mitchell and Mark Hansen (eds), *Critical Terms for Media Studies* (Chicago: Chicago University Press, 2010), pp. 35–48.

Mitry, Jean, *The Aesthetics and Psychology of the Cinema* [1963], trans. Christopher King (Bloomington: Indiana University Press, 1997).

Moholy-Nagy, László, *Vision in Motion* (Chicago: Theobald, 1947).

Molesworth, Helen, '"Pedestrian Color": The *Red Paintings*', in David Frankel (ed.), *Robert Rauschenberg* (New York: Museum of Modern Art, 2016), pp. 118–25.

Monaco, Paul, *How to Read a Film: the Art, Technology, Language, History and Theory of Film and Media* (Oxford: Oxford University Press, 1981).

Montagnini, Leone, 'Quando Wiener era di casa a Napoli', *La Rivista del Centro Studi Città della Scienza* (21 March 2016), <http://www.cittadellascienza.it/

centrostudi/2016/03/quando-heisenberg-e-wiener-erano-di-casa-a-napoli> (last accessed 23 December 2018).

Moore, Rachel, *Hollis Frampton – (nostalgia)* (London: Afterall Books, 2006).

Morando, Sergio (ed.), *Almanacco Letterario Bombiani 1963. Civiltà dell' imagine* (Milan: Bompiani, 1962).

Morando, Sergio (ed.), *Almanacco Letterario Bombiani 1962. Le applicazioni dei calcolatori elettronici alle scienze morali e alla letteratura* (Milan: Bompiani, 1961).

Moravia, Alberto, *Boredom* [1960], trans. Angus Davidson (New York: New York Review of Books, 1999).

Moravia, Alberto, 'È esplosa pura l'arte di Antonioni' [1970], in Michelangelo Antonioni, *Zabriskie Point* (Bologna: Cappelli Editore, 1970), pp. 11–16.

Moravia, Alberto, *La noia* (Milano: Bombiani, 1960).

Morin, Edgar, *L'Esprit du temps: essai sur la culture de masse* (Paris: Grasset, 1962).

Morin, Edgar, *The Stars* [1957], trans. Richard Howard (London: John Calder, 1960).

Morris, Catherine and Clarisse Bardiot (eds), *9 Evenings Reconsidered: Art, Theatre, Engineering* (Cambridge MA: MIT List Visual Arts Center, 2006).

Mulas, Ugo, Alan Solomon and Michele Provinciali, *New York: The New Art Scene* (New York: Holt, Rinehart, Winston, 1967).

Mulas, Ugo, *La fotografia* (Turin: Einaudi, 1973).

Mulvey, Laura, *Death 24x Second: Stillness and the Moving Image* (London: Reaktion, 2006).

Mumford, Lewis, *Art and Technics* (London: Oxford University Press, 1952).

Mumford, Lewis, *Art and Technics* (London: Geoffrey Cumberledge, publisher to Oxford University Press, 1952).

Munier, Roger, *Contre l'image* (Paris: Gallimard, 1963).

Münstenberg, Hugo, *The Photoplay: A Psychological Study* (New York: D. Appleton & Co., 1916).

Murray Schafer, Richard, *The New Soundscape: a Handbook for the Modern Music Teacher* (Don Mills ON: BMI Canada, 1969).

Nagib, Lúcia and Anne Jerslev (eds), *Impure Cinema: Intermedial and Intercultural Approaches to Film* (London: IB Tauris, 2014).

Nagib, Lúcia and Anne Jerslev, 'Introduction', in Lúcia Nagib Anne Jerslev (eds), *Impure Cinema: Intermedial and Intercultural Approaches to Film* (London: IB Tauris, 2014), pp. xviii–xxxi.

Nardelli, Matilde, 'End(ur)ing Photography', *Photographies* 5/2 (2012), pp. 159–77.

Nardelli, Matilde, 'Leafing through Cinema', in Steven Allen and Laura Hubner (eds), *Framing Film: Cinema and the Visual Arts* (Bristol: Intellect, 2012), pp.127–45.

Nardelli, Matilde 'Some Reflections on Antonioni, Sound and the Silence of *La Notte*', *The Soundtrack* 3:1 (2010), pp. 11–23.

Nascimbeni, Giulio, 'Il cronista meccanico comincia a muovere gli occhi', *Corriere della sera* (30 May 1964), p. 4.

Neale, Steve, 'Art Cinema as Institution', *Screen* 22/1 (1981), pp. 11–39.

Nijsen, C. J., *The Tape Recorder: A Guide to Magnetic Recording for the Non-Technical Amateur* (Eindhoven: Philips, 1964).

Novati, Maddalena, 'The Archive of the "Studio di Fonologia di Milano della Rai"', *Journal of New Music Research* 30/4 (2001), pp. 395–402.

Nowell-Smith, Geoffrey, *L'avventura* (London: BFI, 1997).

Nowell-Smith, Geoffrey, *Making Waves: New Cinemas of the 1960s* (New York: Bloomsbury, 2013).

O'Brian, Gleen, 'Interview: Andy Warhol' [1977], in Kenneth Goldsmith (ed.), *I'll Be Your Mirror: The Selected Andy Warhol Interviews, 1962–1987* (New York: Carroll and Graf, 2004), pp. 233–64.

Ongaro, Alberto, 'An In-Depth Search' (1975), in Michelangelo Antonioni, *The Architecture of Vision: Writings and Interviews on Cinema*, ed. Marga Cottino-Jones (Chicago: University of Chicago Press, 2007), pp. 344–5.

Ottieri, Ottiero, 'Automazione', in 'Vocabolarietto dell'Italiano', *Almanacco Letterario Bompiani 1959* (Milan: Bompiani, 1958), p. 149.

Ottieri, Ottiero, *Donnarumma all'assalto* [1959] (Milan: Garzanti, 2004).

Ottieri, Ottiero, *The Men at the Gate*, trans. Ivy Marion Rawson (London: Victor Gollancz, 1962).

Païni, Dominique (ed.), *Lo sguardo di Michelangelo: Antonioni e le arti* (Ferrara: Fondazione Ferrara Arte, 2013).

Païni, Dominique, 'Ritratto di cineasta in veste di pittore', in Dominique Païni (ed.), *Lo sguardo di Michelangelo: Antonioni e le arti* (Ferrara: Fondazione Ferrara Arte, 2013), pp. 21–41.

Parigi, Stefania, 'L'avventura de *I vinti*', in *Michelangelo Antonioni. I vinti*, Raro Video DVD and booklet (n.d.), pp. 5–32.

Parr, Martin and Gerry Badger, *The Photobook: A History*, vol. 2 (London: Phaidon, 2006).

Pasolini, Pier Paolo, 'The "Cinema of Poetry"' [1965], in *Heretical Empiricism*, ed. Louise K. Barnett (Bloomington: Indiana University Press, 1988), pp. 167–86.

Pease, Allison, *Modernism, Feminism and the Culture of Boredom* (Cambridge: Cambridge University Press, 2012).

Peirce, Charles Sanders, *The Collected Papers of Charles Sanders Pierce*, 8 vols, vol. 2: *Elements of Logic*, ed. Charles Hartshorne and Paul Weiss (Cambridge MA: Harvard University Press, 1932).

Petro, Patrice, 'After Shock/Between Boredom and History,' in Patrice Petro (ed.), *Fugitive Images: From Photography to Video* (Bloomington: Indiana University Press, 1999), pp. 265–84.

Petro, Patrice, *Aftershocks of the New: Feminism and Film History* (New Brunswick: Rutgers University Press, 2002)

Petro, Patrice, 'Historical *Ennui*, Feminist Boredom', in Vivian Sobchack (ed.), *The Persistence of History: Cinema, Television, and the Modern Event* (New York: Routledge, 1996), pp. 187–200.

Phillips, Adam, *On Kissing, Tickling, and Being Bored* (Cambridge MA: Harvard University Press, 1993).

Pickering, Andrew, *The Cybernetic Brain: Sketches of Another Future* (Chicago: University of Chicago Press, 2010).

Pinkus, Karen, 'Antonioni's Cinematic Poetics of Climate Change', in Laura Rascaroli and John David Rhodes (eds), *Antonioni: Centenary Essays* (London: BFI/Palgrave, 2011), pp. 235–53.

Pinkus, Karen, 'Empty Spaces: Decolonization in Italy', in Patrizia Palumbo (ed.), *A Place in the Sun: African in Italian Colonial Culture from Post-Unification to the Present* (Berkeley: University of California Press, 2003), pp. 299–319.

Pirandello, Luigi, 'Will the Talkies Abolish the Theatre?' [1929], trans. Nina Davinci Nichols, in *Shoot!* [1926], trans. C. K. Scott Moncrieff (Chicago: University of Chicago Press, 2005).

Plebe, Armando, 'Forma e contenuto nel linguaggio filmico', *Filmcritica* 142 (February 1964), pp. 127–34.

Pocci, Stefano, '*Lascia o raddoppia* (Milan, 1959)', trans. Laura Kuhn (April 2011) <http://johncagetrust.blogspot.com/2011/04/lascia-o-raddoppia-milan-1959.html> (last accessed December 2019).

Pomerance, Murray, 'Notes on Some Limits of Technicolor: The Antonioni Case', *Senses of Cinema* 53 (December 2009) <http://sensesofcinema.com/2009/feature-articles/notes-on-some-limits-of-technicolor-the-antonioni-case/> (last accessed 14 March 2019).

Quaresima, Leonardo, 'Making Love on the Shores of the Rivero Po: Antonioni's Documentaries', in Laura Rascaroli and John David Rhodes (eds), *Antonioni: Centenary Essays* (London: BFI/Palgrave, 2011), pp. 115–33.

Ragona, Melissa, 'Hidden Noise: Strategies of Sound Montage in the Films of Hollis Frampton', *October* 109 (Summer 2004), pp. 96–118.

Rancière, Jacques, *Aesthetics and Its Discontents* [2004], trans. Steven Corcoran (Cambridge: Polity Press, 2009).

Rao, Giuseppe and Pietro Contadini, in collaboration with Archivio Storico Olivetti, *Olivetti Elea 9003. La sfida al future di Adriano Olivetti, Roberto Olivetti, and Mario Tchou* (2001–8), documentary film.

Rascaroli, Laura and John David Rhodes (eds), *Antonioni: Centenary Essays* (London: Palgrave Macmillan/BFI, 2011).

Rascaroli, Laura and John David Rhodes, 'Interstitial, Pretentious, Alienated, Dead: Antonioni at 100', in Laura Rascaroli and John David Rhodes (eds), *Antonioni: Centenary Essays* (London: Palgrave Macmillan/BFI, 2011), pp. 1–20.

Remes, Justin, *Motion(less) Pictures: The Cinema of Stasis* (New York: Columbia University Press, 2015).

Resnais, Alain and Alain Robbe-Grillet, 'Last Words on *Last Year*' [1962], in Harry M. Geduld, *Film Makers on Film Making: Statements on Their Art by Thirty Directors* (Bloomington: University of Indiana Press, 1967), pp. 164–74.

Resnais, Alain, 'Trying to Understand My Own Film' [1962], in Harry M. Geduld (ed.), *Film Makers on Film Making: Statements on Their Art by Thirty Directors* (Bloomington: Indiana University Press, 1967), pp. 155–63.

Rhodes, John David, 'Abstraction and the Geopolitical: Lessons from Antonioni's Trip to China', in Elena Gorfinkel and Tami Williams (eds), *Global Cinema Networks* (New Brunswick: Rutgers University Press, 2018), pp. 53–76.

Richieri, Giuseppe, 'Television from Service to Business: European Tendencies and the Italian Case', in Phillip Drummond and Richard Patterson (eds), *Television in Transition: Papers from the First International Television Studies Conference* (London: BFI, 1986), pp. 21–35.

Richter, Hans, 'The Film as An Original Art Form' [1955], in P. Adams Sitney (ed.), *Film Culture Reader* (New York: Cooper Square Press, 1970), pp. 15–20.

Riskin, Jessica, *The Restless Clock: A History of the Centuries-Long Argument over What Makes Living Things Tick* (Chicago: University of Chicago Press, 2016).

Rizzardi, Veniero and Angela Ida De Benedictis (eds), *Nuova musica alla radio. Esperienze allo Studio di Fonologia della RAI di Milano, 1954–1959* (Rome: RAI-Eri, 2000).

Robbe-Grillet, Alain, *For a New Novel: Essays on Fiction* [1963], trans. Richard Howard (New York: Grove Press, 1965).

Robbe-Grillet, Alain, 'Time and Description in Fiction Today [1963], in *For a New Novel: Essays on Fiction* [1963], trans. Richard Howard (New York: Grove Press, 1965), pp. 143–56.

Roberts, John, *The Art of Interruption: Realism, Photography, the Everyday* (Manchester: Manchester University Press, 1998).

Rocha, Glauber, 'An Aesthetic of Hunger' [1965], trans. Randal Johnson and Burnes Hollyman, in Michael T. Martin (ed.), *New Latin American Cinema* (Detroit: Wayne State University Press, 1997), pp. 59–61.

Rodman, Selden, *Conversations with Artists* (New York: Devin-Adair Co., 1957).

Rodowick, David N., *The Crisis of Political Modernism: Criticism and Ideology in Contemporary Film Theory* [1988] (Berkeley: University of California Press, 1994).

Rodowick, David N., *The Virtual Life of Film* (Cambridge MA: Harvard University Press, 2007).

Rohdie, Sam, *Antonioni* (London: BFI, 1990).

Rosenberg, Harold, 'Rothko', *New Yorker* 46 (6–28 March 1970), p. 94.

Ross, Kristin, *Fast Cars, Clean Bodies: Decolonization and the Reordering of French Culture* (Cambridge MA: MIT, 1995).

Rossellini, Roberto, 'Cinema: Nuove prospettive di conoscenza' [1963], reprinted in Galvano della Volpe, *Teorie e prassi del cinema in Italia, 1950–1970* (Milan: Gabriele Mazzotta, 1972), pp. 59–72.

Rothko, Mark, *The Artist's Reality: Philosophies of Art*, ed. Christopher Rothko (New Haven: Yale University Press, 2004).

Rothko, Mark, *Writings on Art* (New Haven: Yale University Press, 2006).

Roud, Richard, '*The Red Desert*', *Sight and Sound* 34 (Spring 1965), pp. 76–80.

Rubino, Rubino, 'Bruno Munari Versus Programmed Art: A Contradictory Situation, 1961–67', in Pierpaolo Antonello, Matilde Nardelli and Margherita Zanoletti (eds), *Bruno Munari: The Lightness of Art* (Oxford: Peter Lang, 2017), pp. 89–112.

Russell, Ben (ed.), *Robots: The 500-year Quest to Make Machines Human* (London: Science Museum/Scala Arts and Heritage, 2017).

Russolo, Luigi, 'The Art of Noises: Futurist Manifesto' [1913], in Luigi Russolo, *The Art of Noises*, trans. Barclay Brown (New York: Pendragon Press, 1986).

Sadoul, George, 'Puro come *La notte*', *Filmcritica* 106–107 (February–March 1961), pp. 912.

Sarris, Andrew, 'No Antoniennui', *The Village Voice* (29 December 1966).

Scaldaferri, Nicola, *Musica nel laboratorio elettroacustico. Lo studio di fonologia di Milano e la ricerca musicale negli anni Cinquanta* (Lucca: LIM, 1997).

Schaeffer, Jean-Marie, *L'image précaire du dispositive photographique* (Paris: Seuil, 1987).

Schaeffer, Pierre, *In Search of a Concrete Music* [1952], trans. Christine North and John Dack (Berkeley: University of California Press, 2012).

Schaeffer, Pierre, *Traité des objets musicaux. Essai interdisciplines* (Paris: Éditions du Seuil, 1966).

Schoonover, Karl, 'Antonioni's Waste Management', in Laura Rascaroli and John David Rhodes (eds), *Antonioni: Centenary Essays* (London: BFI/Palgrave, 2011), pp. 254–75.

Schoonover, Karl, *Brutal Vision: The Neorealist Body in Postwar Italian Cinema* (Minneapolis: University of Minnesota Press, 2012).

Schoonover, Karl and Rosalind Galt, *Queer Cinema in the World* (Durham NC: Duke University Press, 2016).

Schoonover, Karl, 'Wastrels of Time: Slow Cinema's Labouring Body, the Political Spectator and the Queer', *Framework: The Journal of Cinema and Media* 53/1 (Spring 2012), pp. 65–78.

Scrivano, Paolo, 'Signs of Americanization in Italian Domestic Life: Italy's Post-war Conversion to Consumerism', *Journal of Contemporary History* 40/2 (2005), pp. 317–40.

Seckler, D. G., 'The Artist Speaks: Robert Rauschenberg', *Art in America* 54/3 (May–June 1966), p. 84.

Shinkle, Eugénie, 'Boredom, Repetition, Inertia: Contemporary Photography and the Aesthetics of the Banal', *Mosaic* 37/4 (December 2004), pp. 165–83.

Siegel, Michael Loren, 'Identification of a Medium: *Identificazione di una donna* and the Rise of Commercial Television in Italy', in Laura Rascaroli and John David Rhodes (eds), *Antonioni: Centenary Essays* (London: Palgrave/BFI, 2011).

Silverman, Kaja, 'Growing Still', in Susanne Gaensheimer (ed.), *James Coleman* (Monaco: Hatje Cant, 2002).

Simmel, Georg, 'The Metropolis and Mental Life' [1903], in *The Sociology of Georg Simmel*, ed. and trans. Kurt H. Wolff (New York: The Free Press, 1964).

Simondon, Gilbert, *On the Mode of Existence of Technical Objects* [1958], trans. Cécile Malaspina and John Rogove (Minneapolis: Univocal, 2017).

Singer, Marilyn (ed.), *A History of American Avant-Garde Cinema* (New York: The American Federation of Arts, 1976).

Sisto, Antonella C., *Film Sound in Italy: Listening to the Screen* (Basingstoke: Palgrave Macmillan, 2014).

Sitney, P. Adams, ed., *The Avant-Garde Film: A Reader of Theory and Criticism* (New York: Anthology Film Archives, 1978).

Sitney, P. Adams, 'Structural Film' [1969], in P. Adams Sitney (ed.), *Film Culture Reader* [1970] (New York: Cooper Square Press, 2000).

Smith, Patrick S., *Andy Warhol's Art and Films* (Ann Arbor: UMI Research Press, 1986).

Smithson, Robert, 'A Tour of the Monuments of Passaic, New Jersey' [1967], in Jack Flam (ed.), *Robert Smithson: The Collected Writings* (Berkeley: University of California Press, 1996).

Sontag, Susan, *Against Interpretation and Other Essays* [1966] (London: Penguin, 2009).

Sontag, Susan, 'Against Interpretation' [1964], in *Against Interpretation and Other Essays* [1966] (London: Penguin, 2009), p. 314.

Sontag, Susan, 'One Culture and the New Sensibility' [1965], in *Against Interpretation and Other Essays* [1966] (London: Penguin, 2009), pp. 293–305.

Sontag, Susan, *On Photography* [1977] (London: Penguin, 2002).

Sorlin, Pierre, *Les Fils de Nadar. Le 'siècle' de l'image analogique* (Paris: Éditions Nathan, 1997).

Sottsass, Ettore, 'Paesaggio elettronico', *Domus* 381/8 (August 1961), pp. 39–46.

Spacks, Patricia Meyer, *Boredom: The Literary History of a State of Mind* (Chicago: University of Chicago Press, 1995).

Spigel, Lynn, *Make Room for TV: Television and the Family Ideal in Postwar America* (Chicago: University of Chicago Press, 1992).

Spigel, Lynn, 'Media Home: Then and Now', in *International Journal of Cultural Studies* 4/4 (2001), pp. 385–411.

Spurrell, Katie, 'Interview with Furio Colombo', in Oliver Wick (ed.), *Mark Rothko* (Milan: Skira, 2007), pp. 208–9.

Steimatsky, Noa, *Italian Locations: Reinhabiting the Past in Postwar Cinema* (Minneapolis: University of Minnesota Press, 2008).

Steimatsky, Noa, 'Pass/Fail: The Antonioni Screen Test', *Framework: The Journal of Cinema and Media* 55/2 (Autumn 2014), pp. 191–219.

Sterne, Jonathan, *The Audible Past: Cultural Origins of Sound Reproduction* (Durham NC: Duke University Press, 2003).

Steyerl, Hito, 'In Defense of the Poor Image', *e-flux journal* 10 (November 2009) <https://www.e-flux.com/journal/10/61362/in-defense-of-the-poor-image/> (last accessed 15 April 2019).

Stimson, Blake, *The Pivot of the World: Photography and Its Nation* (Cambridge MA: MIT, 2006).

Stulik, Dusan C. and Art Kaplan, *The Atlas of Analytical Signatures of Photographic Processes: Half-Tone* (Los Angeles: The Getty Conservation Institute, 2013).

Sutton, Damian, *Photography, Cinema, Memory: The Crystal Image of Time* (Minneapolis: University of Minnesota Press, 2009).

Svendsen, Lars, *A Philosophy of Boredom*, trans. John Irons (London: Reaktion Books, 2005).

Szarkowski, John, *The Photographer's Eye* (New York: Museum of Modern Art, 1966).

Tassone, Aldo, 'Conversation' [1985], in Michelangelo Antonioni, *The Architecture of Vision: Writings and Interviews on Cinema*, ed. Carlo Di Carlo, Giorgio Tinazzi and Marga Cottino-Jones (Chicago: University of Chicago Press, 2007), pp. 230–44.

Tassone, Aldo, 'Conversazione' [1985], in Michelangelo Antonioni, *Fare un film è per me vivere. Scritti sul cinema*, ed. Carlo Di Carlo and Giorgio Tinazzi (Venice: Marsilio, 1994), pp. 204–15.

Tassone, Aldo, *I film di Michelangelo Antonioni: Un poeta della visione* (Rome: Gremese, 2002).

Thomas, François, *L'Atelier d'Alain Resnais* (Paris: Flammarion, 1989).

Thompson, Emily, *The Soundscape of Modernity: Architectural Acoustics and the Culture of Listening in America, 1900–1933* (Cambridge MA: MIT, 2002).

Thurman-Jaies, Anne and Martin Hellmold (eds), *Art Photographica: Fotografie und Künstlerbücher* (Bremen: Neues Museum Weserburg, 2002).

Tinazzi, Giorgio, 'The American Experience', in Michelangelo Antonioni, *The Architecture of Vision: Writings and Interviews on Cinema*, ed. Marga Cottino Jones (Chicago: University of Chicago Press, 2007), pp. 313–18.

Tobe, Reneé, *Film, Architecture and the Spatial Imagination* (London: Routledge, 2016).

Toohey, Peter, *Boredom: A Lively History* (New Haven: Yale University Press, 2011).

Tomasulo, Frank P., '"The Sounds of Silence": Modernist Acting in Michelangelo Antonioni's *Blow-Up*', in Cynthia A. Baron, Diane Carson and Frank P. Tomasulo (eds), *More Than a Method: Trends and Traditions in Contemporary Film Performance* (Detroit: Wayne State University Press, 2004), pp. 94–125.

Turing, Alan, 'Computing Machinery and Intelligence', *Mind* 49 (1950), pp. 33–60.

Turvey, Malcolm, *The Filming of Modern Life: European Avant-Garde Film of the 1920* (Cambridge MA: MIT, 2011).

Turvey, Malcolm, Hal Foster, Chrissie Iles et al., 'Round Table: The Projected Image in Contemporary Art', *October* 104 (Spring 2003), pp. 71–96.

Twyman, Michael, *Printing 1770–1970: An Illustrated History of Its Developments and Uses in England* (London: Eyre and Spottiswoode, 1970).

Vaccari, Franco, *Fotografia e inconscio tecnologico* [1979], ed. Roberta Valtorta (Turin: Einaudi, 2011).

VanDerBeek, Stan, 'Culture: Intercom and Expanded Cinema, a Proposal and Manifesto', *Film Culture* 40 (1966), pp. 15–18.

Vasil'evich Parin, Vasiliĭ and R. M. Bayevskiy, *Introduction to medical cybernetics* [1966] (Washington: NASA Technical Translation F-459, 1967).

Vergine, Lea, *Il corpo come linguaggio* (Milan: Prearo, 1974).

Visalberghi, Aldo, 'Industria culturale e società', in *Pirelli. Rivista d'informazione e tecnica,* 'Televisione e Cultura' 14/1 (January–February 1961), pp. 25–31.

Vitale, Raffaella, *Michelangelo Antonioni Schedatura e analisi del fondo pittorico custodito presso le Gallerie di Arte Moderna e Contemporanea di Ferrara*, Tesi di Laurea (Venice: University of Venice, 2014).

Vitello, Paul, 'Stefan Kudelski, Polish Inventor of Recorder that Changed Hollywood, Dies at 83', *New York Times*, 31 January 2013, <http://www.nytimes.com/2013/02/01/business/stefan-kudelski-inventor-of-the-nagra-dies-at-83.html> (last accessed 6 October 2017).

Wade, John, *A Short History of the Camera* (Watford: Fountain Press, 1979).

Wagstaff, Christopher, 'The Media', in Zygmunt G. Baransky and Rebecca J. West (eds), *The Cambridge Companion to Modern Italian Culture* (Cambridge: Cambridge University Press, 2001), pp. 293–310.

Walter, William Grey, *The Living Brain* (London: Gerald Duckworth & Co., 1953).

Warhol, Andy and Pat Hackett, *Popism: The Warhol '60s* [1980] (London: Hutchinson, 1981).

Weiss, Allen S., 'Frampton's Lemma, Zorn's Dilemma', *October* 32 (Spring 1985), pp. 118–28.

Weiss, Jeffrey, '*Temps mort*: Antonioni and Rothko', in Oliver Wick (ed.), *Mark Rothko* (Milan and London: Skira and Thames & Hudson, 2007), pp. 44–55.

White, Anthony, 'Bruno Munari and Lucio Fontana: Parallel Lives', in Pierpaolo Antonello, Matilde Nardelli and Margherita Zanoletti (eds), *Bruno Munari: The Lightenss of Art* (Oxford: Peter Lang, 2017), pp. 65–87.

Whittle, David W. [interviewed by Sandra Johnson], 'NASA Johnson Space Center Oral History Project', oral history transcript of interview on 6 February 2006, pp. 1–56, <https://historycollection.jsc.nasa.gov/JSCHistoryPortal/history/oral_histories/WhittleDW/WhittleDW_2-16-06.pdf> (last accessed November 2019).

Wick, Oliver, '"Do they negate each other, modern and classical?" Mark Rothko, Italy and the Yearning for Tradition', in Oliver Wick (ed.), *Mark Rothko* (Milan and London: Skira and Thames & Hudson, 2007), pp. 5–25.

Wick, Oliver (ed.), *Mark Rothko* (Milan and London: Skira and Thames & Hudson, 2007).

Wiener, Norbert, *Cybernetics: Or Control and Communication in the Animal and Machine* (New York and Paris: John Wiley and Sons/Hermann et Cie, 1948).

Wiener, Norbert, *The Human Use of Human Beings: Cybernetics and Society* (London: Eyre and Spottinswoode, 1950).

Wiener, Norbert, *Introduzione alla cibernetica*, trans. Dario Persiani (Turin: Einaudi, 1953).

Wiener, Norbert, *La cibernetica*, trans. Otto Beghelli (Milan: Bompiani, 1953).

Williams, Raymond, *Television: Technology and Cultural Form* (London: Fontana, 1974).

Wollen, Peter, *Signs and Meaning in the Cinema* (London: Secker and Warburg, 1969).

Worringer, Wilhelm, *Abstraction and Empathy: A Contribution to the Psychology of Style* [1908], trans. Michael Bullock [1967] (Chicago: Ivan R. Dee, 1997).

Wyndham, Francis, 'Fotografi di moda dell' East End [1965], in Goffredo, Fofi, Ernesto Franco, Philippe Garner and Walter Moser, *Io sono il fotografo. Blow-Up e la fotografia fotografia* (Rome: Contrasto, 2018), pp. 106–35.

Zavattini, Cesare, 'Some Ideas on the Cinema' [1952], *Sight and Sound* 23 (October–December 1953), pp. 64–9.

Žižek, Slavoj, *Looking Awry: An Introduction to Jacques Lacan Through Popular Culture* (Cambridge MA: MIT Press, 1991).

Index

CPSIA information can be obtained
at www.ICGtesting.com
Printed in the USA
BVHW052213210123
656830BV00009B/472

9 781474 444405